FULLY REVISED AND UPDATED

The MOUNTAIN SKILLS
Training Handbook

FULLY REVISED AND UPDATED
MOUNTAIN SKILLS
Training Handbook

PETE HILL MIC FRGS and
STUART JOHNSTON MIC

David and Charles

A DAVID & CHARLES BOOK
Copyright © David & Charles Limited 2000, 2002, 2003, 2004, 2006, 2008, 2009

David & Charles is an F+W Media Inc. company
4700 East Galbraith Road
Cincinnati, OH 45236

First published in the UK in 2000
Reprinted 2002, 2003

First paperback edition 2004
Reprinted 2006, 2008

This new edition 2009

Text copyright © Pete Hill and Stuart Johnston 2000, 2002, 2003, 2004, 2006, 2008, 2009

All updates to the 2009 edition by Pete Hill

All photographs © Pete Hill and Derek Croucher 2000, 2002, 2003, 2004, 2006, 2008, 2009

Illustrations by Ethan Danielson, copyright © David & Charles 2000, 2002, 2003, 2004, 2006, 2008, 2009

Pete Hill and Stuart Johnston have asserted their right to be identified as author of this work in accordance with the Copyright, Designs and Patents Act, 1988.

A catalogue record for this book is available from the British Library.

ISBN-13: 978-0-7153-3165-1 hardback
ISBN-10: 0-7153-3165-5 hardback

Printed in China by RR Donnelley
for David & Charles
Brunel House   Newton Abbot   Devon

Commissioning Editor: Neil Baber
Editorial Manager: Emily Pitcher
Desk Editor: Emily Rae
Assistant Editor: Joanna Richards
Senior Designer: Jodie Lystor
Production Controller: Ros Napper

Visit our website at www.davidandcharles.co.uk

David & Charles books are available from all good bookshops; alternatively you can contact our Orderline on 0870 9908222 or write to us at FREEPOST EX2 110, D&C Direct, Newton Abbot, TQ12 4ZZ (no stamp required UK only); US customers call 800-289-0963 and Canadian customers call 800-840-5220.

PUBLISHER'S NOTE
Throughout this book 'he' has been used to avoid awkward constructions such as 'he/she', 'his/hers' and so on. All the techniques covered are equally applicable to men and women.

Contents

KARABINERS

Screwgate karabiners have been referred to in a variety of places throughout this work. It is assumed that, as soon as they have been clipped, they will be screwed in to the locked position. Also, as HMS or 'pear shaped' karabiners are essential for the smooth running of certain systems, these have been highlighted in the text. If 'HMS' is not mentioned, then a standard 'D' shape will suffice. Please note that the authors do not encourage the use of karabiners using a single motion automatic security system for the gate locking procedure.

SLINGS

Sling lengths are shown in both imperial and metric measurements. This is due to slings being commonly referred to in the UK by their circumference in feet, but also allows for them to be referred to by their manufactured size where they are measured doubled, in other words the flat length. Thus, a four foot sling would also be called a 60cm sling.

Foreword

Mountaineering is about enjoyment and recreation, meeting physical and often mental challenges in the extremes of our rich and varied landscape. Learning the skills of mountaineering has often been done through trial and error somewhere on the knife-edge between adventure and misadventure.

Guiding others in the mountains is an old and honourable profession, and man's ingenuity, modern equipment, accurate maps and related paraphernalia have made it into a sophisticated business. The UK has one of the most developed systems of instructor/leader awards and the number of qualified instructors is increasing rapidly. It is therefore very appropriate that this book should be published pulling together the themes of each of the awards into one book. It is worth having a look at some of the older books on mountaineering techniques to see how far safety and training has moved on. It should also be a reminder that we never stop learning as we operate in an ever-changing environment. It should also be noted that, although these awards are UK based, the skills contained within are universal.

The Mountain Skills Training Handbook provides a wealth of up-to-date material that reflects current thinking and practice around the world. When 'playing' in the outdoors there is often not a clearly defined way of doing things. The skills clearly illustrated and explained in these pages have to be practised and require sound judgement applied appropriately. Good judgement is born out of experience usually combined with a good handful of epics. Successful professional instructors like Pete and Stuart have an added talent, and that is the ability to communicate and make learning an enjoyable experience, even in the worst of conditions.

The Mountain Skills Training Handbook is an excellent, practical and entertaining guide for the recreational and professional mountaineer alike.

Nigel Williams, Glenmore Lodge

The revised edition

Time has flown since the first edition, and techniques have moved on in a variety of areas. This update is typical of Pete and Stuart's commitment to their sport, and ensures that the book remains an important work of reference for anyone involved in, or wishing to become involved in, the outdoors.

Pete and Stuart have moved on apace since the original publication, and they now both run their own companies, offering instruction and consultation at the highest level and of the highest quality. That there are now so many very good and highly qualified mountain leaders and instructors in the UK is a reflection of how important the learning progression is, and the original book has gone in no small way to contribute to that. Combine that with the increasing number of qualified individuals and centres offering training and assessment at National Governing Body level in the UK, and you can see that there is a wealth of experience available. Pete and Stuart have linked into that and made the skills available to all, not just the aspiring instructor but to anyone who likes to walk, climb or head into the mountains, whatever the season.

These days, careful judgement and making the correct decisions when on the hill or the crag are paramount when viewed from a leadership context, and it is only by spending time with different groups in different environments that the skills of efficient leadership can be practised and perfected. Much the same is true of the technical skills needed by leaders and instructors, and as such we should never be so bold to say that we know everything, for there is always the ability to gain further knowledge as new skills are introduced and old skills are adapted to new ways of thinking.

As with the 2000 original, this updated version is an excellent and practical guide to those skills needed by leaders and instructors, and it offers an essential guide as to how techniques have developed over recent years.

Nigel Williams, Glenmore Lodge.

Introduction

The incentive for this book has come from mountaineers, both active and aspiring. We are frequently asked where the skills that we teach can be found in printed form; that is, presented in a practical, down-to-earth manner and easy to relate to. Although many instructional books exist on the market, we have found none that fitted these criteria, as all too often publications rely on the quantity rather than the quality of the information, making it difficult to extract the relevant techniques.

We believe that this book fills that gap. It presents skills in an easy-to-read manner, and we have phrased it in the same way as we might teach; thus it is practical, informative and completely up to date.

The contents are aimed at both the beginner and active mountaineer. We decided to start at a level that assumes a little walking or climbing experience, and have not dwelt on the practicalities of the softer skills such as choosing a rucksack or buying a compass – there are plenty of other books to perform that task. Instead, those technical skills relevant to modern-day mountaineering are introduced straight away, and a logical progression is made.

We hope that you enjoy studying the book, and would encourage you to take it out in the hills to be used as a reference when learning techniques, for it is only after repeated practice that skills can become second nature.

Pete Hill and Stuart Johnston
Scotland, 2000

The revised edition

We are very pleased to be able to update the contents of the original *Mountain Skills Training Handbook*. The first version has done phenomenally well, even being translated into a number of other languages including Russian and Czech! It has given us a lot of pleasure knowing that the book has helped a substantial number of candidates through their NGB awards, as well as being a useful source of reference for anyone who simply enjoys walking and climbing in the mountains for their own pleasure.

Although we have reviewed the entire contents, not everything has changed. Ideas come and go, techniques alter and equipment designs advance. However, the basic core skills of safety and leadership remain substantially the same, and it is these skills that remain paramount for the mountain leader and instructor.

We hope that you get as much out of this version as others have from the original. Remember that there are many ways to complete a task and still come out with the same result, so make sure that you look at all of the options when deciding upon a technique or skill that you feel is suited to any given situation, and remain open-minded about other ways of doing things. In that way you will always be able to take on board new ideas and skills, enhancing not only your own knowledge but also the safety and quality of experience of anyone in your charge.

Have a great time on the hill, it would be good to bump into you some day.

Pete Hill and Stuart Johnston, 2009.

The Committee of the Association of Mountaineering Instructors recommends this book as a relevant and up-to-date work, valuable to both aspirant and experienced mountaineers.

PART ONE

Mountain Leadership Skills

This section covers a number of the essential skills needed by anyone taking walking groups out into the hills. Some of the techniques are relevant to both summer and winter conditions.

Navigation

River Crossing

Security on Steep Ground

Emergency Evacuation

Navigation

This chapter details a few ideas, both about teaching and about practising navigation. Compass skills are briefly mentioned, in order to help the novice find direction (!) and make a start. It would serve the reader well to obtain a specialist navigation book from the library, in order to delve more deeply into the basic skills of finding his way.

NAVIGATION TOOLS

Scale

The scale is the relationship of distance on the map to the distance on the ground, generally given as a representative fraction such as 1:50,000, 1:25,000 etc. This means that one unit on the map represents 50,000 of the same units on the ground. For example, 1cm on the map is 50,000cm, or 500m, on the ground. Using this formula you can now easily add and divide map scale to actual ground distance with a high degree of accuracy.

The Compass: What Type?

The best and most convenient compass for mountain use should be simple in design and layout. The practicality of handling it while wearing gloves in foul weather should also be a consideration.

Choose one with good direction-of-travel arrow markings along with base-plate line markings for taking bearings. The compass should also be robust, accurate, light and versatile. In addition, its base plate needs to be transparent with a housing that doesn't move too easily, and it should have two-degree divisions around the rim.

The length of your attachment string (discard the one provided by the manufacturers and add your own – a boot lace is ideal), should be no less than 40cm. A magnifying glass helps with studying small map features, and a Romer scale helps with measuring and taking accurate grid references.

OBSERVATION

It is worth noting that a mirrored sighting compass has many limitations for mountain navigation, as well as short-base-device compasses, and they are not recommended for serious use.

TIP

Compasses can be tricky to hold still on plastic or laminated maps. If you put an elastic band around the base plate next to the housing, you will find that the compass is much easier to keep in position as the band helps it to grip on the slippery surface.

Taking a Bearing

■ Identify position A where you are, and position B where you wish to travel to.
■ Using the edge of your compass or coloured line on the base device, place the compass between A and B. Ensure that the compass direction-of-travel arrow is pointing to position B.
■ Holding the compass firm and being careful not to move it off position, turn the compass housing so that the grid north arrow and lines in the compass housing point north on the map and run in parallel with the map grid lines.
■ You have now taken a grid bearing.
■ Correct for any magnetic variation to align

you with true north; this variation will be highlighted at the top of the map or located at the map key. This is now a magnetic bearing.

Walking on a Bearing

■ Place the compass flat in the palm of your hand in front of your body.
■ Align the floating needle with the north arrow marked on the compass housing.
■ Make sure at this point that the compass is in front of your body.
■ Using the direction-of-travel arrow on the base device, sight ahead a short way, maybe only a few metres, and observe a feature to walk to (boulder, clump of grass, etc.), walk to it, then stop and repeat the process, always keeping the needle pointing to the north mark on the housing.

Good navigation comes with experience and practice, and the mark of a good navigator is having the ability to combine these techniques with a high degree of accuracy.

Walking on a Bearing Without Stopping

This needs practise, but can become easy to do.
■ Line up the compass as above, and sight on your first feature.
■ Walk towards the feature but, as you approach it, let your compass needle settle.
■ Line up your compass with your first feature, look through it and locate another feature on the same line.
■ Now ignore the first feature and walk towards the second. As you approach it, repeat the process of lining up, looking through it and keeping moving.

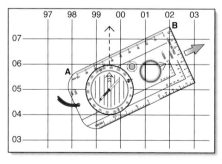

The compass and the map when taking a bearing

OBSERVATION

A compass is an extremely useful piece of kit, but it can have its accuracy compromised. Be careful, when walking on a bearing, that no metallic objects are influencing the needle. Items that do so include ice axes, metallic rock elements, trekking poles, cameras and, bizarrely, under-wired bras. It is also important to consider where to store your compass when at home. A common place to keep outdoor kit is under the stairs, but this is often where the power supply comes into the house, creating strong magnetic fields which can alter the balance of the needle.

Accuracy is the most important factor and, although it is handy to be able to keep moving, if you feel that you need to stop then you must do so – do not be tempted to blindly walk on if you have any doubt that you may have sighted on the wrong feature.

TIP
Magnetic variation varies from country to country, and can be different in various areas of the same country. It is important to know what the variation is (this will be marked on the key of the map) and how to make the calculation. In the United Kingdom, for example, the variation has to be added to the grid bearing, to give a magnetic bearing. A useful way of remembering this is that the world is bigger than the map, so, when taking a bearing from the map, make the number bigger, i.e. add the variation. When going from the world to the map, the map being smaller, make the number smaller.

Grid References

Knowing how to accurately take a grid reference is extremely important, if for no other reason than to be able to report the site of an accident accurately. The diagram shows how to go about it. Remember the phrase 'along the hall and up the stairs', as this should help you get the sequence of numbers right. Also, prefix the numbers with the map-sheet letter, which will make the reference unique.

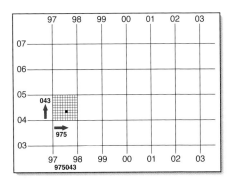

Working out a grid reference

CALCULATING DISTANCE

Pacing and Timing

These are techniques used when navigating in poor weather conditions, when it is extremely important to know how far you have travelled and for how long you have been walking.

Pacing

Pacing is having a known amount of double paces for 100m. This is achieved by measuring 100m on the flat. Start walking and count every double pace, for instance every time your right foot hits the ground. The total that you reach, probably somewhere around 60 to 70 double paces, will only be for walking on the flat in ideal conditions. This number of paces will change as soon as you start going uphill, are wearing a heavy sack, have different boots on, are crossing differing terrain such as deep snow or boulder fields, or have the wind against you, etc. Time should be taken to find out these variables, and note the change in your stride.

Timing

One of the best formulae to use is known as 'Naismith's Rule'. When planning ahead, it is worth noting that you may find yourself tiring when a few hours into a journey, so it is wise to plan for a slower pace. Should you be travelling uphill, then you probably may not walk as fast.

In addition to the formula overleaf add one minute for every 10m contour line of ascent. In the early stages of a trip, 30 seconds per contour may be sufficient. When descending, there is no need to add time for contours, unless the going gets steep. Other factors that will influence your time include:

- tiredness
- weather
- steep ground
- conditions underfoot
- using a rope
- using trekking poles
- not wearing crampons when appropriate
- wearing crampons when inappropriate
- poor navigation skills
- poor route choice
- physical fitness
- when there's nothing to sight on
- when unsure about the point you are leaving from
- when lost.

Speed k.p.h. / Distance m	2	3	4	5	6
50	1.5	1	45 secs.	36 secs.	0.5
100	3	2	1.5	1.2	1
200	6	4	3	2.4	2
500	15	10	7.5	6	5
1000	30	20	15	12	10

Naismith's formula

ESSENTIAL NAVIGATION TECHNIQUES

Attack Points

This technique is used when you intend to go to a small feature, say a small knoll by which you are camped. If you were navigating from some distance away, the chances are that you may find yourself way off target at the end of the leg. By splitting the one leg into two, and first travelling to a larger feature nearer to your objective, such as a big lake, you would have reduced the margin for error considerably. This would leave a short distance to walk, resulting in greater accuracy, to the final objective.

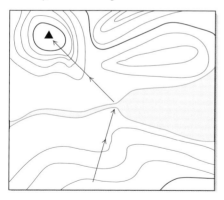

An attack point

Aiming Off

If aiming for a stream junction, for instance, in poor visibility, the chances are that you will end up one side or other of your intended destination. In poor weather, it would be difficult to decide in exactly which direction to travel to reach the junction. Aiming off is a most useful technique, with which you purposely aim a few degrees to the uphill side of the objective. When the stream, in this case, is reached, you would then know in which direction to turn to follow it to the junction.

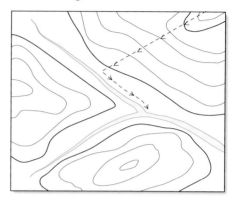

Aiming off

Boxing

Should you come across an obstacle in the way of your bearing such as a large gully cutting back some way into a cliff-top, it can be avoided by aligning your compass needle 90 degrees from your bearing then following this for a measured distance, say 50m, until the obstacle is cleared. Now walk on your original bearing for a measured distance past the obstacle, then stop and realign your compass needle 90 degrees and walk the same distance back. Continue on the original line.

Boxing

Dogleg

This is when there is a huge, dangerous feature that we wish to avoid. Take a bearing and follow it over a set distance past the danger then take a new bearing to rejoin the original direction.

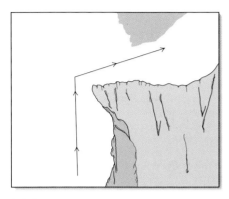

A dogleg

Slope Aspect

This is when you check the direction in which the slope faces, by using your compass. It can be a useful tool for relocation in poor visibility.

Take a bearing directly up or down the slope, then, having corrected for any magnetic variation, place the compass on the map in the area you have been walking, maintaining the north arrow in the compass housing parallel with grid north on the map. Move your compass across the map, maintaining north to north, in the area that you suspect you may be. Where the lines on the base device of the compass cross

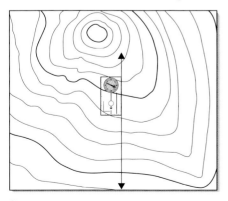

Slope aspect

the slope at exactly 90 degrees will indicate your approximate position. However, you will still need to find out how far up the slope you are, and there may be other possible positions relevant to your current slope aspect that need to be eliminated.

Collecting Feature

This is a large, obvious feature a short distance behind your intended destination that will immediately indicate that you have overshot your target. A collecting feature could be a change in slope, the edge of a cliff (care needed in winter or in poor visibility) or a river. A point will then be identified as an attack point, as mentioned previously.

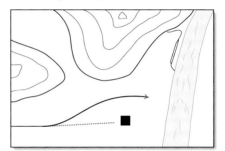

Collecting feature

Hand-railing

This is a simple technique, which allows ground to be covered rapidly. It is the act of following an obvious feature, such as a river or an area of major contour change, to help lead you to your destination. This may be gained by 'aiming off', the feature 'hand-railed', and then an 'attack point' used to reach your final objective. Navigation is often the linking of a series of line features (hand-rails) together to form a route.

Winter Considerations

Although navigational techniques are very similar from summer to winter, there are a few points that need to be borne in mind when travelling under winter conditions. For instance, features to sight on can be hard to find, and it may be necessary to have your partner travel ahead of you to give you something to sight on.

White-out conditions occur when the sky, cloud and ground merge into one blank sheet, and it is very disorientating to be out in these conditions. Your eyes have nothing to focus on, and it is all too easy to travel too far or too close to an edge and simply walk over a drop. One technique that is useful is to make a snowball and throw it in front of you. This serves two purposes: firstly it makes a mark in the snow, thus giving your eye something to focus on and a point you can use as a feature; secondly, it may help to determine if you are close to an edge by simply making a mark for a short distance and then disappearing.

Great care must be taken when hand-railing a steep edge, as there is a chance that it will be corniced. A technique that will make this safer is to use a rope. One person ties on the end, and follows the edge; at least two others tie in a minimum of 10m away from the edge, and walk on a parallel route. This means that if the one closest to the drop should fall, they will be counterbalanced by the others.

Another problem in winter is estimating distance travelled, even when using timing and pacing. A climbing rope may well be to hand, and there is a very good chance that this will be 50m in length – simply use this, tied round you, as a distance guide. Very great accuracy can be gained, and this is useful when travelling on complicated terrain necessitating many bearings to be taken and legs to be followed.

Roped up near to a corrie rim when handrailing

NIGHT NAVIGATION

It is important to be able to confidently, and competently, navigate during the hours of darkness. This may be because your day is taking longer to complete than originally estimated, you have started early in the morning to maximize the available daylight hours, an injury in your party has necessitated you to move off the hill at night, plus a myriad of other reasons.

All the standard navigational skills should be well practised, with particular attention to skills such as aiming off, attack points, pacing and the like. Below are a few pointers that should help your night navigation session, in particular when working with a group.

■ Use a head torch that is suitable for the job. Styles with three or four LEDs are fine for reading in bed at night, but for navigation go for the brightest, allied with the longest battery life, that you can. A multiple LED configuration, along with a spot-light facility (often facilitated by swinging a lens that concentrates the beam into place), are ideal.

■ Be seen. Attach florescent strips to your rucksack, head torch battery pack and rear of your helmet. These strips can be bought on an adhesive reel from cycling shops.

■ Make sure that all of your group have their torches on when you are on the move. This not only stops people from tripping over when using their so-called 'night vision' (which rarely works), but it also makes your group-management easier. It is simplest to be able to glance over your shoulder and count lights than to wait for various figures to loom out of the darkness.

■ If you need to leave the group in one spot for a moment to check on a feature, make sure that at least two members keep their torches on and face the direction you are heading. This makes it far easier to locate them again. If you do not tell them to do this, they will all turn their torches off and sit down for a rest as soon as you leave, making finding your way back trickier.

■ If you are trying to make out a feature in the distance and your beam doesn't quite reach, have everyone point their torches at the same point. This increase in brightness may well do the trick.

■ Alternatively, get everyone to turn their torches off and wait a short while. You will regain around 90 per cent of your night vision within a minute or so, and previously invisible features will become easier to discern, in particular the outlines of ring contours and large land forms.

> **TIP**
> Cover both sides of your map with clear plastic, available from stationers. Cutting the map down to a usable size before doing this also helps. Commercially laminated maps are available, but the plastic is often so thick that they crack at the folds after relatively little use. Those covered with the thinner laminate from the stationers will last a lot longer.

River Crossing

It may happen that, having enjoyed a day out in the hills, you find your return route blocked by a river whose waters are swollen by a cloudburst in the hills many miles away. That river stands between you and your objective. It is tempting to include just one word in this chapter that sums up river crossing in its entirety – DON'T!

It cannot be emphasized enough that river crossing should be avoided as far as possible. If it means a huge detour to find a bridge, then that must be the first choice. If there is no chance of finding a dry crossing point, then sitting out the night should also be considered, allowing the river a chance to abate. River water levels subside almost as fast as they rise, so the wait might not be that long.

The following procedures are for when there is no other option, the river must be crossed, and the decision to do so has been taken.

■

CROSSING POINTS

Consideration should be given to the suitability of any given crossing point. There will be less flow above a junction, where the river splits into two, rather than below. Bends are best avoided, as the outside bank will tend to be undercut, and the water will be deeper on the outside than the inside. A widening is a better place to cross than a narrowing, as the same volume of water will be spread over a larger area.

Easier gradients are worth looking for, as there is a good chance that the water will be moving slower across flatter areas of terrain, perhaps splitting into a number of branches or 'braidings'. Areas of trees are best avoided,

as there is a chance of fallen branches lying unseen under the water, and to slip and be caught by one of these would certainly mean being dragged under. An area with small islands can help, as can individual boulders. These will often create a back-wash, creating an area of slack water which can be used as a rest point. Consider also the bed of the river. Sandy chippings are easier to maintain footing on than rounded greasy boulders.

The consequences of a slip must be considered. Would this result in being gently washed to the bank somewhat further downstream, or is there a waterfall, log jam or waterchute nearby downstream? And what is happening upstream? Is it still raining hard, and does this mean that there is a risk of half of your party crossing and the other half being stranded by the ever-rising water level?

EQUIPMENT CONSIDERATIONS

Two very useful pieces of kit are trekking poles and a rope. The use of both of these are discussed below, but if they are not to hand then this may make a difference to the crossing method that you choose.

PREPARATION

Rucksacks are surprisingly buoyant for a time, so they should be prepared by rolling up and securing the top enclosure. Waist belts should be left undone and shoulder straps kept loose – there is an argument for just having one shoulder strap on, but this may add to instability when in the water. Chest straps should not be used. Boots should be worn on all but the sandiest of river beds, but socks should be removed in order to keep the worst of the water off them and, more importantly, to provide a quick way of warming up feet when on the other side. It makes sense to wear the minimum of clothing, storing it safely in your rucksack, and if the weather is cold to then put on waterproofs, both top and bottom, do them up and make sure that pockets are fastened.

Remember to brief all party members as to what is needed from them, as communication is often difficult from one bank to another when water is travelling fast. An important point to remember when crossing a river, using any of the techniques described, is to lessen the chance of the water knocking you over by facing upstream where possible. If facing downstream, the force of the water would push at the back of the knees and cause them to bend, throwing you off balance.

One Person Crossing

Face upstream, holding the pole in front of you with one hand on top of its grip against your chest and your other hand well down the shaft, so that you create a strong triangle. Move each foot, one at a time, and resist the temptation to place it too close to the other. Then move the pole back to the apex of the triangle. Ensure that you have a secure footing and pole placement before moving on.

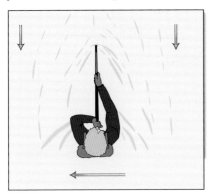

One person crossing with a trekking pole

> **TIP**
> Should you slip and be washed downstream, the best position to adopt is on your back, head upstream with your feet downstream, ready to fend off any obstructions. Make sure that your group understand this as well.

Two People Crossing

The most secure method is a variation of the single-person system.

■ One person takes up position as above, the second stands behind him, also facing upstream, securely taking hold low down of the shoulder straps of the first's rucksack and leaning in to give support. Progress is made by shuffling as above.

■ A second method, when no poles are available, is for both people to stand at right angles to the flow facing each other, taking a firm grasp of each other's shoulder straps. Feet are kept wide, allowing a four-point stable base to be maintained. It is important to ensure that both stay sideways on to the flow – if one turns to face into it, the other will have a good chance of his knees being bent forwards by the flow.

River flow

Holding on to waist

Two people crossing with trekking pole

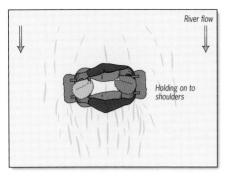

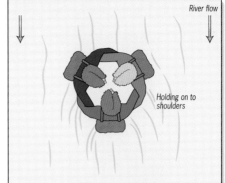

Two people crossing without a pole

Three People Crossing

Once again, the best method is to stand one behind another and shuffle across in a line, the front person using a pole for support.

■ The three should firmly grasp each other's shoulder straps, keep their legs wide, and shuffle across, the person on the downstream side coordinating movement and keeping the group in line.

■ If there are no poles to hand, a huddle can be made. The strongest person will be on the downstream side facing the flow. The second strongest will be positioned with his back to the direction of travel, the third will face across the river. It is unavoidable at this point having two people with their knees a little vulnerable to the flow, but good measured movements and support from each other will help counter this.

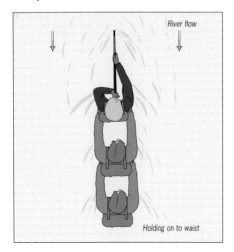

Three people crossing with a trekking pole

Three people crossing without a pole

Crossing with a Group

Depending upon your group's abilities, you may wish to cross as one large team, rather than split down into individual sections. There are two ways to organize this.

■ Firstly, the simplest method is, as before, to stand in a long braced line behind the leader with a pole. However, if more than four or five people are trying to cross, it becomes very difficult to coordinate the movements of each person. Inevitably the line will get out of true and present a larger surface area to the flow, with the subsequent chance of someone being knocked over.

■ A better method is to construct a group wedge formation. The strongest person goes at the front, with extra support from a pole if possible. Two people go behind him, then three, then another three, and so on, not having more than three abreast. The weaker members, in this instance, will go in the middle of the pack, receiving support from the others. Shoulder straps are grasped, and the movement of the group is once again controlled from the front.

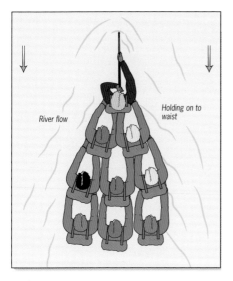

The group wedge

Roped Crossing

There are two types of roped crossing that we will look at here, the tensioned diagonal system and the 'V' system. Broadly speaking, we would suggest the tensioned diagonal for times when the water is flowing very slowly, thus the rope is being used more as an aid to balance than as security against being washed away, and the 'V' system in a situation where, if the person crossing stumbles, they will be washed downstream a distance and thus need a high degree of support and security from the rope.

Tensioned Diagonal

A secure stance is taken by a strong group member (often the leader), who sits down and braces themselves upstream of the intended crossing point, possibly assisted by others holding them in place around their waist. The next most experienced team member uses the rope for support while crossing in a pendulum-type manner. Once across, they take up position diagonally downstream, and then secure the rope above the water (shoulder height to those crossing), by bracing themselves and taking up a waist belay. The rope is then pulled as tight as possible between the two people.

Subsequent group members can then cross one at a time downstream of the rope, holding

on to it with both hands and using it for support. The last person across can then use the rope for support in a pendulum fashion.

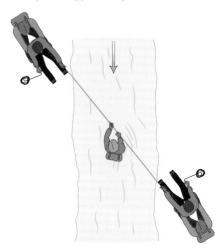

The tensioned diagonal, crossing from right to left

OBSERVATION

You should never secure the rope for a tensioned diagonal crossing around a boulder or tree. Should anyone lose contact with the rope and be heading downstream, the rope may be your only method of retrieving them. You will lose valuable rescue time undoing it from the fixed anchor and jeopardise the safety of the group member in doing so.

TIP

Ropes under tension are very hard to hold, so it is advisable to wear gloves in most cases.

The 'V' System

Remembering that ropes and water DO NOT mix, the 'V' system is the simplest technical rope system to learn and set up. The positioning of the crossing must be carefully considered, taking into account all of the above points, and ensuring that the bank on either side of the crossing point allows unrestricted movement up and down it for some distance. Remember also:

■ NEVER tie off the rope on either bank
■ NEVER field the rope from a sitting position

– it is important to be mobile at all times
■ NEVER try to pull a fallen person upstream – he will immediately be pulled underwater
■ NEVER tightly tie the person crossing into a loop. If a loop is used, there must be plenty of space for them to escape from it (see overleaf)
■ NEVER let the rope fall into the water
■ NEVER have any extra knots in the rope
■ NEVER wear a rucksack if using a tie-in loop, and avoid when using a waist-wrap.

TIP
Mark the centre of the rope with tape or proprietary rope-marking ink, to ease the process.

Holding a waist-wrap

The 'Z' grip. Gloves would normally be worn

Locate the centre of the rope. The first to cross – usually not the leader but a well-briefed and reliable person – takes a waist-wrap, holding on to the small loop with one hand or the other.

When the first and the last person are crossing using the waist wrap, they should always be on the outside angle of the rope, otherwise they will become entangled if they were to slip. For instance, if the group is crossing the river from right bank to left they will start by standing on the left hand side of the rope, with the loop from the wrap also being held in the left hand. The last person to cross will make sure that they are to the right of the rope, holding the loop in their right hand. Everyone else will be held in the 'V' shape from upstream, so it does not matter which hand they hold the loop in, and they are always clear of the rope should they slip.

■ One person takes station upstream of the crossing point, another positions himself downstream. The upstream person braces himself and provides support to the person crossing by means of the rope, holding it snugly with a 'Z' grip. The first may then cross, facing upstream. Should he lose his footing, the upstream belayer immediately runs downstream along the bank, the second belayer taking in the rope as he also moves downstream, and the fallen person is washed towards them. It is important that at no time is the rope held tightly on the upstream side, as anyone fallen could be pulled under.

■ Assuming the first person crosses successfully, he shuffles the centre of the rope back over to the first side. The rope is best held high above their heads when doing this, to keep it clear of the water. The downstream person on the original bank can throw any spare rope across, and the person on the far bank takes up position opposite the first belayer.

■ The second person to cross now takes a waist-wrap, and receives support from either bank as he crosses, one belayer giving support until he reaches the centre, then the belayer on the far bank takes over. Should this person fall in, the belayer giving support at that moment immediately runs downstream past him, pulling in on the rope as he goes, in order to bring him in to the side. The other belayer must allow sufficient slack on his rope to let this happen unhindered, but not to the extent that his rope either enters the water or is let go. Once the crossing has been successfully made, the centre is then pulled back across for subsequent group members.

■ When only one person is left on the original bank, he pulls the centre across, takes a waist-wrap, throws his end of the rope across to a person on the opposite bank who takes up position downstream as for the first crossing, and the final member joins the rest.

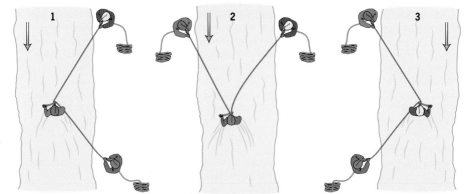

The 'V' system

TIP

To get the end of the rope across the river to the first person who has crossed, it is usually better to use a 'flick' rather than a throw. Take in almost all the rope until the person on the opposite bank can just pinch the very end between their fingers. They hold this up high and you sharply tug the rope towards you, which flicks the rope efficiently across the water.

OBSERVATION

Following the crossing, chances are that your group will be wet and cold, and possibly quite tired. You should take time to ensure that all members are fit before moving on: getting inside a group shelter and having a food and drink break is a very sensible idea, and it does wonders for morale.

Waist Wrap V Large Loop

We recommend the waist-wrap as the best attachment method for a roped river crossing. This gives a reasonably secure attachment for the person crossing, but also allows them to escape from the system should the rope become snagged upstream for some reason, as they can release the rope by letting go with their securing hand. The drawbacks of the waist-wrap are the difficulty for some people to hold on to a thin rope in cold conditions, and the consequences of them being washed downstream should they let go. However, extreme care should be exercised if deciding to use a large diameter loop as the attachment point for a roped crossing. If the person loses their footing and gets washed downstream and a trailing end of the rope becomes lodged below surface level under a boulder or around a branch, the person will be pulled under the water in an instant.

Security on Steep Ground

This chapter introduces the techniques necessary to provide a group with safe passage over an unexpected rocky hazard, either when in ascent or descent.

◼

GROUP MANAGEMENT ON AWKWARD TERRAIN

The simplest method of providing security to a group member on a simple step is by providing 'hands on' confidence, using their rucksack as a handle to get hold of as a back-up whilst they negotiate a step up or down. Note that this is only for the distance of a move or two, such as may be found on a boulder obstacle on a short section of an otherwise easy path, anything longer may require the use of a rope. Considerations are as follows:

◼ your safety is paramount. Thus, never be in a position where a slipping person could land on you or knock you over

- with few exceptions, you will not be able to 'catch' someone who slips. Your job is to prevent them from slipping by providing confidence and demonstrating moves, and by then fielding them from above or below by holding them in place or decelerating them if they do slip
- get the group to tighten their rucksacks and do up the chest straps. This makes them easier to use as a holding point
- the base of the shoulder strap and the haul loop between the shoulders are the best places to hold, although any area will do.
- base the decision as to where to operate from on the hazard. If you help from the bottom, will the person be out of reach for the last section of the move, thus vulnerable to a slip? Perhaps the better scenario here would be to assist from the top, so that they are only unprotected for the first short distance before you can reach their rucksack
- your positioning, whether you are assisting from above or below, needs to be stable and not in the way of the person's progress
- if pushing the base of the rucksack from underneath, don't push too hard or the person's balance will be compromised
- holding someone's foot onto a slippy hold helps, as does making an improvised hold by bending your leg and letting them stand on your knee
- if you are going to grab hold of anything other than the rucksack, such as clothing or even a push from the rear, make sure that you have told the person what you are going to do so that there is no misunderstanding.

Using a rucksack as a handle when negotiating a tricky step

OBSERVATION

Note that it is often the most confident person in your group that will be prone to having an accident, as they leap from rock to rock with scant consideration for the consequences. Conversely, the nervous person, even though they may take up more of your time and attention, will be moving slower, have a lower centre of gravity and will carefully consider each move before making it.

Techniques Prior to Rope Deployment: Steep-ground Management

It is worthwhile exploring various options when managing the security of people on steep ground prior to deploying a rope. The leader of a group should always have this at the forefront of his thinking when faced with a situation:

- consider an alternative route
- look for a line of least resistance through the steep ground
- check out the route prior to committing your group to it
- ensure that the leader can easily cross the ground themselves
- keep the least able group member near to the leader
- explain to the group what you are doing.
- eep close together
- brief the group on relevant terrain-crossing skills
- the leader can use his downhill arm to secure the weak group member by holding snugly on to his rucksack strap, thus providing support and reassurance
- should more than one group member require assistance, then only one person should be led at any one time, while the others wait in a safe area
- it is vital that the leader instructs the group members on how to balance and scramble on awkward terrain. Should the ground be steep, wet and grassy, then the leader must consider an alternative route as this sort of terrain is extremely hazardous.

For all mountain leadership ropework, an excellent method of carrying the rope is inside a stuff sack. The rope can be piled in with a short tail left protruding. Should the rope be needed, pulling on the tail will give enough rope to use and will be more efficient than coiling or flaking it.

CONFIDENCE ROPING

What is Confidence Roping ?

A method used to secure a nervous, tired or injured person while descending, ascending or traversing a short section of ground. This type of roping is unplanned and is an emergency procedure. When a rope is deployed a leader must work very fast, and only experience, skill and knowledge can ensure a smooth transaction of rope management and group safety.

Where Would I use it ?

It can be used on any type of terrain, from scree slopes to short sections of snowy ground. There are two very important considerations when confidence roping. Firstly, the leader must be confident in his ability to safely cross the terrain. Secondly, as confidence roping only looks after one party member at a time, the rest of the group must also be completely happy and able to continue unaided. It must be emphasized that any danger sensed by the person being roped – such as the feeling of walking on angled wet grass and the assumption that a slip will turn into a catastrophic fall – should be imaginary. If there is a real danger to the leader or a group member, different tactics or route choice should be used.

Firstly, provide reassurance to the person. Just being close to them will help. Position yourself on their upslope side and hold on to their rucksack shoulder strap, low down just above where it reaches the main compartment. Having their shoulder straps snug and hip belt and chest straps done up helps with keeping the rucksack stable and more controllable.

With your arm slightly bent, walk along with them, holding their weight slightly via the shoulder strap. This makes them feel that they are less likely to slip or fall outwards, speeds them up and helps you cross that particular section of ground. If this technique is not suitable, or the terrain continues for some distance, deploying the rope may be a better option.

Method

- The rope can be readied before it is needed. Feed it into the top of a rucksack, ideally inside a stuff bag, with a few inches of the rope tail protruding. To deploy the rope, pull on the tail end. You will require around 3m.
- With their rucksack hip belt undone, tie the end around the person's waist. This should be secure but not too tight, as the knot will have to move from side to side of the person as you zigzag. Do up their hip belt underneath the rope to prevent it sliding down.
- As close to the person as appropriate, between a few centimetres to a metre, grasp the rope with your palm down and the rope to the person emerging from the little-finger side of your hand. Bend your hand straight, gripping the rope with two 90 degree bends in it. This gives you a firm grip (far stronger than holding it straight through your hand with the load coming out by your thumb). This is a 'Z' grip (see page 19 for a photo).
- Should there be any excess rope between hand and rucksack, some butterfly coils can be positioned through the rucksack waist belt.
- The arm holding the rope is positioned at a right angle with the elbow bent, so it can now act as a shock-loading mechanism, as it moves forwards and backwards maintaining tension.
- The body position of the leader is important, leaning slightly into the slope to counter any outwards pull, using the edges of the boots to create extra purchase on slippery ground.
- To aid grip, tie a small 'disappearing' knot in the rope. This gives it more bulk, making it easier to hold when gripped just under the knot, with the rope to the person emerging from the little finger side of your hand (see photo). This knot is solid when held below, but when pulled from above the knot, it undoes itself, useful if more rope needs quickly paying out. NEVER PLACE YOUR HAND THROUGH A LOOP ON THE ROPE. If you do, there is a chance of being pulled over by the person you are safeguarding.

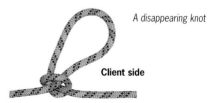

A disappearing knot

Client side

Pulling the rope from the rucksack

Method: Moving Together

Once you decide on which direction you wish to travel, you need to think about the direction of pull from the knot tying off at the client.

- The knot tying off the client should always be on the uphill side of the client. This is important to assist with the tensioning of the rope between client and leader.
- To change direction the leader gives the client clear instruction to stop, the leader swaps hands and then turns into the new position.
- The client now turns into the new position, facing uphill when making a turn, and either you or he slides his waist-loop knot round to the uphill side.
- This process should be repeated when changing direction; with practice this technique is very quick to become slick.
- The uphill arm of the client is often best positioned in front of the rope to the leader, allowing him to use his arm to support himself, particularly if he should slip or stumble.

Winter Considerations

In winter the transfer of hands requires some care as you will have your ice axe positioned in your uphill hand. To change direction and transfer smoothly, both leader and client stop.

Moving when confidence roping

23

Security on Steep Ground

This technique is for one person at a time. The rest of the group must be happy traversing the terrain and you need to be sure that they will be OK on that terrain. If you ask a group if they are OK, they will invariably say 'yes', even if they feel worried and vulnerable, often so that they do not lose face in front of other group members. Thus, **you** must decide if they are OK, not them. Obviously, if they say 'no' then that clearly indicates that you are on the wrong terrain, but your observation of them – speed, posture, if they have stopped chatting, using hands etc. – should influence your final decision about their safety.

1 The leader must be uphill of the person at all times.
2 It is important that the waist tie is snug so that the loop cannot slip down over the client's hips, and he feels as though he is receiving support.
3 The leader must never take hand coils.
4 If the client slips, the leader must be able to hold him without compromising his own balance and safety.

The leader tells the client to take a good firm stance. Then, while maintaining tension on the rope, he places his ice axe under the arm holding the rope, changes direction by turning to face downhill, then retrieves the axe from under what is now the uphill arm with the uphill hand. This transfer is very quick when practised.

The client now turns around facing up-slope, using the ice axe for support, and slides the waist loop knot round to the new uphill position.

Another method on easy terrain is to place your ice axe into the snow, then transfer as for summer and pick up the axe with the uphill arm.

OBSERVATIONS
1 While managing a party on steep ground the leader should coach the correct methods for use of feet and balance (and ice axe if appropriate), and not march along pulling the person with him. Reassurance will go a long way in growing someone's confidence.
2 When managing a party on steep icy slopes or steep wet-grass terrain, always consider the consequences should someone slip: are there rocks at the bottom, are there hidden outcrops, how far will someone travel before stopping?
3 If the leader is in any doubt as to the safety of the party, then he should look for an alternative descent or ascent. Good judgement is based on experience.

This is a section dedicated to the solving of problems that may occur when crossing mountainous terrain with a group of friends or clients. The classic example is, when descending, finding your way blocked by a very short but greasy slab of rock, with an unpleasant landing at the bottom. Rather than spend a lot of time in re-ascent or searching for a way through, you may elect to lower your group with the security of a rope, then follow by abseil. Another reason may be finding your way barred by a short section of steep ground while ascending, with little option but to cross it.

It must be said that the descent scenario is the more likely, as this could well be encountered on a concave section of slope, at the end of the day when the group is tired, the light is fading and the possibility of motivating your group to go uphill again almost non-existent. In ascent, however, you are far more likely to see the steeper section from a distance, and be able to make an alternative route choice.

Even when leading groups in the hills under normal summer conditions, carrying a rope is a very sensible thing to do. For the sake of most trips, a 30m length of 9mm or similar diameter dynamic rope is ideal. Longer than 30m adds to the overall weight and shorter makes it impractical for many tasks. Similarly, if it is thicker it just adds more weight, if it is much thinner, say around 8mm, it becomes very hard to handle effectively when under load. It is important, though, to treat the rope as part of the first-aid kit – that is, there is no intention of deploying it. If you are intending to use the rope that will mean that you are aware of the hazards that exist on your route and have either made a bad choice for the day, or are entering scrambling terrain which is another discipline entirely.

Finally, remember that the safety of your group is paramount. Never lower your group in darkness when you are not sure if they will reach safety, always be 100 per cent happy about the security of your anchors, and, if your abilities and the situation dictates, be prepared to sit out the night.

ABC

An essential fundamental of any belay system is the ABC – anchor, belayer, climber. It is vital that they are all in a straight line, both vertically and horizontally, and that the rope to the belayer

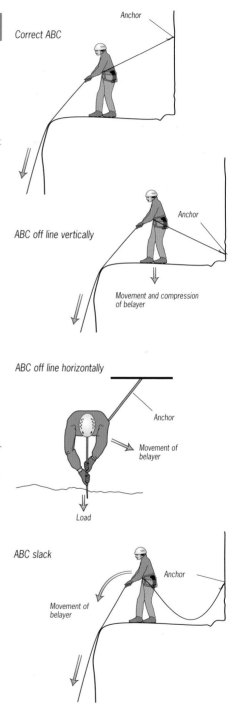

Correct ABC

ABC off line vertically

Anchor

Movement and compression of belayer

ABC off line horizontally

Anchor

Movement of belayer

Load

ABC slack

Anchor

Movement of belayer

from the anchor is tight. If one or more of these criteria are not in place, either the belayer or the climber, and possibly both, could be injured in the event of a fall. You should always consider the ABC, whether rigging the simplest of systems using the rope alone, through to setting up a technical, multi-anchor rig. The diagrams opposite clarify the ABC scenarios.

Anchors

It goes without saying that the security of your anchors must be beyond question. Having selected a likely-looking anchor, maybe a large boulder, and after considering such factors as direction of pull and a suitable stance, start with a visual inspection. Is it part of the mountain-side, or is it simply perched on other rock or turf? Progress then to tapping the boulder, and then to kicking it. If you do this with one hand on the rock, you will be able to feel any vibration and movement transmitted through it. Try to move the boulder with a rocking action.

When testing an anchor, ensure that you are trying to move it in the direction of loading – for instance, it is useless kicking into the hillside if the boulder is loose in an outward direction. Always bear in mind your own safety when checking an anchor, as standing directly below a large loose block and giving it a wobble is a recipe for disaster.

OBSERVATION

Deciding to use an anchor for a direct belay is a huge judgement call, as if by any chance you had missed that the anchor would fail under load, and it does so, the result would be catastrophic. For this reason we highly recommend that you become totally confident with your ability to choose solid anchors to be used indirectly, before progressing to using direct anchors. Remember that every technique, or variation of, that we show can be used with an indirect anchor, and the safety margins are consequently that much higher.

Group Safety

Although your attention will be taken up with organizing the lower or scramble, do not neglect your group. As soon as the rope is deployed, your group will be feeling somewhat uneasy, so reassurance is important. Make sure that people are positioned in an area that is safe

for them to be in, and get them to sit down. Stopping your group halfway up a steep, black, dripping slab is not the mark of a good and attentive leader. Consider also members' safety when you or others are overhead. Having them huddled at the bottom of a gully, at the top of which you are trying to shift a 7-tonne granite boulder, is completely unacceptable.

Attaching to an Anchor

There are many ways to attach yourself to an anchor point; the most relevant are given below. Overhand knots are extremely useful and quite acceptable; the bowline may also be considered for some applications.

If using a thread (such as a tree or two boulders securely butted together):

- pass the end of the rope through and tie a re-threaded overhand knot (in a similar fashion to the re-threaded figure of eight). Then tie an overhand knot further down the rope to create a loop to step into
- if tied on to the end of the rope, a bight can be passed through the thread and back to the waist tie-in loop, and then connected with an overhand knot or figure of eight on the bight.

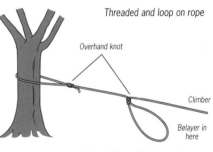

Threaded and loop on rope

Overhand knot

Climber

Belayer in here

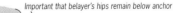

Important that belayer's hips remain below anchor

Bight of rope to waist loop using figure of eight knot

Rope to climber

Threaded bight to waist tie-in

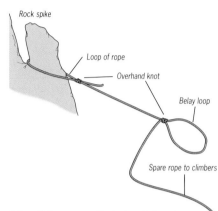

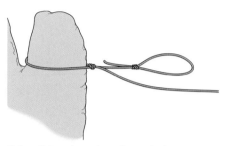

Spike with loop dropped over from waist tie

Spike with loop over and belay loop further down

If Using a Spike:

■ if not tied on to the rope, a large loop can be tied in the end of the rope using an overhand knot on the bight, it then being placed over the spike. A second overhand knot can then be tied further down the rope to create a loop to step into.

■ if attached round the waist, either loop the rope around the spike and attach it to yourself by using an overhand knot or figure of eight on the bight, or tie a loop in the rope and drop it over the rock.

If using a system that has a loop around a spike or thread and another for you to step in to, it can be tricky to end up where you intended to after it

The overhand knot adjustment method

has been tied. To make this easier, attach yourself with a little extra slack in the rope. This can be pulled in and tied in an overhand knot (ensuring at least 30cm of end) between yourself and the anchor, allowing for perfect length each time.

THE OPEN LOOP SYSTEM

This is the simplest, quickest to set up and easiest to adjust of all the methods described. It is, quite simply, a large loop of rope (initially tied to be on the generous side, as this aides final adjustment), that is dropped over a spike or used as a thread, secured with an overhand knot (it is ESSENTIAL that a figure of eight is NOT used here, as it could unroll and fail). The belayer then sits inside the loop (NEVER stand with this system), the loop is tightened by moving the overhand knot towards you which is then pulled snug itself.

A System for Both Spikes and Threads

Known as the 'Spider knot', this system is extremely quick and efficient if practised. Loop the rope around the spike (or through the thread), and grasp the two lengths at the point from which you wish to belay. Fold the ropes back on themselves, so that you are now holding four pieces of rope. Tie an overhand knot in them to create a loop to belay from. Step into it, and, with a little practise, you will be able to tie it the right size first time. You have now created both an anchor attachment and belay point by tying just one overhand knot.

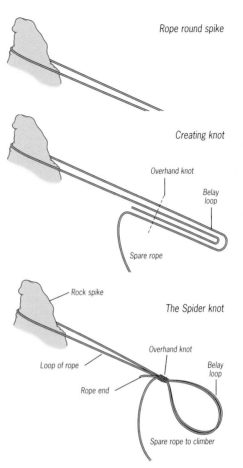

The open loop system

Rope round spike

Creating knot

Overhand knot

Belay loop

Spare rope

Rock spike

The Spider knot

Overhand knot

Loop of rope

Belay loop

Rope end

Spare rope to climber

OBSERVATIONS

Although there are many variables, our suggestion is to become confident with the open loop system, as well as the method of tying the end of the rope to the anchor and then stepping into a loop further down the rope. These two will cover just about every belaying situation you are likely to come across in the mountains. The former is simple and quick to arrange, the advantage of the latter is that it uses less rope should the anchor be some distance away.

There are obviously many different possible styles of belaying. However, to avoid confusion, stick with the two simplest. These are the open loop system, and the system where you tie the end around the anchor and then make a second loop to step in to. If you know these you will most likely be able to tie yourself to any anchor. However, there are disadvantages to each:

• the open loop system uses up a lot more rope than the single strand system if the anchor is a long way back from the stance
• the single strand system will have a lot more stretch in it when some distance from the anchor, so adjusting it correctly is important.

The 'Punter' knot

This can be tied very quickly on to a rope and used in either ascent or descent. Its advantage is that it can be adjusted to fit a variety of waist sizes very quickly, without the need to re-tie the knot for each person. It should be tied first with a single figure of eight knot, then finished with half a triple fisherman's knot

(the same as a double but with one more wrap around the rope), leaving 15cm (6in) of tail. The fisherman's is mobile and will slide along the rope, and the figure of eight is there as a 'stopper' knot, so that the wearer will not be crushed if they fall and the knot tightens around them.

Place the loop around the person and slide the fisherman's along. The figure of eight should be adjusted to be at a point where the rope is very snug around them but any additional loading, such as if they slip, will mean the figure of eight will stop the fisherman's tightening around them further.

You may find that the figure of eight has to be adjusted slightly for each person if they are of varying waist sizes. If you are going to be using this technique in ascent, show the group how to adjust the knot before you start up.

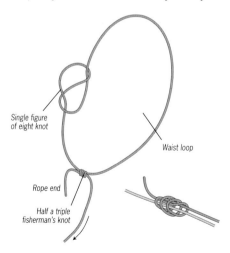

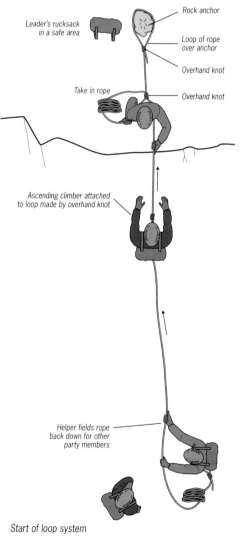

Security on Steep Ground

Ascent of a Rock Step with a Group in Windy Conditions

The simplest way to solve this, once a stance has been taken, is to throw down the end of the rope with a loop tied in it, either an overhand knot on the bight, or a 'punter' knot (see diagram below). The problem with this, is the difficulty in high winds of delivering the the rope to where it needs to go. There may also be another problem in that the knotted end of the rope could jam out of reach in an awkward position. The following is a way of organizing the ropework in a manner that should help negate nearly all problems.

■ Organize your group in an area away from any danger of falling debris.

■ Tie the rope around the waist of a reliable person, ensure that it is flaked out tidily on the ground, and either tuck the other end through your rucksack waist belt, or tie it round you.

■ Scramble up a short distance to a suitable ledge or stance and anchor yourself.

■ Identify an area near to you that you consider completely safe for your group to be on when they untie from the rope, and mark it with your rucksack. Pull up all of the slack rope between yourself and the person tied on.

■ Allowing enough rope for people to reach the safe area, tie an overhand knot in the rope to create a loop. This is then pulled back down by the person at the bottom. Keep the rope

high and off the rock at this stage, to stop any chance of it snagging.

■ A group member steps into the loop, and it is adjusted by the helper.

■ Using a waist belay (or a direct belay in some circumstances), bring the climber up to you and across to the safe area. Ensure that he is not, at any time, unwrapping himself from the belay system, and that he will not end up leading on steep ground behind you.

Leader's rucksack in a safe area

Rock anchor

Loop of rope over anchor

Overhand knot

Take in rope

Overhand knot

Ascending climber attached to loop made by overhand knot

Single figure of eight knot

Waist loop

Rope end

Half a triple fisherman's knot

The 'Punter knot'

Helper fields rope back down for other party members

Start of loop system

- Get him to sit down and slip off the loop. This is then pulled back down by the helper, and another group member placed into it.
- Continue like this until all members but one are up, and finally bring up the last person, the helper, who is already attached.

OBSERVATION

It may be appropriate, in some situations, to adopt a braced sitting position with your heels dug in or feet against a rock and the rope low down around your back, when safeguarding a group member, but without being attached to an anchor. However, there must be careful consideration as to whether this technique is suitable in each individual case. For instance, it may be fine to use the rope with this style of belaying when helping the group down a short sloping grassy step where there is no real chance of a fall, but it would be entirely inappropriate to perform the same technique at the top of a steep rock step where the rope will likely be fully loaded for some of the time, with the consequences of a slip being dire. Only experience and careful consideration of each situation will tell you whether the technique can be employed or not, and if there is any doubt whatsoever, always go for an anchor system instead.

Down-climbing

This will be by far the commonest way of safeguarding your group in descent over an awkward step. If it is too far for them to safely climb down unassisted, and this may only be one or two moves in length, then you should deploy the rope to avoid any mishaps. The set-up at the top of the step would be the same as usual, obviously looking after your own security. Once you have your person attached to the rope, take it in nice and snug and, as they start to climb down the section, gently feed the rope out to them. Don't pay it out but rather let them drag it from you, so that you are holding around 50 per cent of their body weight. This makes them feel more secure and also reduces the chance of them slipping any distance if they lose their footing. You could have both of your hands on the dead rope to aid control, and let the rope through with a gentle shuffling motion.

If the ground to be descended is not climbable, perhaps a slimy slab set back some

way from vertical, you could use the same method of belaying but the person would be 'down-slithering'! Sitting down, or better still sideways on one of their hips, you pay the rope out and gravity and slippery moss does the rest! This is a very effective way of descending, but make sure that it is not too steep and they will never have all of their weight hanging on the rope, as this would be very uncomfortable.

Lowering

This is a means of getting your group down an overhanging or extremely steep step. However, it should only be considered as a last resort, as it takes time to construct properly, uses a lot of rope and can be difficult to control.

It will be best carried out as a direct belay, but an indirect belay will be far more common. The diagrams demonstrate both types.

In an indirect scenario, you will be pulled forward by the weight of the person being lowered as well as back against the anchor. Thus, wearing a rucksack will protect your kidneys and having some extra padding, such as a rucksack insert or spare clothing, pushed into the front of your tie-in loop will save your abdomen from bruising. ABC is critical, so make sure that you are tight on the anchor before starting. Gloves and long sleeves are essential, and you can have both hands on the dead rope to make controlling it easier.

Ideally, you will be belaying a little higher than the edge over which your person is descending, which means that the system can be loaded before they get to the steep section. Encourage them to hold on to the knot in front of them and to adopt an abseil-type position so that you have full control. Let the rope through slowly, ensuring that you do not speed up or control will be lost, and once they are at the bottom have the person walk back into your view and onto a safe area before releasing them.

To use a direct belay, such as a boulder as shown in the diagram, a waist belay can still be taken to help rope control. Brace yourself with one foot forward and lean back slightly to avoid being pulled over. If the person being lowered is a lot heavier than yourself, you may need to tie on to an anchor to avoid being pulled over.

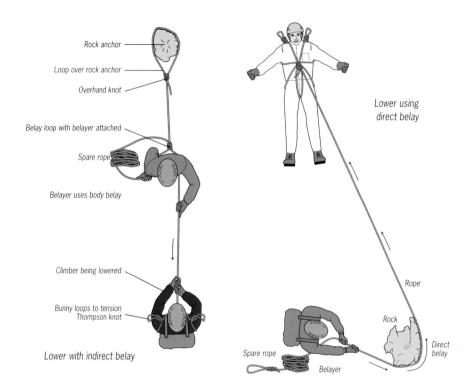

Rock anchor

Loop over rock anchor

Overhand knot

Belay loop with belayer attached

Spare rope

Belayer uses body belay

Climber being lowered

Bunny loops to tension
Thompson knot

Lower with indirect belay

Lower using
direct belay

Rope

Rock

Direct
belay

Spare rope

Belayer

THOMPSON KNOT

If you have exhausted all the alternatives (which would be a hard thing to do in most cases), this is the standard knot for lowering, but it should NEVER be used for climbing, either up or down, as the leg loops drop down and catch behind the knees. Ensure that the knot is adjusted to be by the sternum for each person, and the rope to the lowering system is coming out of the top of the knot. To avoid having to re-tie the knot for each person, make the first one over-generous and take up the slack by tying 'bunny's ears' at the shoulders. Ensure that they are tied just in front of the shoulder, where the person lowered can reach to untie them again. Having the person bend forward and holding the knot up by their sternum as you tie the bunny's ears helps to keep the whole system snug, which it should be once they straighten up again.

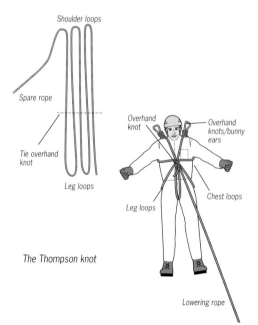

Shoulder loops

Spare rope

Tie overhand
knot

Leg loops

Overhand
knot

Overhand
knots/bunny
ears

Chest loops

Leg loops

Lowering rope

The Thompson knot

OBSERVATION

There are two options for getting your group down steep ground; down-climbing or using a lower with a Thompson knot. A Thompson knot is a useful technique to have in your 'tool box', but at least 95 per cent of situations can be solved with down-climbing or down-slithering and these should be considered first. Once you decide to use a Thompson knot, time disappears rapidly, briefings take longer and the resultant belay method is likely to be quite painful and hard to control.

TIPS

The knot uses a lot of rope so ensure that you have enough for the procedure by tying a Thompson knot and then dropping the other end of the rope, the one that you will anchor with, over the edge. Providing there is plenty touching the ground to allow you to tie on to the anchor, you know that there is enough rope.

When safeguarding a descent, try to have both hands on the dead rope. Cross your free hand over the rope running to the person being lowered or down-climbing and hold the rope just below the main controlling hand.

Controlling a lower with both hands on the dead rope

OBSERVATION

Note the difference between direct and indirect belays, particularly when using them in a mountain leadership situation with the rope alone. With a direct belay the anchor takes 100 per cent of the load. Thus, if there is a problem with the anchor, you are likely to find out with consequential serious injury. Because you are part of the system in an indirect belay, if an anchor is not 100 per cent sound (which it should be), and the system is loaded, as you take some of the load from the anchor via the waist belay it is protected from failure.

This is not a reason to use less-than-perfect anchors when deploying an indirect belay system, but shows why one may be chosen over the other. You must judge the strength of any anchor, to be beyond question.

ABSEILING

Abseiling, in this situation, is ONLY for the leader. Other members of your group should down-climb or be lowered over the obstruction, then you follow by abseil descent.

Once you have deployed the rope, there are a number of options open to you. The simplest is to simply grasp the rope, with a twist on the downslope arm, and slide down to your group. Gloves with a good grip are obviously important, and it is not appropriate for steep terrain. However, for a quick descent of moderate ground it is totally appropriate.

For many years, the 'classic' abseil has been the standard way of approaching a descent. However, another method has recently been introduced that is more user-friendly, being less painful, easier to control and having less chance of being fallen out of. Introduced as the South African abseil, it can now be referred to as the 'new classic', as it is surely destined to become.

The only disadvantage is that it requires the rope to be doubled, whereas the older version can be performed on a single thickness. However, as abseiling on a single thickness means that you will be abandoning the rope, the chances of needing to abseil like this are hopefully few and far between.

The Classic Abseil

■ Stand over the ropes. Assuming a right-handed person, pick the ropes up, bring them across your chest from right hip to left shoulder, pass them behind your neck (make sure your collar is up), down under your right arm and into your hand. You may wish to take a wrap around this arm to help control.

Taking an arm wrap for descending the rope

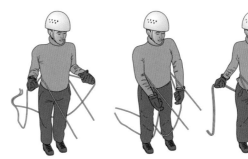

Classic abseil   *The 'New classic' or 'South African' abseil*

■ The other hand holds the ropes where they emerge at crotch level, and it is essential that you do not let go as you could flick upside down, due to the low attachment point.
■ Descent, along with the understandable pain that a high percentage of users feel, is eased if you adopt a slightly sideways posture.

The New Classic
■ Stand between the ropes and pick them up.
■ Cross them over behind your back and bring your hands forward.
■ You now have a loop of rope on either side of you so step one foot over each and grasp the ropes together behind your legs.
■ Bring them up together to be held, palm up, in the right hand if you are right-handed, and in the left hand if you are not.
■ Your other hand can be used for balance but does not need to be used for control, unless you really want to.

This method creates a good deal of support for you, and can be used with a rucksack on, with the ropes being crossed over behind it, which makes it very comfortable. Try to keep a stable position while descending, sitting back out from the rock.

Deploying and Retrieving the Abseil Rope
Throw the rope overhand down the step, after it has been flaked backwards and forwards and divided into two sections for throwing, using the end section first. In windy weather, aim upwind of the target area to allow for drift.

It is important to retrieve the rope after you have used it, and it may take some time. If the back of your anchor is not perfect, pad it with moss, sticks and leaves so that the rope runs easily and will not jam. If there is a chance of the rope catching, you may need to cut off an appropriate length (if you don't have a knife, pounding it with a rock will work). Thread this around the

anchor, tying it with a double fisherman's knot. Thread your abseil rope through this, thus avoiding any chance of jamming. Be aware that moving rope-upon-rope creates a lot of heat, and melts easily, but as the two sections of rope will only be moving once you retrieve the main rope, this will not be a concern.

TIP
As long as both sides of the rope reach the ground, the middle does not need to be at the anchor. This will give you less to pull through when retrieving it.

OBSERVATIONS
You may need a group member to help you pull on the rope to retrieve it. In addition, having another person flick the other end of the rope in a series of arcs (a bit like a sine-wave) will also help reduce friction. Altering your position, perhaps standing far out from the base of the descent or off to one side, may also help.

Within mountaineering, anything called 'classic' hurts! A 'classic' abseil hurts, a 'classic' belay hurts, and a 'classic' route will be a dank, dripping-green terrifying chimney with no runners, first climbed in the 1800s.

TIP
A good way to carry your leadership rope, say 30 metres of 9mm diameter, is to feed it into an old stuff sack (keep 15cm (6in) of end sticking out for convenience). Add to this bag a 16ft (240cm) sling, an HMS screwgate and a pair of gloves (glazier's gloves, the type with a criss-cross sticky palm, are excellent), and you have a kit to deal with the majority of problems that require a rope to solve them. In a leadership situation the rope is classed as part of the first aid kit, and so it should be carried but hopefully never used.

Emergency Evacuation

WHAT IS EMERGENCY EVACUATION?

Emergency evacuation is exactly as it sounds – the removal of a casualty in order to position him in a safer place where first aid can be carried out, or a short-distance carry to move him to an area that is more suitable for awaiting the arrival of a rescue team.

It must be emphasised that any improvised carry in the mountains can only be over a short distance, often no more than a couple of hundred metres, and the method of carry will be dictated by:
- the equipment available
- the manpower available
- the nature of the casualty's injuries
- the nature of the terrain to be crossed
- any extreme weather conditions.

It is important to consider each of these points in turn in a realistic manner when practising, when training mountain leaders and when at a real incident.

OBSERVATIONS

Many people carry trekking poles these days, and they have many benefits when travelling in the mountains. However, consideration should be made as to when they become a hazard, and at the following times they should be packed away or held with the wrist loops removed.

1 When acting as a leader on steeper terrain, they should be packed away. Neither you nor your group would benefit if you slipped, and you need to be ready to help a group member should they need assistance.

2 When crossing a boulder field, wrist loop should be removed to prevent injury.

3 When crossing a river, wrist loops should be off.

4 When traversing a narrow path, wrist loops should again be removed. It is possible to catch a trekking pole between your legs and trip.

5 In winter, care should be taken that the stability offered by using poles does not get you on to ground where an ice axe should be deployed instead.

Equipment Available

With very few exceptions, you will not be taking to the hills with a purpose-designed mountain-rescue stretcher. You will also very rarely be out on the hills with a couple of 2.5m lengths of timber, much beloved of leader-training courses! Granted, you may be in a forested area that has the potential to provide poles suitable for improvised carry construction, but think back to when you were last in that situation.

However, you may well have some trekking poles available, which are rather flexible when used on their own but can be lashed together with tape from your first-aid kit to provide a much stronger and stiffer implement. You should also have with you a group shelter, a couple of heavy-duty plastic bivi bags within the group, a first-aid kit, probably a rope and a mobile phone. As well as this, you will have additional seasonal kit, such as spare clothing, ice axes, and so on.

The Casualty's Injuries

This is the most important factor determining if, how, and how far, a casualty is moved. Back and neck injuries are obviously a far more serious problem than a broken wrist.

The Nature of the Terrain

This must be considered, as it is counter-productive to organize a side-by-side carry and then to be faced with a steep narrow path where it is only possible to proceed in single file. Conversely, to arrange a weird and wonderful rope-stretcher system requiring many people to carry it, when the ground underfoot is flat hard snow, is somewhat more tiresome than simply putting the casualty on a bivi bag and dragging him over the ground, injuries permitting.

Never underestimate the effort it takes to move a person from one place to the next. This will only ever be over a short distance and consideration must be given to the fitness and well-being of both yourself and the rest of your party when organizing a carry – you are no good to the casualty if you exhaust yourself. Similarly, watch out for your back when lifting; lift by pushing up with the legs and not by straightening your back when holding a weight.

EVACUATION TECHNIQUES

From the many possible variations, the following is a selection of the most practical evacuation techniques. The skill here, as in so many things, is having a good working knowledge of three or four possibilities, and being able to recognize where each should be deployed. It goes without saying that professional training in first-aid techniques is essential, and should be considered by any walker or mountaineer.

Thought should be given to the nature of the injuries before deciding on the final method of evacuation, and the process of getting the casualty onto the carry. For instance, someone with a lower-leg injury may well be perfectly capable of assisting by lifting his weight with his arms. Alternatively, two people clasping hands (making an interlocking hook with your fingers) and 'scooping' the casualty up between them is very quick and effective over a short distance. The following assumes that simply picking up the casualty and progressing with him on a simple hand carry is not an option.

Scenario: the casualty has been injured in an area threatened by stone-fall. You must move him a short distance for his and the rest of the group's safety.

Method 1

Place the casualty on a bivi bag or some other smooth material. Drag them! This is surprisingly effective on grass or heather, although you should watch out for hidden boulders. Care should be taken on snow that an easy drag does not become a terrifying toboggan ride as the slope steepens!

Method 2

Place the casualty lengthways on a plastic bivi bag. The object is now to roll in the sides of the bag to hip-width to provide purchase for carrying. This can be done by rolling the edges in around trekking poles, pieces of heather, or indeed anything that will give the plastic a little bulk and make either side's rolled section bulkier and thus the carrying easier. A rope, run up and down each side makes for a comfortable carry.

We thoroughly recommend this method.

Bivi-roll carry

OBSERVATION

Method 2 is far more practical than the often-taught practice of placing stones at various points along the bivi bag and securing a rope or slings around these to provide a handle system. The size of the bag, thus the carrying surface, is much reduced.

TIP

A silver foil 'space' blanket, either pre-taped into place on a plastic bivi-bag or deployed as needed, makes a very efficient 'thermal wrap' system for keeping the casualty warm. Place an opened-out bivi bag on the ground, then a layer of fleeces under where the casualty will lay. The silver blanket goes on top of this, preferably taped to another plastic bivi bag. Once the casualty is on the silver blanket and adjoining bivi bag, wrap it round them and secure it in place with the tape from your first-aid kit. Make sure that you are not inhibiting their airway. The final bivi bag, the one on the ground, can then be used as a carry system if needed. They will then stay warm for the evacuation or whilst help is summoned.

Method 3

Tape together three or more trekking poles to strengthen them. Two group members of similar height stand side by side wearing rucksacks, and the poles are pushed through the shoulder-strap lower attachment point. The poles are padded to make a seat, and the casualty is helped on to this. He is supported by placing an arm around the back of each of the carriers, who in turn hold on to the casualty in a similar manner.

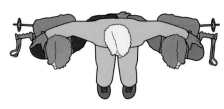

Pole/sack carry

Method 4

If a rope is carried, it can be organized in tied-off coils, and half of the coils given to two group members of similar height. Standing side by side, they place the coils over their outside shoulders with the tied-off section at the lowest point between them. The casualty can sit on this, and be supported in a way similar to that described in Method 3 opposite. The rope coils should be padded at the relevant points for the casualty, and for the carriers if they are to travel any distance.

It is also possible to arrange a one-person split rope carry, although padding becomes a priority for the casualty! Separate the coils so that you have half in each hand. The casualty steps into this and you can then lift him wearing the rope like a rucksack. The casualty is easier

to pick up if he can be positioned on a suitable boulder at the right height, and the rope should be padded at the relevant points – the casualty will tell you where these are!

Method 5

A piggy-back is hard to do for any distance, but it can be improved with the use of a rucksack. Pack the lower half of the rucksack with firm objects and empty the lid. The casualty can now be picked up (with help from a suitable boulder and other group members) and end up sitting on the packing. This acts like a seat and gives a generally very comfortable carry for both parties. The only drawback is that they are quite high, which can be unnerving on difficult ground. However, this is a very good carry requiring the minimum of equipment and is to be recommended.

Method 6

This method requires three carriers and the use of trekking poles or similar, but is the comfiest for both the casualty (injuries permitting) and the carriers. We recommend this method for slightly longer-distance carries on good terrain.

Tape trekking poles together to make two strong carrying poles. Using a spare fleece or waterproof jacket, pull the arms through to

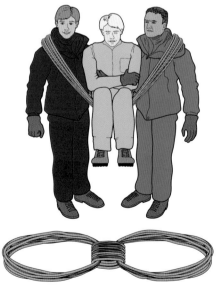

Two-person split rope carry

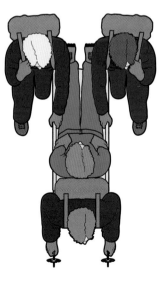

Three person pole carry

OBSERVATIONS

Designate jobs for the rest of the group. There will most likely be kit to carry, at least the casualty's, and having a person or two out in front of the carry party making route choice decisions will save a lot of detouring and falling down pot-holes and the like.

Even with a minor injury, a child is likely to be more distressed than an adult with a similar injury. However, if the nature of the injury allows a carry to take place, and having taken into account all first-aid considerations, evacuation is often easier due to the weight difference. It may be possible to evacuate a light person a considerable distance.

All of the other methods mentioned are valid, as long as you do not expect other children to be part of the carrying operation. The following may also be considered: a one-person split rope carry, as detailed above, will often be the quickest and simplest to arrange, obviously well padded. In some cases, a small child can be carried by a method similar to the above, but by using a rucksack. With the sack off, he steps in with a leg through each of the shoulder straps. The rucksack is then put on as normal.

the inside, do up the zip, and pass the poles through the arms so that they are running down the inside of the garment. All three carriers wear rucksacks. Insert two pole ends into the lower rucksack strap attachment points of one carrier from the back. This person will be at the front of the carry. One trekking pole then goes into the inside shoulder strap of each of the two rear carriers. The casualty can then sit on the jacket, his back being supported by the lead carrier.

The Rope Stretcher

It is quite possible, as long as there is a rope in the party, to construct a stretcher that is capable of comfortably supporting a casualty. A rope stretcher, though, has a number of drawbacks that may limit its use, not least that it is time consuming to make, and requires a lot of people to carry it even a short distance. However, it is useful to know how to construct one, and, of the various methods possible, we will concentrate on a version that uses clove hitches. A flat area of ground will help in its construction.

■ Ideally, a 50m rope will be used, although it is possible to use a shorter rope if that is all that is to hand (seeing as 30m is the norm

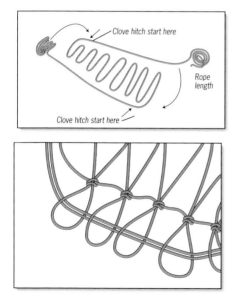

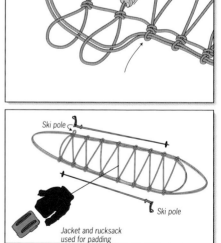

The rope stretcher

for mountain leadership situations, this length will more likely be to hand). Starting with the centre of the rope, lay it out on the ground in a series of loops, six to ten either side of the centre, depending on the size of the casualty. These loops should be kept reasonably close together, and follow the contours of the casualty; close for the head and legs, wider for shoulder and hips. Once the loops have been laid out, run the rope past either end to make a handle, then back down the opposite side. Now it is possible to start connecting the stretcher together. Tie a clove hitch on the side rope, and pass through the end of the corresponding loop. Repeat this for all of the loops on either side.

■ Now run the spare rope across the top and bottom ends of the stretcher, and thread it through the loops protruding from the clove hitches. Continue doing this until most of the rope has been used up, then securely tie the ends off. Push the clove hitches flush with the threaded rope and ensure that all attachments are tight. The basic stretcher is now finished. The base should be padded with mats, spare clothing or rucksacks, making sure that there is no chance of the casualty disappearing through gaps in the rope-work.

■ The stability of this basic design can be greatly increased by threading trekking poles through the clove hitches as well as the rope. This makes the stretcher far easier to carry, as well as being a lot comfier for the casualty.

PART TWO

Technical Skills for Summer and Winter Climbing

This section describes a variety of technical skills and techniques for use in summer and winter climbing and mountaineering.

Knots	Changeovers
Forces and Vectors	Lowering
Tying in	Abseiling
Belay Methods	Short Roping
Rock Climbing	Improvised Rescue Techniques
Summer/Winter Multi-pitch	Single-pitch Climbing Sessions

Knots

Rarely does a subject bring forth as much fear or discussion as the subject of knots – what is the best for what application, which way is it best tied and so on. The number of essential knots needed for both summer and winter mountaineering and climbing is in fact relatively small. We have concentrated here on the knots that we regularly teach, a lot of which are transferable to various applications. The skill here is to be aware of the situations in which they can be usefully deployed.

Rewoven Figure of Eight

The figure of eight is one of the most useful knots, and it is the standard way of tying onto a harness. It is very simple to construct, and has a recognisable shape when complete. The loop created by tying the knot should end up the same size as the abseil loop of your harness – slightly less than fist size. The knot should be finished with half a double fisherman's stopper knot, pushed up snug to the fig eight when tightened, with the end of rope that emerges being 5–10cm long. The habit of tucking the rope end back through the '8' to lock it off should be avoided, as it can cause complete failure under certain conditions.

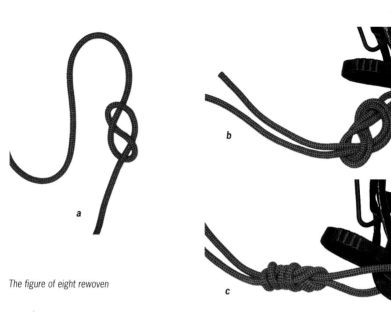

The figure of eight rewoven

OBSERVATION

We recommend tying a half a double fisherman's knot snug against the figure of eight rewoven when tying on to a harness. The function of this knot, in this particular case, is not to increase the strength of the figure of eight but to demonstrate that enough tail has been left so that the main knot cannot unravel. In theory, a tail of rope the same length as is used to tie the fisherman's could be left hanging down, and some people like to do this. However, there is a chance of this loose tail being inadvertently clipped into protection, particularly when the leader is close to the rock and under stress, which would obviously prove both useless and dangerous in the event of a fall. Thus, a stopper knot and a short tail is recommended.

Figure of Eight on a Bight

This is an excellent knot for belaying, relevant for all climbing and scrambling situations. It has the benefit of possessing dynamic properties, meaning that it will tighten slightly when loaded, thus taking a proportion of any shock loading away from the anchor points. It should always be considered first when constructing an anchor system.

Start with a 60cm bight of rope through the harness tie-in loop. This means that when the

knot has been tied, there will be approximately 30cm of tail left, important for its security.

A little practice is needed in order to tie the knot in such a manner as to not introduce any slack into the rope between yourself and the anchor, but it will be time well spent.

The figure of eight on a bight

Double Figure of Eight

This knot is sometimes used as a rope method of bringing two anchor points down to one, but has now been somewhat superseded by the use of slings. Its main application, however, is in the rigging of rope systems, particularly bottom-rope rigs, and when used for these it is excellent. It allows a double loop to be used at the top-pulley karabiner section, thus increasing its strength and security. Its main advantage,

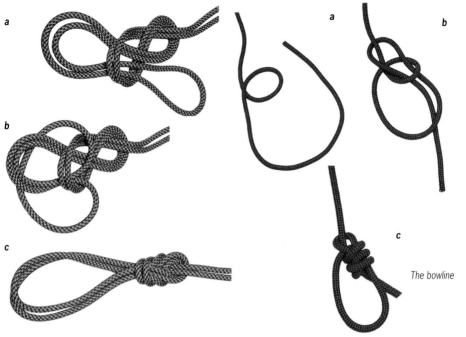

The bowline

Double figure of eight

though, is that it is very easy to untie even when it has been repeatedly loaded. It is important that both loops are clipped, either individually or together, otherwise there is a possibility that one could pull the other through when loaded.

Bowline

The bowline has been superseded in many cases by the figure of eight. It does, however, still have its place for a number of applications. One of its main plus points is that it is easy to untie once it has been loaded. It is sometimes used as a knot for tying onto the harness and, because of the ease with which it undoes, it is a useful knot for situations where a lot of falls are expected to be taken, such as when working a route on a crag or wall.

One of the main minus points is the position of the stopper knot on the inside section of the tie-in loop when it is used on a harness. This can get in the way of any subsequent knots and karabiners which need to be tied or clipped in. A stopper knot is essential with the bowline. Indeed, it could be said that the bowline is not complete until it has one as,

> **TIP**
> For situations of extreme loading, such as repeated long falls or a heavily used tied-off abseil rope, a double bowline may be appropriate, as it will undo even easier than the standard version. This is tied by making two loops initially, one on top of the other, and completing the knot as normal. Once again, it is essential that a half a double fisherman's stopper knot is tied, as this greatly increases the security of the knot overall.

under certain circumstances, a kink in the rope can cause the knot to undo and fail, as could loading the internal diameter and not the main suspension rope.

The Clove Hitch

This is one of the most frequently used knots (see below), and is an essential tool for both summer and winter mountaineering. Its main use is as an anchor knot, where its ease of adjustment can be a big advantage over other systems. With a little practise, it can be easily tied with one hand.

It is best that an HMS karabiner is used with the clove hitch, as this will allow the knot to sit in the correct configuration. For this reason, it is important that only one knot is used per karabiner – the habit of clipping two or more clove hitches into one karabiner is potentially dangerous and should be avoided. It should also be noted that the correct way to clip the knot is with the load rope nearest to the back bar of the karabiner, along its strongest axis.

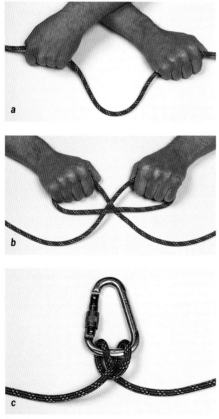

The clove hitch

The Italian Hitch

This is an extremely useful knot, as it can be used for belaying, abseiling and rigging. For general climbing use, its main purpose is as a back-up should a belay device be dropped from a stance, for example.

However, for group-activity use, the Italian hitch comes into its own as a belaying knot, allowing a huge flexibility in system design and operation. The knot is controlled from in front, as opposed to a belay device which must be controlled from behind. Maximum braking is obtained by having the ropes parallel on the load side of the karabiner. This means that the braking system on a top-rope set-up, for instance, can be rigged some distance back from the cliff edge, with the person controlling the system anchored well in front of it. The climber, upon reaching the top, is then still well protected as he walks away from the edge.

Care must be taken to ensure that the controlling rope at no time runs across the sleeve locking the gate of the karabiner. If it touches, there is a chance it could unscrew the gate open, resulting in complete loss of control. Particular care should be taken when abseiling.

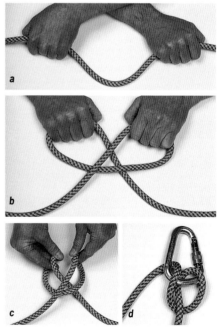

The Italian hitch

Locking Off an Italian Hitch

There are a number of reasons why you would wish to lock off the Italian hitch. This could be when rigging a releasable abseil maybe, or when securing a second on a multi-pitch climb. An excellent and most useful feature is that the hitch can be locked off and released when the rope is under full load. The locking off procedure consists of two types of knot, a slippery hitch and a half hitch, of which two are tied. Start the process with about 60cm of bight and you will be left with the correct tail length of 30cm when finished.

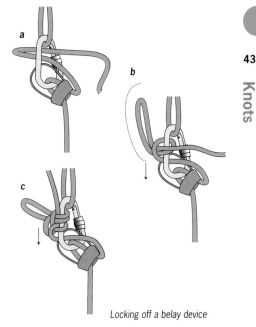

Locking off a belay device

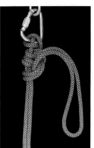

Locking off an Italian hitch

The Overhand Knot

This simple knot is used for a variety of tasks, such as tying off the end of the rope after tying into the harness, for equalizing slings, and it is an indispensable tool for the mountain leader.

Locking Off the Belay Device

This is done in a similar manner to the Italian hitch lock off, except that the knots are tied around the back bar of the karabiner, avoiding the gate. This must be practised before it is needed, unlocking as well as locking off. The finished product should have two half hitches; one is shown on the diagram for clarity.

The overhand knot

The Alpine Butterfly

This knot has been overlooked in recent years, as the overhand knot has gained favour. However, we feel that the butterfly is extremely relevant for a number of situations, such as in the rigging of group-abseil and bottom-rope systems, and for short-roping.

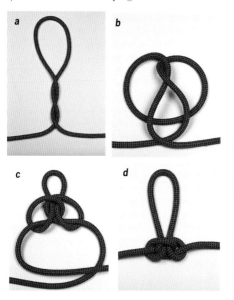

The Alpine butterfly

Double Fisherman's Knot

This knot is used more for construction of equipment than while on the move. However, it can be utilised on the hill to join together two ends of rope to make an improvised sling during retreat, for example, or for joining the ends of an Abalakov thread.

The double fisherman's knot

The Lark's foot

The lark's foot is a relatively weak knot. It can be used to join two slings together, as long as it is arranged to sit like a flat reef knot, but this will weaken the sling by at least 50 per cent, even more if the joined slings are of different sizes or materials. This is a situation where either a longer sling or a screwgate karabiner should be used.

The commonest use for a lark's foot is when attaching a sling onto a harness to use as a safety line or 'cowstail'. In this situation, the sling can be either threaded through the leg loop and waist-belt central points, taking the same line as the abseil loop, or simply around the abseil loop itself. At all costs, avoid shock-loading any system that has a lark's foot in it.

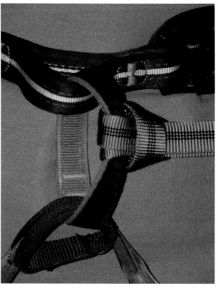

A sling lark's footed on a harness for use as a cowstail

The Tape Knot

This knot (opposite) originated as a way of constructing slings, in the days before sewn slings were readily available. It is now rarely seen, and can be considered mainly as a knot for emergency procedures. It is often a good idea to carry a couple of 3m lengths of tape in the rucksack, for use in case a retreat has to be made from a winter route, for instance. The tape knot is then the best way of securing the sling around an anchor. This knot is not appropriate for use with spectra or Dyneema slings, as they are slippery and will pull through under load.

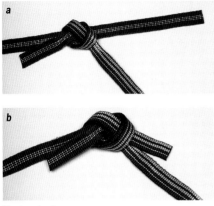

The tape knot

The Reef Knot

This knot (below) has two main uses – for carrying the rope, and for creating a way of stopping a double fisherman's from tightening up when abseiling. Although simple, it is very easy to tie incorrectly. The best way to remember how to tie it is 'right over left, left over right', which describes the route taken by the rope when starting with the right-hand end. Both ends should then be pulled to help tighten the knot.

The reef knot

The Parisian Baudrier

This is a method of making an improvised chest harness, particularly useful in an emergency situation. The knot is in fact a 'sheet bend', and it is important that it cannot slip tight around the casualty. You will find that you need one, possibly two 8ft (120cm) slings (joining them at the back of the casualty) to tie it. The resulting loop could be attached to their climbing rope with a French Prusik which will keep an

unconscious person upright, but you will be able to slide the Prusik loose should you need to tip them over to clear their airway.

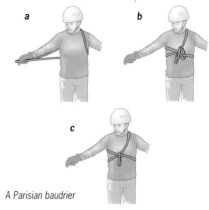

A Parisian baudrier

Prusiking Knots

The following two knots have taken over from the original Prusik knot. This has lost favour due to its propensity for jamming when under even a small load, especially on wet ropes, and its difficulty of operation. However, the generic name 'Prusik' has been retained to describe the loop with which the knots are tied; and the act of using the loops to ascend the rope is, and will be for evermore, known as 'Prusiking'.

The loops, two should be carried, are best tied from 6mm kernmantle cord, and they should measure 50–55cm long when tied with a double fisherman's knot.

French Prusik

This will be the most regularly used of the two knots described here. Its major advantage over the Klemheist is its ability to be released while under load, an essential property when abseiling or performing emergency procedures. When

forming the knot, take care not to include the double fisherman's in the coiled section, and ensure that the knot wrapping is neat when completed.

The French Prusik

Klemheist

This knot is similar in appearance to the French Prusik, the main difference being that only one loop of rope connects to the karabiner, unlike the French's two.

This knot is very difficult to release under load, thus making its use somewhat different to that of the French Prusik.

The Klemheist

A Tibloc and a Ropeman

Forces and Vectors

Before we proceed much further, there are a few technical terms and figures that need to be understood.

■

KiloNewton

The Newton is a unit of force that has as its basic components mass, length and time. The Newton is equivalent to the force required to produce an acceleration of one metre per second per second on a mass of one kilogram, with this acceleration being what we experience when we fall off a climb. 1000 Newtons equal one kiloNewton (kN). Thus a piece of climbing equipment with a 25kn stamp on it would have a strength rating equivalent to 25,000 Newtons.

Many manufacturers test their ropes to a rating of 12kN, as this is seen as the maximum force that the human body can take. A climber experiencing anything over 4kN when taking a fall is likely to experience a good deal of discomfort.

Impact Force

This is the loading taken by various sections of the protection system, particularly the highest runner, if you fall off. The lower the impact force the better, the higher the impact force the more chance there is of injury or equipment failure.

Reducing the impact force is important, particularly where runners or anchors are poor, as could be the case in winter. Using a rope that is rated with a low impact force will help, as will adopting a dynamic belay technique. Straightening the run of the rope by using appropriate length extenders lets it stretch when loaded, and having your belayer lift up to a metre from the ground is advantageous (although they may take some convincing!). Kit such as shock-absorbing slings and karabiners with built-in rollers, and even using a figure of eight knot instead of a clove hitch, all go towards reducing the impact force.

Fall Factor

Fall factor = length of fall ÷ length of rope deployed.

The fall factor is the name given to the sum of the equation used to calculate the hardness, or severity of loading, of a fall. The higher the value the more severe the fall will have been. For most rock and ice climbing situations, the highest fall factor obtainable is '2', the lowest is '0'. It can only be fully calculated when climbing in a multi-pitch situation, as on a single pitch route the ground will get in the way.

The calculation comes in two versions, the 'Theoretical Fall Factor' and the 'Actual Fall Factor'. The latter is a much more complicated equation, which takes into account such variables as the line that the rope takes between runners, the friction inherent between placements and the effect of it rubbing over rock or ice. It is the former that is commonly used and which we will concentrate on here.

If you have, as an example, run out 2.5 metres of rope from the belayer and have not placed any protection, a fall of 5 metres could result. Using the above calculation, we come up with a fall factor of 2, an unpleasant experience.

If you now climb up 5 metres but place a runner at 2.5 metres and fall off, the fall factor is now 1. This gives much less stress on the belay system, not to mention yourself.

You can see that it is important to reduce the fall factor as much as possible when leaving a stance, and placing gear immediately will go a long way to protecting the belay system and subsequent runner placements and to reduce the fall factor.

Be aware that fall factors with a value higher than 2 can occur in some situations, such as on Via Ferratas and some industrial rigs, but these are outside the scope of this book.

Vectors

This is the angle that a sling, belay rope or similar make when all the load bearing points meet, such as when equalizing two anchor points or forcing a sling over a spike, for example. The wider the angle the weaker the overall system will be as the load on each anchor will be increased. The diagrams demonstrate some variations.

The relationship between angle and loading percentage

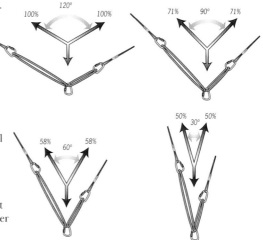

The relationship between sling angle over a spike anchor and the loading in kilograms

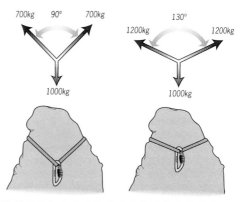

A NOTE ON SLINGS

Choose the correct thickness of sling for the job. If a sling is going to be subject to repeated use and some abuse, go for the widest weave available and leave the super-thin Dyneema slings for technical rigs on routes. All slings have their strength compromised when abraded, and the thinner the sling the less abrasion has to take place to severely compromise its strength – **NEVER** rub a sling to and fro around a boulder to seat it.

As previously discussed, slings that have a lark's foot tied in them lose a minimum of 50 per cent of their strength and far more in certain situations. Thus, never use one with a lark's foot in it where it can be shock loaded, such as a cowstail when you are standing above the point on the anchor to which it is clipped.

Slings are also prone to melting through if a rope runs through or over them, with Dyneema again being the most fragile. This has a melting point of 145 degrees centigrade, with nylon and polyester melting around 230–260 degrees centigrade. Keep all moving parts, in particular the rope, away.

Tying into a harness

Belay Loop

By tying in you have created a belay loop that will accommodate your belay device. When belaying you should always use your tie-in loop as the attachment point. Avoid attaching your belay device directly to the abseil loop, unless you have not tied in, such as may be the case when bottom roping or using a climbing wall. Attaching to the rope loop ensures that any loading will be handled dynamically, that the harness is loaded correctly, and will make some emergency procedures, such as escaping the system, easier to complete.

Tying in

Tying in is the term used for attaching the rope to your harness. When tying into a harness, you should be careful to follow the manufacturer's recommended guidelines. We would always recommend a harness type that has a loop linking your leg loops to the waist belt. Alpine-style harnesses without an abseil loop or those requiring the rope to be tied in to make a secure attachment point are not recommended.

■

The Knot

When tying into the harness, we recommend that you use a rewoven figure of eight with a stopper knot. When completed, the tie-in loop should be the same size as the abseil loop on your harness. If using a bowline with a stopper knot, you need to ensure that the stopper is properly butted against the bowline.

TYING ON TO ANCHORS

ABC

Consideration of the anchor – belayer – climber line is essential whenever constructing an anchor system. A description of ABC is included on page 24.

Single Anchor

Before tying on to a single anchor, you should ensure that the anchor is completely sound. This means testing by inspecting, tapping, pushing, pulling and kicking it. There should be absolutely no question as to its strength.

Within Reach

This means you are within reach of the anchor. Clip a clove hitch into the HMS screwgate karabiner.

By tying off in this fashion, you can easily adjust your position on the stance by simply adjusting the clove hitch, maintaining tension between the anchor and your harness.

Single anchor within reach

Out of Reach

Establish where you need to belay from. Clip the rope to a screwgate karabiner clipped into the anchor. Take up your position and tie off into your belay loop using a figure of eight on the bight. When tying the figure of eight, start with a bight of rope 60cm long; this will ensure that the correct tail length is left once the knot has been completed.

It is also possible to use a clove hitch clipped into an HMS screwgate karabiner positioned at your belay loop. This has an advantage of being easy to adjust. However, the figure of eight has dynamic properties, which means that it will tighten somewhat when loaded, thus reducing the amount of shock-loading transmitted to the anchor in the event of a fall. It also does not require the use of any extra equipment. The figure of eight should always be considered as first choice.

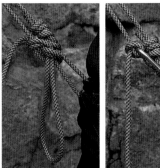

Single anchor out of reach

Single anchor out of reach using a clove hitch at the harness

Multiple Anchors

A multiple anchor is the use of two or more points of attachment to the rock or ice at a stance. It is used whenever security cannot be guaranteed by just one anchor, or when one substantial anchor is out of line to the possible direction of loading. The important point to remember about any multiple-anchor system is that there must be no chance of one anchor point being shock-loaded if the other fails for some reason. To ensure this, equalized-tension methods have evolved of tying into multiple anchors by using both the rope and slings.

49

TIP

Never compromise the integrity of your anchor by 'making do', with placements or your belay position.

OBSERVATION

When tying off with a figure-of-eight knot you should ensure that when you take a bight of rope from the live, you must include the dead rope leading to the ground when making your turns. In other words, tie the knot around the two lengths of rope that form the loop. Once the knot has been tied, pull it snug by pulling on all four sections of rope independently. An indication that it is firm enough is when no daylight can be seen through the knot.

A figure of eight will absorb energy better than many other knots, as the knot will reduce in size when loaded, helping to reduce the forces transmitted to the anchor.

To tension the rope while standing or sitting in position, lean a few inches towards the anchor and tie the knot with the ropes from the anchor pulled snug. When you lean back into position, the rope will be correctly tensioned.

Within Reach Using Rope

Clip one HMS screwgate karabiner to each anchor point. Taking the rope from your harness tie-in loop, clip on to the first point using a clove hitch. Leave a little slack, and clip a clove hitch into the second point. Tie off the rope back to your harness using a figure of eight on the bight. Adjust the clove hitches to equalize the tension on both sections of rope leading to your harness. The anchor is now said to be equalized.

Tying in

Two anchors in reach

Two anchors out of reach

One in reach and one out of reach anchor

Out of Reach Using Rope

This is a repeat of tying into one anchor using a figure of eight on a bight. Clip the rope into one anchor, bring it back to your harness and tie a figure of eight on the bight. Then simply repeat the process for the second anchor. Practise will ensure that both rope lengths are tied with the same tension.

The habit of bringing two clove hitches back to a karabiner on the belay loop is possible but is not the best option, as it loads the karabiner incorrectly and is difficult to adjust.

Variable Anchor Positions

Once the method of tying in using either a clove hitch or figure of eight has been practised and understood, the only limiting factor for attaching yourself to anchors will be the amount of rope available. An anchor system that has one out of reach and one in reach can be easily solved using first a figure of eight, then a clove hitch, and more than two anchors points can be tied into using a variety of these knots.

Using Slings at Multiple-anchor Points

There are a number of reasons why you may choose to attach yourself to a multiple anchor brought to one point with a sling: you may be short of rope, intent on leading the next pitch, be leading clients and need a central attachment point, or wish to use a direct belay method, sharing the load between the anchors. Here is a variety of methods we recommend. They are all very simple, and are to be recommended when leading multi-pitch routes in any season. However, the first two are our personal favourites and will always be our initial choice.

Method One

This is the simplest and quickest. Attach a sling by clipping it into two screwgates at the anchors. Pull both lengths of sling downwards to a point of tension, in the direction of

Overhand knot on the bight

An overhand knot on the sling

loading. Tie an overhand knot in the sling, creating a small loop. Clip a screwgate karabiner into this. This will now be your attachment point. Should one anchor fail then the other will not be shock-loaded.

You can now tie into this central point using either the in-reach or out-of-reach rope method. If you are right next to the anchor, the karabiner in the sling can be simply clipped into your tie-in loop.

Method Two

This is useful if the anchors are a little further apart than for method 1. Tie a loose overhand knot in the middle of the sling, which has the effect of creating two independent loops. Clip one loop into each anchor. Decide on the direction of loading, and equalize the anchors by adjusting the overhand knot.

Clip a screwgate karabiner through both loops above the overhand knot, and attach yourself to this.

Method Three

This method allows adjustment to be made to the system once it is set up. Attach a sling to the first anchor using a clove hitch. Create a short length of slack between both anchors (which can subsequently be used for adjustment if necessary) and attach a second clove hitch to the second anchor. Tie an overhand knot in the sling. This creates a central point for attachment.

Method Four

You will require two slings for this. Clip one sling into each anchor. Pull the slings towards the possible direction of loading and, holding them together, tie an overhand knot near their ends. Clip an HMS screwgate karabiner into both shortened sling sections above the overhand knot. Should the loops below the knot be even and equalized, this will be OK to clip into.

If tying on to three anchor points, a 16ft (240cm) sling is very handy. Clip the sling into all anchor points, gather all sections of the sling together (you will end up with three loops in your hand) and adjust them to the same length. Tie an overhand knot in the loops, and clip a karabiner through this as the attachment point.

Clove hitches on the sling   *Using two slings*

Tying on to three anchors

1 There is a method of arranging a sling with a twist in it so that it is self-equalizing, the karabiner moving with the belayer, and it is often suggested as the best method for use with ice screws to permit constant tension. However, should one anchor point fail, there is no captive knot and the second anchor will be shock-loaded with the chance of it failing. This method should be avoided, any of the above being far more relevant, up to date and safer. If you do choose to use it, tie two overhand knots, one a few centimetres either side of the connection point, The sling can than still adjust but the shock loading, in the event of one anchor failing, will be limited.

2 It should be noted that the integrity of your anchor set-up is based upon the sound placement of your protection, and the direction of pull when loaded.

3 Always avoid using snapgate karabiners singly at anchor points. If snap karabiners are required because no screwgates are available, double them up and position them back to back, as this will reduce the chance of a gate being opened unintentionally.

4 Double and twin-rope systems are quite common when climbing multi-pitch routes. When tying directly into two anchor points, it is worth using just one rope for the two anchors. This has the advantage that the second rope is out of the system, and can be used as a spare rope in an emergency. However, in some situations it may just be easier to use one rope on to one anchor and the second rope on the other.

SELECTING A BELAY DEVICE

There is a vast range of belay devices to choose from, with each one designed differently in its shape and use, so ensure that you choose one that will do the task that you want it to. This will often mean that it will have to double up as an abseil device, as well as possibly being a device for directly belaying clients. Not every belay device will be appropriate for your rope diameter, as some are designed for thin ropes only, while others are designed for up to 11mm ropes. Using the correct gauge of rope with your belay device is essential.

You should ensure that you receive a manufacturer's instructional leaflet when purchasing a device and follow the directions given. Time spent practising with the device before using it on the hill will be well spent.

When using a modern belay device, you are no longer required to have spent a year in the gym working out. Your arm strength plays little part in the use of a belay device when used correctly.

Standard Devices

This heading covers devices that every climber should know how to use. From a simple 'slick' device with few features, through to those designed with grooves through which the rope runs, allowing a more 'grabbing' action to take place, these are the workhorses of climbing and mountaineering belaying and abseiling. Those with built-in grooves, allowing for more rope control on thinner ropes, are to be recommended for the majority of situations.

A variety of slick and grabbing devices

Auto-locking Devices

These devices will be commonly seen at climbing walls and sport climbing venues. As they work by 'clamping' the rope securely, it is difficult to provide a dynamic braking effect, so they should not be used where protection is marginal, such as in winter or on some rock types.

Auto locking belay devices

Self-locking Devices for Instructors

This is a specialist category of devices, and they come in a range of designs and functions. Generally speaking, they are capable of being set up on a direct belay so that one or two following climbers can be belayed at the same time. A big problem with a number of the devices is the difficulty with which a fallen climber can be lowered when all of their weight is on the rope, and this can require the belayer to perform a number of rope tricks to release the device (see direct belay section).

Self-locking instructional devices

Belay Methods

There are many different types of belay devices in the market place, and almost as many techniques. When using the right belay method everything should run smoothly, with the leader and second experiencing no difficulties.

When using an incorrect method for a particular situation problems arise. It is worth asking yourself each time, 'Should the climber slip will I, as the belayer, be able to hold a fall without causing injury to myself and to him?'

This section describes the correct use and appropriateness of the three 'normal' methods. Never forget that no matter how good a belayer you feel that you may be, should your stance position be poor or incorrect then the integrity of your belay system is in doubt and your ability to hold a fall could be impaired. The ABC is critical in all situations.

■

SEMI-DIRECT BELAY

What is a Semi-direct Belay?

The construction of the true semi-direct belay contains four key parts:

1 tie the rope end into your harness thereby creating the belay loop

2 create a single or multiple equalized anchor, whichever is appropriate

3 attach yourself to the anchor

4 attach a belay device to your belay loop. The belay device in the belay loop is ready to be used as a semi-direct belay.

This method absorbs any load through the belay device, the belay loop and the rope to the anchor. It should be noted that the belayer must be tight to the anchor and in line with any possible direction of loading.

Any force applied is taken away from the belayer's body and partly absorbed by the anchor, allowing him to comfortably lock off and pay out the rope when under tension.

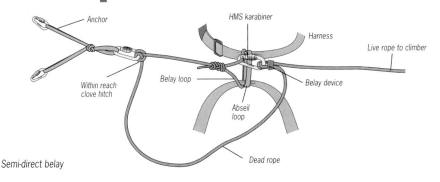

Semi-direct belay

Labels: Anchor · Within reach clove hitch · Belay loop · HMS karabiner · Harness · Live rope to climber · Belay device · Abseil loop · Dead rope

■

There are a number of ways to arrange a direct belay, depending upon the situation. A direct belay is constructed to transfer any load directly to the anchor. The anchor therefore must be able to take a large load without any chance of it failing. The belayer can be attached or unattached to an anchor when controlling the rope, again depending on the situation. There are two common methods.

Method 1: Scrambling Style

You can belay directly by taking the rope round a rock flake, spike, boulder or tree, generating friction along the surface of the anchor. Whichever type you decide to use, it is imperative that the anchor is solid. It is then a matter of holding the rope with both hands and taking in or paying out hand over hand as required.

must always be in front of an Italian hitch for it to work properly. You can now operate the belay, with any loading being transmitted directly through the system to the anchor. A major advantage of this method is that it is simple to lock off the Italian hitch, and remain out of the system all of the time.

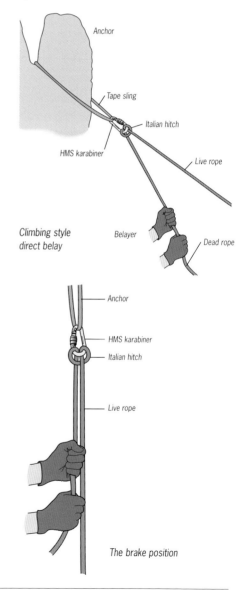

Anchor

Tape sling

Italian hitch

HMS karabiner

Live rope

Climbing style direct belay

Belayer

Dead rope

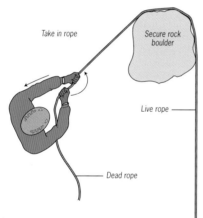

Take in rope

Secure rock boulder

Live rope

Dead rope

Scrambling style direct belay

Method 2: Italian Hitch: Climbing and Lowering Style

When using a single or multi-point anchor system, the direct belay method can still be used. Once you have ensured your own security, clip an HMS screwgate karabiner into the anchor. Orientate it so that the gate faces up and the wider end is away from the anchor, and clip in an Italian hitch. Stand in a comfortable and braced position, remembering that you

Anchor

HMS karabiner

Italian hitch

Live rope

The brake position

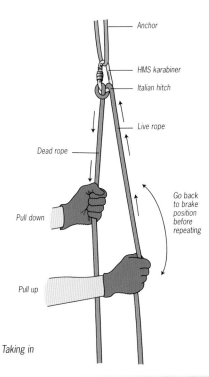

Anchor

HMS karabiner

Italian hitch

Live rope

Dead rope

Pull down

Go back to brake position before repeating

Pull up

Taking in

OBSERVATIONS

This type of friction knot is very simple to use and has a big advantage in that it is very fast to belay with, and so can be used where speed and security are prime concerns. It is common practice to use this method when moving together such as when short roping or when traversing technical ridges where it is often critical to move fast.

1 The most important factor is the strength of the anchor. You should progressively test the anchor before committing to it by first gently tapping it, then shaking it and finally kicking it. However, don't kick it off down the mountain as it may cause injury to your partner, client or others.
2 Before belaying you should ensure that your stance is solid and comfortable, that you are in a braced position, and that there is no chance of the rope lifting off from the anchor as your second reaches you.
3 The direct belay is only advisable when belaying a second, or when lowering. It is usually unsuitable for belaying a leader, unless there has been careful consideration as to the loading direction on the anchor.

WINTER CONSIDERATIONS

In hard snow conditions, it is possible to take a direct belay from a snow anchor. Careful judgement is required, as direct belay anchors must be impeccably solid. The following could be considered as being practical and safe anchors for a direct belay under good conditions:

■ a buried or reinforced axe anchor. The sling must be correctly clove-hitched and great care must be taken to ensure that the load is directed along or below the surface of the snow. A shallow pit a couple of inches deep can be cut at the karabiner position, to ensure that the Italian hitch does not jam if loaded
■ from a dead-man. The above considerations apply
■ from a snow bollard. The rope can be used as a large sling, tying it around the bollard with an overhand knot, figure of eight or bowline.

TIPS

1 Ensure that you flake or place your spare rope in a suitable position so it doesn't knot, snag or drop down the route.
2 The Italian can be locked off using a slippery hitch and two half hitches to secure the second when they arrive at the stance. Alternatively, a second screwgate can have a clove hitch clipped in and the Italian removed.

If you are using two Italian hitches to bring up 2 clients at one time, avoid the hitches jamming against each other by clipping a spare screwgate between the 2 HMS's. This will keep them apart and allow the system to run a lot more smoothly.

Method 3: Instructing and Guiding Style

The use of a self locking belay device (also called a 'direct belay device'), is a very popular and indeed very efficient method of bringing up either one or two clients at the same time. This system invariably uses a direct belay set-up. The device is clipped on to the anchor and the climbing rope/s pushed through the appropriate slot/s, with a free hanging karabiner being clipped into the rope loop/s thus created. A loading on the rope to the climber, which is the higher of the two emerging from the device, causes it to pull the free karabiner tightly into place and down onto the dead rope, jamming it and holding the climber's weight . Note that this is not a hands-free device and the dead rope should be managed all the time. However, it does allow for slick climbing and improved stance management once the technique has been practised.

Load rope

Dead rope

The set-up for a self locking belay device

TIP
You may find that a direct belay device works more efficiently if a karabiner with a 'T' section back bar is used to clip the ropes through at the back of the device. Not only will this grip more readily on freezing or icy ropes, but it can be manipulated up and down by hand to a certain extent when the device is loaded, allowing a little slippage of the rope, possibly enough to avoid having to set up a complicate release mechanism.

OBSERVATION
It is essential to remember that any direct belay system can only ever be as good as the anchor itself. Take great care when selecting suitable anchors, and if there is any doubt as to their integrity, choose a different belay method.

TIP
The higher above you the anchors are, the easier they will be to use, both for belaying and for connecting and managing your seconds. Having a belay point at around or just above head height makes many jobs a lot simpler.

Releasing a Self-locking Belay Device

Some devices incorporate a small hole through which a length of cord can be threaded. Pulling on this can help to release the weight of a fallen climber. If this is not possible you will have to adopt some technical rope tricks.

■ Attach the dead rope to your harness, most likely with an Italian hitch. You may wish to lock this off whilst you are working on the rest of the system.

■ Secure a sling to the karabiner at the back of the direct belay device, run it up though the anchor (probably via a new screwgate) and back down to your harness, clipping it in.

■ Holding tight to the Italian hitch, hang all of your weight on the sling, which will lift the karabiner on the belay device.

■ You can now pay rope out via the Italian hitch.

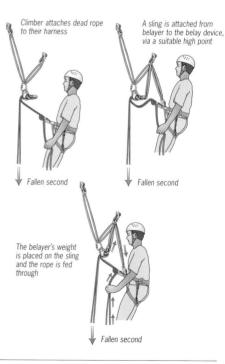

Climber attaches dead rope to their harness

Fallen second

A sling is attached from belayer to the belay device, via a suitable high point

Fallen second

The belayer's weight is placed on the sling and the rope is fed through

Fallen second

OBSERVATION

If you have two seconds, only one of whom needs assistance, you will have to tie the other one off before releasing the device. A large overhand knot on their dead rope will do the trick.

Another method of releasing a loaded direct belay device is to use the slot or hole provided on the device for this purpose. A karabiner is placed into the hole and then used as a handle to tilt the device into a paying-out orientation. Not all devices have this facility, so it is worth choosing carefully when making a purchase.

Doing this is obviously far quicker than rigging a complicated release system involving a sling through the anchor etc. However, be very aware that the load can suddenly come onto the dead rope, so you must be ready. Make sure that the second rope to the other client, if this is relevant, cannot be dropped or control of it lost.

Using a karabiner to release the load on a Reverso 3 belay device

If using slick ropes, it may be an idea to bring the dead ropes up and through a karabiner clipped into the anchor point. This will give some extra friction and a higher degree of control when the load is released.

If you still feel that you will not have enough control, a different method could be employed.

- Place a French Prusik on the live rope/s just below the device, and push it down as far as it will go. This should be connected to the anchor with a 4ft (60cm) sling or similar.
- Clip the dead rope/s into the anchor with an Italian hitch on an HMS karabiner, leaving as little slack as possible between it and the device.
- Work the karabiner at the back of the device up and down so that some rope slips through, putting the load onto the French Prusik.
- When sufficient slack has been eased through, remove the device.
- You can now pull up on the French Prusik to transfer the load on to the Italian hitch, and can lower away.

TIP

It is quite easy to set up an unassisted hoist from a device that is holding someone's weight. Use a Klemheist, Ropeman or Tibloc connected to the live rope below the device, run the dead rope from the back of the device down through this and pull upwards. The device will lock off when you need to move the blocking mechanism down the live rope again. Continue for as far as is necessary.

INDIRECT BELAY

This is often known as the 'waist' or 'body belay'. The rope is taken round the belayer's back and positioned at the top of the hips. A turn of the dead rope is taken round the arm to act as a friction brake should force be applied. It is important that the belayer is tied on to an anchor in such a manner as to prevent them from being pulled off the stance and accidentally releasing the rope. In exceptional circumstances when winter climbing you may only have a bucket seat for security when belaying with this method, but this must only ever be used for belaying someone lower down the slope than yourself and never a leader.

This type of belaying is often the most appropriate in winter where snow and ice anchors may be limited, scarce or of dubious quality, and absorbing the load through the body becomes important to reduce any loading on the anchor.

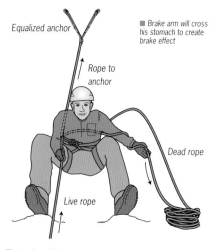

Equalized anchor

■ *Brake arm will cross his stomach to create brake effect*

Rope to anchor

Dead rope

Live rope

The indirect belay

Method

■ Once you have tied on to your anchor and correctly adjusted the tension between it and your harness, sit down and brace yourself with your feet shoulder width apart. Take in the slack rope between yourself and the climber, then arrange the rope round your back above your hips to the front, ensuring that it runs over the top of the rope from the anchor.

■ When using a front attachment harness, it is essential that the rope to the climber is on the same side of your body as the rope from the anchor.

■ The process of controlling the rope during a leader fall is also important. Let the rope slip a little (as it will tend to do anyway as the load comes onto you), bringing your braking arm across the front of your body to increase the friction. This will dilute any shock loading to the system and prevent the belayer from being pulled off his stance.

This technique is applicable to all seasons. However, semi-direct or direct belays may well be more relevant for the majority of situations, particularly in summer.

Take great care to think about the direction that your leader will be taking when you use a waist belay, particularly in winter. It is possible for them to either unwrap themselves from you, or to wrap you tight in the rope in the event of a fall. The diagrams demonstrate these two situations.

TIPS

1 It is essential to wear gloves and have long sleeves when using this method of belay as it is solely dependent on friction; skin is very sensitive and burns easily.

2 You should always have the rope-end secured, either to your harness, with chest coils or with a knot tied in it. This will prevent the accidental loss of the rope and the second, particularly when lowering!

OBSERVATIONS

It is worth noting that whenever you decide to use a body belay there are a number of basic principles you should adhere to:

1 sit down whenever possible, as you can brace your feet to help prevent being pulled off the stance

2 never stand and body belay when not tied on to an anchor

3 always make sure that the rope runs in a straight line from the climber, past you to the anchor. If the rope to the climber and anchor run on opposite sides to your body and a fall is held, severe injury to your spine could occur

4 never take a twist round the live-rope arm. This could result in injury

5 ensure that the rope around your body is running low down behind your back, and that it has not got caught up on your rucksack if worn

6 wear gloves when belaying, even in summer

7 the rope around your body must go over your head, and not be stepped into. It should be resting on top of the rope coming in from the anchor.

TIP

You will find, in particular when using a bucket seat backed up with a buried axe or deadman in winter, that is becomes awkward to pay the rope out to the leader as they head up and above you, as your arm on the live rope gets pulled out to your side as you pay the rope out. To alleviate this, clip a screwgate into the front of your harness and run the live rope through this, so that even when they are pulling the rope up from behind you, you will be able to have both your arms in front of you in a comfortable position.

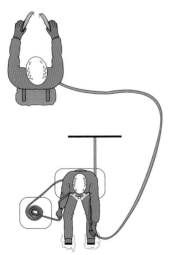

Having climbed up to the belayer's left-hand side, the climber traverses across above them, unwrapping the belay

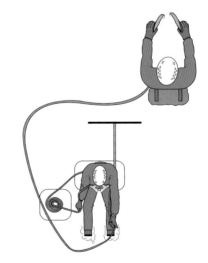

Having climbed up to the belayer's right-hand side and traversed above, the belayer is now tangled in the rope in the event of the climber falling

When attaching your belay device to your harness, always clip it to the loop created by tying on to the rope (at a climbing wall or when bottom roping, however, you may not have tied on, thus use the abseil loop on your harness as the attachment point).

Paying out Rope to Lead Climber

It is important to clip on to the top of your belay loop above the figure-of-eight knot, ensuring that there are no twists and that the rope runs smoothly through the device.

Taking in Rope from a Second

Clip your belay device to your loop below the figure of eight, again ensuring that there are no twists and that it all runs smoothly.

Controlling the Dead Rope

It is important to pay attention before belaying, and to check that the belay device orientation is correct before giving the climber the command

TIP

If, on a multi-pitch route, the belay device needs to be re-orientated when the second arrives at the stance and the anchor points are within reach, they can simply clip themselves to the anchor system before the device is moved. However, if the anchor points are out of reach, this can be attained by the following method. Once the second arrives at the stance, tie an overhand knot on a bight in the dead rope, and clip this loop to your harness tie-in point with a screwgate. The belay device may now be removed, re-orientated, replaced, the overhand knot untied, and the second can now lead through.

to climb. If your rope from the anchor runs to your right side, your right hand should hold the dead rope and vice versa.

To safeguard the climber, it is critical that you never let the dead rope release from your hand, no matter what style of device you are using.

Clipped in to belay a leader

Clipped in to belay a second

Common Belaying Mistakes	Remedy
Always relying on a single anchor.	Single anchors are good as long as they are absolutely solid. Always test them before using. You may get better security with a multiple anchor.
Standing to belay with anchors arranged below waist height.	If no good high anchors can be found, then sit down to belay.
Anchors not equalized.	Adjust the system and check that should one anchor fail the other will not be shock loaded.
Not in line with an anticipated direction of pull.	Redirect the ropes running back to the anchor or adjust your belay stance.
Belay device clipped to abseil loop on harness.	Always clip on to your tie-on belay loop.
Incorrect orientation of belay device.	Ensure that it is in the correct position for taking in and paying out.
Not having free movement of control hand on the belay device.	Extend yourself from the anchors away from the obstruction, or go under the anchor attachment rope and belay on the other side with the correct hand.
Ropes jamming in belay device.	Belay device may be twisted and incorrectly orientated or belay device is too small for the rope diameter. Rope fed to belay device may be kinked or knotted, indicating poor attention to stance management.
Rope not feeding out slack when required.	Using an inappropriate mechanical direct belay device.

OBSERVATIONS

1 It is important that you learn to belay using either hand for taking in the dead rope, as you will not always have a stance position that would allow you to use your strongest hand. It is very possible, if using the incorrect hand, that a shock load would rotate your body and make it very difficult to lock off the belay device.

2 Remember to watch the lead climber as they will require slack rope when clipping into placed protection. Should you not provide enough slack rope you may accidentally pull the leader off route. When taking up your belay position for protecting a leader, ensure that the rope to them is running up the line of the route.

3 Always belay from your tie-in loop, rather than from the abseil loop on your harness, whenever practicable.

Rock Climbing

This chapter looks at a few of the more important considerations when rock climbing, with the emphasis on learning to lead, and the way an instructor may be able to assist by being close by. There is a variety of instructional books that devote many pages to the placement of runners and anchors, and you are directed towards one of these if you are requiring basic information.

■

LEARNING TO LEAD

This section is aimed at preparing the novice to lead by learning through best practice, but the comments within are equally relevant for consideration by anyone undertaking to instruct rock climbing.

Following the experience of climbing on indoor walls, and bottom roping and top roping on a crag, the next stage in the leading process is to practise clipping pre-placed protection on a route. This should take place on a single-pitch crag. To practise this safely for the first time, the novice leader can work on a bottom rope. This method allows him to practise placing and clipping runners without the worry of clipping incorrectly and falling any great distance.

There are three methods to choose from:
1 place all the protection on the ascent while being protected by a bottom rope
2 abseil down the route and pre-place all the protection
3 use an instructor to set it up.

Method

Two ropes will be needed, one for the bottom rope set up, the other for a 'lead' rope used to clip the runners. If learning from an instructor, he will often climb beside you on a fixed rope anchored to the side of your route. This allows him to offer coaching as you climb and to give any assistance should you feel uncomfortable.
■ Once you have arrived at the top of the route, the belayer will gently lower you back down.
■ The trail rope will simply run through the pre-clipped protection as you descend. Now you can untie the trail rope and pull it back through all the pre-placed protection, then

It should be noted that the trail rope used by the lead climber to practise clipping protection should be properly uncoiled and flaked on the ground for it to run smoothly, with the leader's end running from the top of the pile, and it should be close to, and on the correct side of, the belayer.

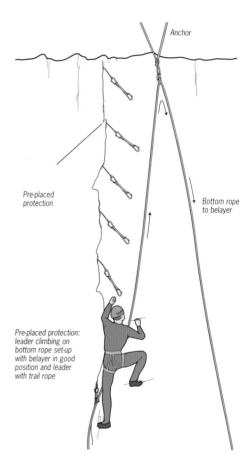

Anchor

Pre-placed protection

Bottom rope to belayer

Pre-placed protection: leader climbing on bottom rope set-up with belayer in good position and leader with trail rope

Clipping pre-placed protection

prepare to climb back up practising the extraction of the protection. Alternatively, if the protection is good you can use it pre-placed and lead whilst clipping the gear.

COACHING NOTE

This is the first progression towards leading, and as such should be made as realistic as possible, erring on the side of safety. For instance, the bottom rope can be left a little bit slack, in order to simulate the feeling of leading. The climber can be allowed to place his own gear, and it can be discussed on the descent with the instructor alongside. If you are instructing, do not forget the role of the second, as he is performing an important task and may feel a little isolated if all of your attention is with the leader.

Learning to Lead Without a Bottom Rope

The next stage is when preparing to lead without the security of a bottom rope. It is advisable to pre-place your protection, either by abseil or by using a bottom rope. Check that the belayer is correctly positioned and has correctly orientated his belay device.

- A good belayer is part of the key to success. The belayer may be anchored at the bottom of the route, using one of the methods for setting up an anchor already mentioned in previous chapters.
- It is also critical that the belayer is belaying close to the base of the route. This is necessary as the further away the belayer is the more chance that the first, and possibly subsequent, protection will pull out, as an outwards pull will be created.
- The leader should be careful as to the position of the lead rope while ascending and clipping. It is very easy for the rope to slip round to the back of your leg, and should you take a fall with the rope in this position then you may be inverted with the possibility of injury. Once the leader gets to the top he should set up an anchor and prepare to belay the second. After the correct call sequence, the second can now climb and extract all of the gear.

Leader climbing with pre-placed protection in place

The rope wrapped around the leader's leg

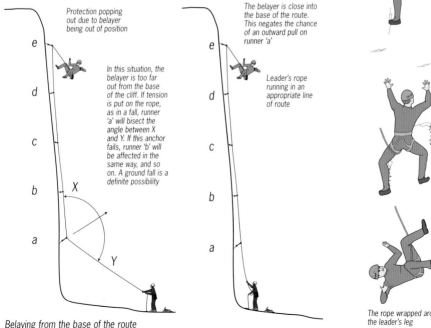

Protection popping out due to belayer being out of position

In this situation, the belayer is too far out from the base of the cliff. If tension is put on the rope, as in a fall, runner 'a' will bisect the angle between X and Y. If this anchor fails, runner 'b' will be affected in the same way, and so on. A ground fall is a definite possibility

The belayer is close into the base of the route. This negates the chance of an outward pull on runner 'a'

Leader's rope running in an appropriate line of route

Belaying from the base of the route

LEADING THE ROUTE

When leading your first route, you will obviously not have any pre-placed protection. If you are concerned about this, it would be wise to abseil the route and place two or three key runners that will act as 'islands of safety' should you need them. Having an instructor beside you on a fixed rope is a definite advantage. It is important to choose a route that is well within your climbing capabilities.

Method

■ Once you leave the belayer, stay calm and focused; your aim is to place protection as soon as possible after leaving the ground and at regular intervals after that. Don't climb past obvious runner placements without making use of them, but also don't use all of your gear up in the bottom few metres of the route!

■ If the climbing is getting too difficult or you haven't placed any protection and are thinking you may fall, remain calm and down-climb before you get yourself into a situation that is difficult to reverse.

■ It is also important to ensure that placed protection is adequately extended, which will avoid unnecessary rope drag and help keep the protection in place.

■ Belaying from the ground is difficult to perform slickly and safely. The rope should be sufficiently slack as to not inhibit the leader as he moves up, but not so slack as to allow him to travel some distance in the event of a fall. The belayer needs to pay particular attention when the lead climber asks for slack rope, possibly for clipping a runner. At this point, the lead climber is vulnerable, from pulling through some slack, failing to clip and falling off. Ensure that slack is given straight away, and the unused slack retrieved when the piece of gear is clipped. The belayer should remain constantly alert, continuously adjusting the rope through the belay device.

■ When you have led the route and reached the top, you may wish to have a rest for a minute or two, in order to clear your mind before bringing up your second. Remember your own safety, and communicate properly with him before proceeding.

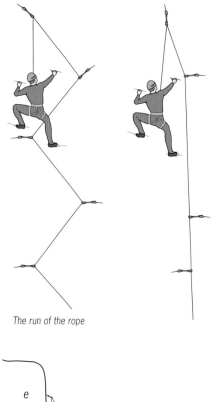

The run of the rope

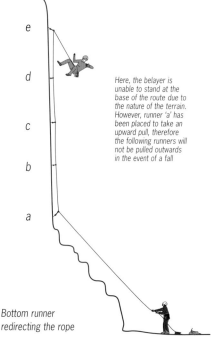

e

d

c

b

a

Here, the belayer is unable to stand at the base of the route due to the nature of the terrain. However, runner 'a' has been placed to take an upward pull, therefore the following runners will not be pulled outwards in the event of a fall

Bottom runner redirecting the rope

It is important to differentiate between the three styles of using ropes. The list below sets out the main pros and cons, and the diagram shows the difference between single/twin roping and double roping.

Single Rope (a full weight rope, designated to be used as a single strand)
PROS
- Simple.
- Light weight.
- Easy for belayer to control.
- Good shock absorbing properties in the event of a fall.

CONS
- Extensive runner extending may be necessary to avoid zigzags.
- All runners have to be clipped, possibility of long fall (see diagram).
- Limited length for complicated anchor set-ups.
- Disastrous if cut in a rock fall.
- Awkward if climbing with more than one second.
- Abseil distance only half the rope length.
- Difficult to protect a second on a traverse.

Double Rope (most likely two lightweight single ropes,thus can be used as a single strand at each runner)
PROS
- Straightens out zigzagging lines.
- Moves are protected with one rope from above and one from below (see diagram).
- Rope available for complicated anchor rigs.
- Rope available for rescues.
- Unlikely for both ropes to be cut in a rock fall.
- More than one second can be easily attached.
- Abseil distance full rope length.

- Good energy absorption in the event of a fall.
- Good for protecting a second on a traverse.

CONS
- Rope handling awkward if just one belayer.
- Heavier than a single rope.
- More runners may have to be carried.

Twin Rope (two thin half-weight ropes, both needing to be clipped into every runner)
PROS
- Ability to abseil full rope length.
- Lighter weight than double ropes.
- Rope handling easier than with double ropes
- One rope left if other is cut by rock fall, albeit half-weight.

CONS
- Heavier than single rope.
- Single strand cannot be climbed on alone.
- Difficult to protect a second on a traverse.
- Placing two ropes in a single lightweight karabiner not recommended

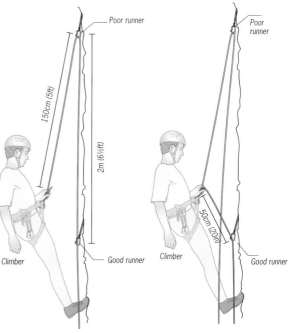

Poor runner

Poor runner

150cm (5ft)

2m (6½ft)

50cm (20in)

Climber

Good runner

Climber

Good runner

Clipping a single rope into a high runner. Distance of fall if runner fails = 3.5 metres

Using a double rope technique. Distance of fall if top runner fails = 1 metre

Rock Climbing

Comments on Gear Placement

This book concentrates on the more technical aspects of mountaineering in all its forms. Therefore, we are not including a chapter on the basic placing of equipment, since this can be read about in great detail in other publications. There are, however, several observations about equipment placements that need to be discussed. The object of this short section is to bring a few of those to light as a series of notes.

- There is a bewildering variety of different items of equipment on the market, both hardware and software, all designed for a particular job, and usually tested to stringent safety standards. All of these items of kit can be dramatically weakened by misuse and abuse, high impact, a load or a fall, corrosion, abrasion, cuts in textile components, prolonged exposure to ultra-violet light, incorrect loading over sharp edges, age, poor storage conditions, temperature, sea water, and chemical contamination. You should make a habit of always inspecting your kit before and after use, and discard any that shows signs of wear and tear, age or overuse.
- It is a matter of personal choice where you carry your kit while on a route. The gear loops on a harness are good, as long as the gear is easily accessible. A bandolier is another option; this is easier to pass over when swapping leads on a multi-pitch route, but it can cause the kit to bunch together making gear selection awkward. A compromise might be extenders on a bandolier, the rest of the kit on your harness. Whichever method you prefer, ensure that the kit is easy to get at and racked in a logical order.
- It is advisable to have a wide range of wire sizes: a set of 1 to 9 is good with an additional set advisable. For carrying the wires, it is best to split them into two sets of 1 to 5, and 6 to 9, clipped to two snap-gate karabiners.
- When placing a piece of equipment, summer or winter, as a running belay or as an anchor, ensure that the direction of load is compatible with the direction of possible loading.
- When a wire has been placed, it is good practice to pull down sharply on the karabiner to which it is connected, to help ensure a good placement and minimize the

chance of it swinging out with the movement of the rope. When seating the wire, only one firm pull is required: constant tugging is to be discouraged. Ensure that the hand that is not pulling has a firm grip on the rock, as a wire that flicks out of a placement when tugged may well send you off balance.

- A camming device with a rigid stem will not be able to be deployed in quite as many situations as one with a flexible stem. Care should be taken to avoid using a rigid-stemmed device in a horizontal crack, where the effect of a fall could snap the shaft.
- Camming devices should not be used on main belay anchors if at all avoidable (which it often is), as they are prone to 'walking' into a crack, which will compromise the make-up of the belay system.
- Care should be taken not to force a camming device too far into a crack as, once the trigger is released, there is a high chance of it becoming irretrievable.

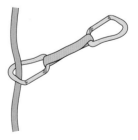

Incorrectly clipped. The rope could unclip from the karabiner in the event of a fall

Extender incorrectly clipped. Movement through the rope will cause the extender to rotate, with the possibility of dislodging the wire placement

Climber

Correctly clipped. The rope will run across the back bar of the karabiner in the event of a fall

Extender correctly clipped

- If there is a danger of a camming device 'walking' into a crack when being placed on the lead, it can be extended by clipping an extender on to the sewn tape loop.
- It is important, before you begin to lead, that you position your karabiners correctly on your extenders. Ensure that the gates are opening the correct way; it is normal to have the karabiners facing opposite directions on each end but this is up to personal preference.
- It is important that the rope runs correctly up through the karabiner, allowing the extender to hang naturally and not twist the gear placement.
- Bent gate karabiners are often seen on extenders. These are designed to make clipping the rope easy; unfortunately, in some circumstances, they allow the un-clipping of the rope to occur in the event of a fall. It is essential that the rope runs in a manner that lets it run across the back bar of the karabiner so that, in the event of a fall, the rope will stay well away from the gate.
- When a piece of gear has been clipped, ensure that neither of the karabiners will have their gates pushed against the rock and opened in the event of a fall. A karabiner's strength is greatly compromised when the gate is in the open position.
- Great care should be taken when using bent gate karabiners on long routes in summer or winter, as it cannot be guaranteed that they will sit in the safest configuration, with the rope running across the back bar as it should.
- Bent gate karabiners should only be used on the rope end of the extender, and never be clipped directly into the protection.
- Wire-gate karabiners have three advantages over solid-gate karabiners. Firstly, only obvious when a number are being carried, they are lighter. Secondly, the gate closure does not rely on an internal spring system, something which could freeze up or fail under certain conditions. Most importantly, however, is the mass of the gate. A solid gate, having a large mass, is susceptible to opening and closing very rapidly when the karabiner is at the top point of a fall, due to the action of the rope running through it at high speed causing vibration. As the gate-open strength of a karabiner is far less than that when it is closed, if the point of critical loading on the

karabiner should coincide with the gate being in the 'open' position (or the gate not being able to close due to karabiner deformation), there is a chance of it failing. A wire gate, having far less mass, will be less prone to opening during vibration, thus increasing the overall strength of the placement. This difference in mass can be felt by tapping the back of each type of karabiner against your hand, with the 'click' of the solid gate showing what happens during a fall – the wire gate should not make a noise at all when tapped with the same force.

- Care should be exercised when using extenders on bolted routes. The karabiner that attaches to the bolt is easily scratched on the inside surface when falls occur, and these abrasions could consequently damage a climbing rope. It is wise to keep a set of karabiners simply for the purpose of using on bolted routes, always using the same krab for the bolt. This could be marked with a piece of tape to show that it is only to be used on the bolt end of an extender.
- Slings are the traditional piece of gear for threading around anchors, but do not forget that wires can be threaded, too. They can be placed in such a manner that the head of the nut sits loosely on top of a constriction, having been placed by first passing the wire loop down through the hole and then clipping it with an extender.
- Often, the first piece of gear on a pitch is placed to avoid ankle injury on the initial moves, thus it may not need to be extended. It might be an advantage to simply clip it with a spare karabiner, increasing the distance for which it will be of an advantage to the leader.

INSTRUCTING LEADING

Overleaf there are a number of pros and cons of soloing alongside a novice compared to a rope-protected ascent when teaching leading. It should be fairly obvious that using a rope for your own security will be the safest, both for yourself and for your student. The importance of having the ability to clip your student to your system should he begin to feel uncomfortable should not be underestimated.

Soloing CONS	Roped Ascent CONS
Need to be competent climbing several grades harder.	Time consuming to set up.
No use to panicking leader.	Needs access to top of route.
Chance of being grabbed by panicking leader.	Rope may be in way of leader.
Chance of being accidentally knocked off by leader.	
Chance of serious injury if fall occurs.	
PROS	PROS
No setting up required.	Complete safety for instructor.
Ease of movement around route.	Ability to clip leader to system if required.

TIP

It is always a good idea for you to place the first runner for a novice client when teaching leading. This not only helps to reduce the chance of a ground fall from the start of the route (even a short slip can cause ankle injury), but also helps to relax them as they adjust to moving on steep ground.

OBSERVATION

Remember that, when you are leading clients in either a single or multi-pitch situation, they will be watching what you do and aspiring to copy it as closely as possible. For that reason, make sure that everything that you do, be it runner placement, belaying techniques, stance management etc, is as sound as possible and always work to current best practice.

ASCENDING THE ROPE

The safest way to teach leading is by using a rope to safeguard yourself. Considering that an average beginner's pitch will be less than 25m in height, the instructor's rope in this case has been doubled, secured to an anchor at the top, and the ends lowered down. The system that we recommend is as follows:

■ a handled ascender is clipped on to the rope at about head height, and this should have a sling on it to create a foot loop. Some adjustment as to the length of this sling can be done with an overhand knot once the system is rigged. As a back-up, a shorter sling may be placed from the ascender to the abseil loop on your harness

■ a screwgate karabiner is clipped into the hole at the lower end of the ascender

■ now put a Grigri, Eddy or similar active auto-locking belay device on the rope below the ascender, and connect it to your abseil loop

■ the dead rope coming from the Grigri is clipped through the karabiner on the ascender, and allowed to hang down free

■ place a foot in the sling, and pull the dead rope from the Grigri tight. Sit in the harness so that the Grigri takes all of your weight, bend your knee and slide the ascender up the rope. As you stand up in the sling (pulling down on the handle of the ascender helps here), pull the dead rope through the Grigri

■ you can now sit back in your harness with the Grigri taking all your weight, and repeat the process.

Ascending the rope using an ascender and a Grigri. The back-up from the ascender to the harness has been omitted for clarity

There are a couple of advantages to this method. First, it is easy to lift your body weight on even the steepest of ground, as you are using a mechanical advantage similar to a hoisting system. Secondly, it is simple to change direction and descend the rope should the need arise. With the Grigri taking your weight, unclip the rope from the ascender, remove the ascender and clip it to one of your gear loops, and descend.

If the ground up which you are climbing is not particularly steep, you may decide to do without clipping the rope through the screwgate on the ascender, just having it running out of the Grigri at your waist. The handle on the ascender (which still needs to be attached to your harness with a sling as a back-up), can be used to pull up on as you take the rope in through the Grigri, and you will also be able to use your feet on the rock to help. You can then sit back in your harness and push the ascender higher, repeating the process.

TIP
The second length of rope, the one that you are not ascending, can be used as a safety line for the leader if the need arose, perhaps if it is proving difficult to find gear placements. Simply tie an overhand knot on the bight into it and clip in an extender for them to use as a runner whilst you help them sort the problem out.

OBSERVATIONS
In ascent, it may be a good idea to tie an overhand knot on the bight every couple of metres on the rope below you. These will act as a back-up in case the system slips or in the event of you having to abseil to a fallen leader, using the Grigri alone as an abseil device.

If you are ascending the rope alongside a novice leader, you need to be equipped to deal with any gear placement problems they may have. Carry a few extenders, a bunch of wires and an assortment of camming devices, as you will be able to hang on your rope and arrange protection far easier and quicker than the leader will be able to do when he is feeling stressed and afraid. Remember that many novice leaders will be grateful if you place one or two key runners for them, so-called 'islands of safety'. This helps keep them focussed and also confirms to you that they are secure at any points of difficulty.

CLIMBING CALLS

Climbing calls have evolved to give clarity to communication between leader and second. It is important that they are called out loudly and clearly, and are not confused by adding non-standard calls within any sequence. If climbing on a busy crag or near other climbers, remember to use your climbing partner's name to avoid potentially disastrous confusion between teams. There may be slight variations when on a multi-pitch route, and it is important to clarify these with your partner before starting out. Indeed, a series of rope pulls may be employed when communication is difficult, perhaps due to the noise of the sea or the wind.

The essential calls are listed below.

TAKING IN – call from the leader that he is pulling up, hand over hand, all of the slack rope between himself and his second.

THAT'S ME – call from second to indicate that all of the slack rope between himself and the leader has been pulled up.

CLIMB WHEN YOU ARE READY – call from leader, which only comes after he has put on his belay device, checked all knots, gates shut and done up, tight on belay, in line with belay and able to brake correctly.

CLIMBING – call from second, but he does not start climbing until he has had the OK from the leader.

OK – call from leader to show that he has heard that the second is about to climb.

TAKE IN – if the rope has not been taken in for some time, or slack rope has been introduced due to unclipping a runner, etc.

SLACK – indicates slack rope is needed, maybe to reverse a move or unclip a runner.
Note: never shout 'take in slack', as these are two countermanding orders. If just the word 'slack' were heard due to the wind, etc, spare rope would be paid out when you were needing it to be taken in.

TIGHT – often called by the second, either when making an awkward move, or when expecting to fall off.

WATCH ME – commonly from the leader, meaning that they are about to make a tricky move and are not totally confident about its outcome.

SAFE – from the leader, to indicate that there is no possibility of him coming to harm. The second will normally say 'safe' at the top of a route to the belayer out of courtesy.

YOU'RE OFF or OFF BELAY – from the second, following the 'safe' call from the leader. (In some countries, 'off belay' is used in place of 'safe'.)

RUNNER ON – from the leader, to indicate that the first runner has been placed and the second must now be ready to hold a fall from a different direction.

BELOW – from anyone who has accidentally dislodged a stone etc. from a crag or route. This call must be shouted at full volume! If you hear the call, do not look up as you may receive a facial injury.

ROPE BELOW – a courtesy call used when lowering or throwing out a rope for abseiling, top roping, etc.

BOLTED ROUTES

Lowering Off From Bolted Routes

Although many bolted or 'sport' routes are furnished with a clip-in style lower-off, many others require you to untie and thread the rope through a welded ring or maillon. Communication is paramount here, as there have been many accidents where there has been a misunderstanding between belayer and climber.

Figure of Eight System – One and Two-bolt Lower-offs

This is the simplest and will deal with most styles of lower-off.
- Clip yourself into the chain or a suitable bolt with a cowstail.
- Pull up a bight of rope and pass it through the ring/s.
- Tie a figure of eight onto the bight of rope.
- Clip this into your abseil loop with a screwgate.
- Untie the rope on your harness and pull it through the ring/s. Tuck this spare end at the back of your harness so that you do not trip over it on the way down.
- Pull yourself close to the lower-off so that your belayer can take in the slack rope.
- Lean out on the rope to test the system.
- After a final check and communication with your belayer, unclip your cowstail and you can be lowered to the ground.

A single-point lower-off

A two-point lower-off

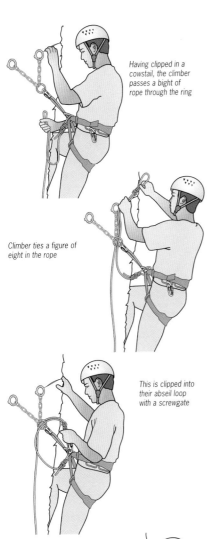

Having clipped in a
cowstail, the climber
passes a bight of
rope through the ring

Climber ties a figure of
eight in the rope

This is clipped into
their abseil loop
with a screwgate

Climber unties from the
end of the rope, pulls
it through, removes
the cowstail and is
lowered off

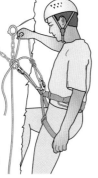

The process of arranging
a lower-off using the figure
of eight method

Tie-in System – One and Two-bolt Lower-offs

If the bolts are too small to allow a bight of rope to be passed through once your cowstail has been clipped in, or if you need maximum rope length, a re-tie system will be appropriate.

- Clip yourself into the chain or a suitable bolt with a cowstail.
- Pull up a bight of rope from about a metre down and tie a figure of eight or overhand knot into it. Clip this into an extender attached to a suitable part of the lower-off. This is to hold the rope secure ensuring it cannot it be dropped down the route.
- Untie from the rope and thread the end through the ring/s.
- Either retie onto the rope or connect it to your abseil loop with a figure of eight and screwgate karabiner.
- Remove the extender and untie the knot on the bight.
- Pull yourself close to the lower-off so that your belayer can take in the slack rope.
- Lean out on the rope to test the system.
- After a final check and communication with your belayer, unclip your cowstail and you can be lowered to the ground.

OBSERVATION

If, on a two-ring lower-off, you are not happy about the state of the bolts, clip yourself into each with separate cowstails, the second perhaps made up from spare extenders.

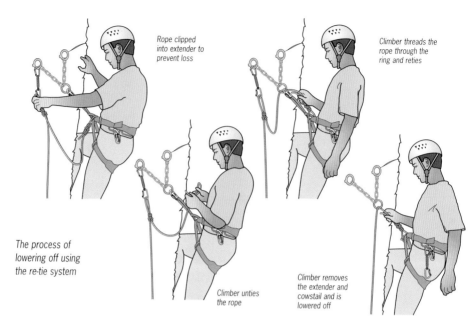

Rope clipped into extender to prevent loss

Climber threads the rope through the ring and reties

The process of lowering off using the re-tie system

Climber unties the rope

Climber removes the extender and cowstail and is lowered off

Summer/Winter Multi-pitch Changeovers

This section will illustrate different methods of route change-overs in both summer and winter conditions. In addition, we will highlight some of the common problems climbers experience, particularly those who are making the transition from summer multi-pitch climbing to winter multi-pitch climbing. When selecting a route, you should consider alternative options in the event that your choice is not suitable for any reason.

What is a Route Change-over?

This is the process of rope management, allowing climbers to alternate between leads or for one climber to lead the entire multi-pitch route.

Planning Your Trip

■ The weather: the effects on you and your partners.
■ Avalanche forecast: potential hazards at the chosen venue.
■ Route choice: consider the length and how long it will take.
■ Daylight: is there enough or is an early start/late finish inevitable?

■ Maintain flexibility: is the route in condition?
■ Equipment: personal and team needs.
■ Climbing ropes: single- or double-rope techniques.
■ Adopt a rope system: how many people are climbing; rope management.
■ Climbing partners: their experience; are you instructing or guiding?

Once you have carefully planned your trip the next stage is to consider whether you have the appropriate skills, techniques and equipment to do a route.

STANCE MANAGEMENT

One of the key areas that may often slow down climbing teams is poor stance management. Climbers often become benighted on routes because they have simply moved too slowly.

What is a Stance?

A stance is a position on a cliff face where you have chosen to stand or sit by attaching and tying yourself to an anchor, most often used to belay your partner up or down.

What is Stance Management?

Stance management is one of the most important aspects of climbing. When climbing multi-pitch routes, it is crucial to get your ropes organized and seconds positioned correctly. This allows the seconds to belay safely and the leader to climb smoothly. This is achieved by adopting a rope method appropriate to your situation.

Managing your Stance includes:

- location of stance
- equipment required
- rigging appropriate anchor/s
- tying yourself on
- positioning yourself for belaying
- preparing a position for seconds/thirds
- belay-device orientation
- position for spare rope taken in
- climbing calls
- on arrival at stance, positioning and locking off your second/third
- preparing the dead rope and belay-device orientation for leader climbing on.

EQUIPMENT

Careful consideration must be given when choosing your belay device, making sure that it is suitable for the job and appropriate for the diameter of rope/s that you intend to use. In an instructing situation, a self-locking belay device may be chosen, as this will give the flexibility to set up direct belay systems if the ground and anchors are suitable.

OBSERVATION

Bear in mind, when working out the time that it will take you to complete a route, that your clients may well be climbing a good deal slower than yourself due to lack of experience, nervousness etc. Thus a route that may take you and an experienced companion 2 hours to complete could take 4 to 5 hours with two seconding novices. It is important to be flexible when climbing and to be able to adapt the objective to suit the pace of the climbers, and to work well within your own comfort zone.

TIP

When leading on long or complicated routes, use runners to take the rope in the direction that you want the clients to climb. Thus, runners are not being just used for your own protection but are also there to 'lead' your clients along the correct line of the ascent.

Method One – One to One

Scenario: the route will be climbed swapping leads. The route continues up the wall behind the stance.

- The leader constructs and connects himself to an anchor system.
- The leader ensures that the belay-device orientation is correct. This means that any loading should not allow the live and dead ropes to cross at the device, which could potentially cause a lack of friction, affecting the device's ability to lock off the rope, or for the rope to jam. Ensure that the dead rope is being placed in an accessible position, very close to the belayer.

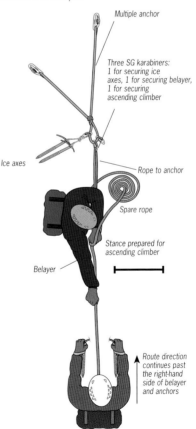

Multiple anchor

Three SG karabiners:
1 for securing ice axes, 1 for securing belayer, 1 for securing ascending climber

Ice axes

Rope to anchor

Spare rope

Stance prepared for ascending climber

Belayer

Route direction continues past the right-hand side of belayer and anchors

Climbing one to one

- When the second arrives at the stance, he secures himself by either clipping into the anchor, or by the belayer tying a big overhand knot on the bight on the dead rope close to the belay device. If the device needs re-orientating, the second should clip into the anchor while the belayer unclips and re-clips the device.
- The belayer passes the equipment to the new leader.
- The belayer now ensures that his stance is appropriate to the direction that the new leader will be taking and the climb continues.

OBSERVATIONS

1 Often, instructors will have two people climbing together while belaying them independently. To achieve this, careful selection of the belay device is important as is the position of the spare rope taken in. If two people can climb one above the other safely, then this will save a lot of time.

2 On some routes, climbers may have enough space to climb side by side, which will help prevent debris from falling onto others. Alternatively, seconds may need to move one at a time on each pitch to reduce the hazard from falling debris. In winter climbing, a stance should be located in a reasonably safe position, protected from falling debris dislodged by the lead climber or another climbing party above.

3 To achieve a smooth transition on multi-pitch changeovers, you should consider trying relevant techniques in a controlled situation. A steep route is no place to be when practising for the first time.

1 In winter the leader should secure his ice tools, either to the anchor or in a safe position near the stance.

2 It is important to have a ledge well prepared, not only for the leader and second to stand on, but sufficient in size to allow the rope to be flaked onto it. In some situations, it may be that a separate ledge is dug in the snow to accommodate the rope.

Method Two – One to One

- With this method, the leader, upon reaching the stance, prepares an anchor as normal. However, he also pre-places the first piece of protection on the next pitch, clipping the rope to the second through this.
- The leader will then take up a belay position facing into the rock, with the rope running from his device, up through the runner, and down to the second. When the second arrives at the stance, he has simply to take the gear from the belayer, and continue climbing. No re-orientation of any part of the system is needed.
- This method, though not always possible, is to be recommended. Anchors capable of taking an upward pull should be considered, in case the system needs to be escaped for any reason.

One to Two

Scenario: you are climbing a winter gully with two clients. You will be leading all of the pitches. You have decided to use a direct belay method for both of your seconds. Two ropes will be used.

- The leader arrives at the stance and creates an anchor, clipping into it and using it as a runner as he prepares the stance for the seconds.
- Two screwgate karabiners are placed in the central point of the anchor system. These will be used by the seconds as anchors.
- The leader ties on to the anchor and prepares for belaying.
- When the seconds arrive they should be stacked in order of climbing, close together and one above each other, or side by side.
- The leader should be positioned in such a way as to be on the outside of the seconds when they arrive at the anchor.
- When the seconds arrive at the stance, both dead ropes should be run through so that the lead rope runs from the top of the pile.
- The seconds then belay the leader. Both seconds may belay the leader, or just one using a rope through the belay device while the other rope trails and is hand fed by the other second.

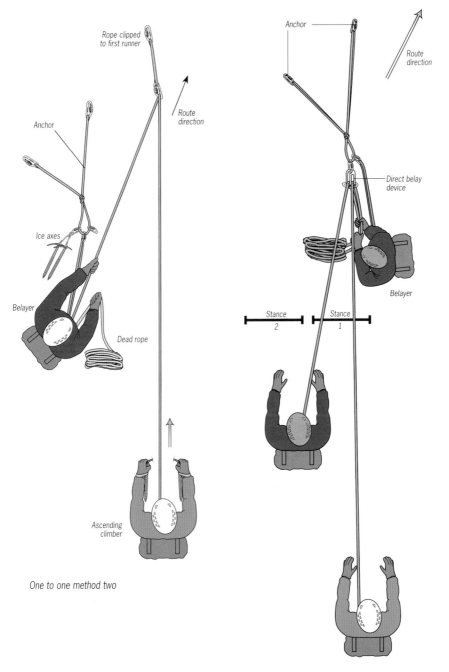

Rope clipped
to first runner

Anchor

Route
direction

Ice axes

Belayer

Dead rope

Ascending
climber

One to one method two

Anchor

Route
direction

Direct belay
device

Belayer

Stance
2

Stance
1

A leader brings up two seconds

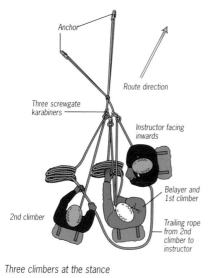

Anchor

Route direction

Three screwgate karabiners

Instructor facing inwards

Belayer and 1st climber

2nd climber

Trailing rope from 2nd climber to instructor

Three climbers at the stance

One to Three

Scenario: you are leading a group up a buttress route of a moderate grade. Two ropes are being used.

Method of Attaching Three Seconds to Two Ropes

■ The leader ties on to one end of each of the ropes.

■ Two of the climbers tie on to the other ends using a rewoven figure-of-eight knot.

■ The third climber ties on approximately two to three metres from one of the other climbers. First tying an isolation loop, he must then use either a rewoven overhand knot with the tail loop clipped back into the belay loop using a screwgate karabiner, or a rewoven figure of eight on the bight (using a screwgate karabiner to clip in should be discouraged when climbing), see picture on page 92.

■ It is important to advise the person tied on part-way up the rope that he must not climb past the isolation-loop knot; also, that the two seconds climbing together are briefed to maintain the distance between them.

OBSERVATIONS

Method Two – One to One

It should be noted that it is extremely important to place a runner above the stance as soon as possible when in a multi-pitch situation. This helps to reduce the shock loading to the system and avoids a factor-two fall occurring. The placing of an early runner should be of prime concern.

One to Two

1 The leader should remember to instruct the seconds on how to extract climbing protection from both the anchor and while on the route. Organizing equipment extracted from the route is important so that expensive and much-needed gear does not get lost.

2 Should you have two seconds climbing together on two ropes, either have them climbing one above the other at not too great a distance between them, or have them both climb side by side. You should think about objective dangers, such as falling debris, in winter conditions.

3 In most cases you may choose to belay your seconds one at a time, or, when the first arrives at the stance he could belay the last climber. One person should prepare the rope for the next pitch while the other belays the final climber.

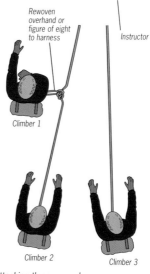

Rewoven overhand or figure of eight to harness

Instructor

Climber 1

Climber 2

Climber 3

Attaching three seconds

On Arrival at the Stance

- The leader creates an anchor, secures himself, and clips two HMS screwgate karabiners into the central point in readiness for the arrival of seconds.
- He then prepares the belay device and calls the seconds to climb in the pre-arranged climbing order. The rope with one climber attached is taken in first, as he will often be climbing faster than the two.
- The first second is clipped into one of the HMS's, in a position next to the belayer.
- When the final two climbers arrive at the stance, clip them into the second HMS using the short section of rope between them, so that they are counterbalancing each other.
  A clove hitch could also be tied here if thought necessary.
- Flake the ropes and run them back through.

OBSERVATION

When two climbers are moving together in winter, especially when sharing the same rope, there is a danger of injury through contact with each other's axe or crampons. It is essential to train in the art of ice-axe and crampon use before attempting a route, and to employ a full briefing about maintaining the distance between each other.

Stance Management: Common Problems

Whether climbing for fun, or professionally instructing, you should always ensure that your partner or client understands your stance management system and procedures. Should any seconds be unsure as to what is required of them, or lack training with interpretation of procedures, then problems and serious delays will arise.

Think about problems that you have experienced while organizing your stance: do the same problems recur again and again?

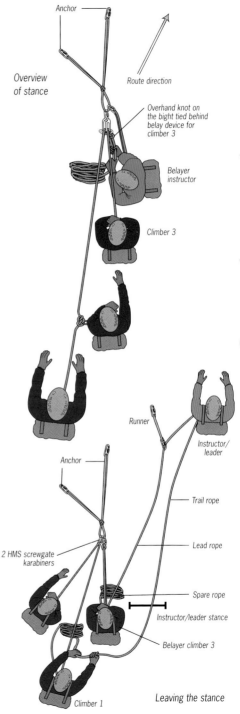

Overview of stance

Anchor

Route direction

Overhand knot on the bight tied behind belay device for climber 3

Belayer instructor

Climber 3

Runner

Instructor/ leader

Anchor

Trail rope

Lead rope

2 HMS screwgate karabiners

Spare rope

Instructor/leader stance

Belayer climber 3

Climber 1

Leaving the stance

Problem	Cause	Remedy
Ropes twisted at the stance.	Leader positioning seconds incorrectly inhibiting direction of travel of leader.	Leader positions seconds to the inside of route and stacks in order of climbing.
Rope running between seconds at stance.	Inefficient check of belayer and poor belaying. Dead rope stowed in wrong position.	Consideration should be given to the position of the person belaying the leader and the location of the dead rope.
Seconds and leader can't hear climbing calls.	Poor location of stance, inefficient briefing in climbing call interpretation.	Stay in sight of seconds shorten the pitch length in bad weather, check and understand climbing call terms.
Debris falling down on seconds.	Poor location of stance, poor route choice, poor technique, seconds dislodging debris on to each other.	Good location of stance protecting seconds from the line of debris, improved route selection, improved technique, ensure that seconds moving together maintain a short maximum distance.
Seconds drop the dead rope down route which then jams.	Inefficient stowing of dead rope and inattentive belaying.	Good stance management skills. In winter, dig a bucket or ledge for the rope.
Seconds incorrectly positioned at the stance.	Leader not having prepared climbing order, creating rope twisting and confusion. The seconds depart from the stance in the wrong sequence.	Good stance management; on arrival the leader positions themselves on the outside edge of the stance and route direction then prepares for seconds arrival.

Aim	Need	Action
Remain in sight of seconds.	Choose an appropriate and safe location for the stance.	Consider the level of second experience. Ensure that you can see the seconds, and that they can hear your calls.
Rig an equalized anchor.	Create a multiple anchor that allows the leader to carry on through with minimum disruption to the system.	When instructing and leading you may decide to avoid rigging the anchor with spare rope and simply use a tape sling to create a central clip point.
Safety of yourself.	Tie yourself on at the anchor before you call "safe" to the belayer.	Ensure that your position at the stance is appropriate and is suitable for the climbing order of the seconds.
Stance and anchor prepared to accommodate the seconds.	In winter you should dig or cut slots in the snow / ice for the seconds to stand or sit in, and then position them in climbing order.	Prepare screwgate karabiners in correct orientation at the anchor central point of clipping prior to seconds arriving at stance.

Aim	Need	Action
Prepare a position for the dead rope.	Ensure that the rope taken in will be stowed at the appropriate position for the belayer.	Arrange the rope neatly on the ledge, round your leg or over your anchor attachment point. In winter, cut a slot or dig out a hollow in the snow to place it in.
Ensure that you have an appropriate belay device, and that it is orientated correctly.	Be familiar with your belay device. Check that it is orientated for taking in and paying out the rope.	Learn how to lock off the belay plate to safeguard seconds on arrival at the stance prior to clipping on to anchor.
Preparing take-in rope for leading on.	Re-flake the rope.	The leader's rope should now be running from the top of the pile. The second attaches the rope to their belay plate. Leader climbs on.

OBSERVATION

When allowing your client to retreat down a section of route and head back down to a stance, bear in mind that they will most likely have stripped all of the gear from it before moving off to start to climb. Can you trust them to re-rig the anchor? If not, it may be much better and safer to bring them up to you by using a combination of encouragement, tight rope and rope tricks, such as assisted and unassisted hoists.

Lowering

Lowering is a method used to protect the descent of a group member or members. There are a number of techniques; this section will illustrate two of the commonest methods using a direct belay.

Where is it Used?

It is often used when traversing complicated ridges or descending routes where short, steep walls may be encountered. Instructors and guides around the world will use these techniques regularly, as it is often faster to lower the climbing party than to have everyone abseil independently.

Prior to lowering a climber, you must first ensure that your rope will reach the bottom of the cliff and that a safe area is available for your party once they take the rope off. In the event that no safe area can be located at the bottom of the cliff, two options are open to you:
1 manage the descent using multi-pitch techniques
2 find an alternative route.

Method 1: Using a Belay Device

Find a suitable direct anchor away from the immediate cliff edge. This will provide more space for controlling the dead rope, and will ease organizing the group's descent. It is important that the leader be positioned below the anchor and that they are tied on.

- Once you have located an anchor/s, bring it/them to one point using a sling.
- Tie an overhand knot in the sling about 10cm from its end, creating a small loop. Beware of sling angles; less than 90 degrees is fine. Clip one HMS screwgate karabiner into the small loop, and one screwgate into the main part of the sling. Ensure that the HMS is positioned correctly, with the gate facing upwards and the wide end pointing down hill.
- Fix the belay device to the HMS on the small loop.
- Flake the rope out and secure one end to the anchor so that it does not accidentally fall down the cliff.
- Tie a figure of eight on the bight on the other end, and clip an HMS screwgate karabiner into it.
- Clip the rope into the belay device. Now, clip the dead rope up and back into the screwgate in the main part of the sling.

Lowering

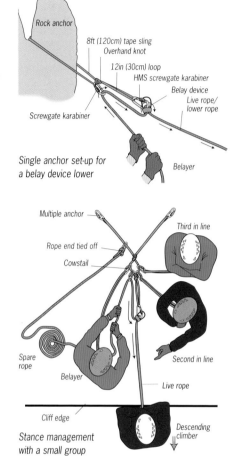

Rock anchor

8ft (120cm) tape sling
Overhand knot

12in (30cm) loop
HMS screwgate karabiner
Belay device
Live rope/
lower rope

Screwgate karabiner

*Single anchor set-up for
a belay device lower*

Belayer

Multiple anchor

Third in line

Rope end tied off

Cowstail

Spare
rope

Belayer

Second in line

Live rope

Cliff edge

Descending
climber

*Stance management
with a small group*

■ Clip the figure-of-eight loop onto the harness abseil loop of the descending climber. Tying them in for longer descents is also an option.
■ Position the descending climber below the belay device, hold the dead rope using both hands and lower the climber down.

By using this method you will create a 180 degree angle that is easily lockable and releasable while under tension. This additional friction allows comfort and smooth control when lowering.

Method 2: The Italian-hitch Lower

The Italian-hitch lower is an ideal technique when lowering climbers over a short section of rock, snow or ice. Unlike the belay-device lower, only one HMS screwgate karabiner is required.

OBSERVATIONS

1 It should be noted that the person controlling the rope must not be positioned above the belay device but should remain in front of it to maintain control.
2 The belayer should always tie himself on at the cliff top so he can comfortably observe the descending climbers; this can be easily organized using a sling from anchor to harness.
3 Always lower slowly as the lower rope will experience abrasion when moving under tension over rocks.
4 It may be necessary to place a protective cover between the rock edge and the rope, such as a rucksack or stuff sack.

■ Establish a solid anchor system, brought to one point with a sling.
■ Clip an HMS onto the sling in the direction of load, and ensure that the gate is facing upwards with the wide end pointing downhill.
■ The leader should position himself down-slope of the anchor and be tied on if appropriate.
■ Flake out the rope, tying one end onto the anchor, and prepare the other end for clipping onto the abseil loop of the climber about to descend.
■ Clip an Italian hitch into the HMS.
■ Clip the rope end to the climber or tie them on if appropriate.
■ The leader should hold the dead rope with both hands for lowering, and be wearing gloves. Again, it is important that the belayer is on the down-slope side of the anchor, in order to create the correct amount of friction.

OBSERVATIONS

It is essential that anyone connected to the anchor with a cowstail is below the attachment point, as the anchor, sling and lark's foot must not be shock-loaded in any way.

It is obviously critical with either type of lower that the belayer controlling the descent does not let the rope release at any time. Problems that can lead to this occurring include: lowering too fast and losing control; the belayer being incorrectly positioned; and the rope diameter not being appropriate to the lowering device, in other words too thin.

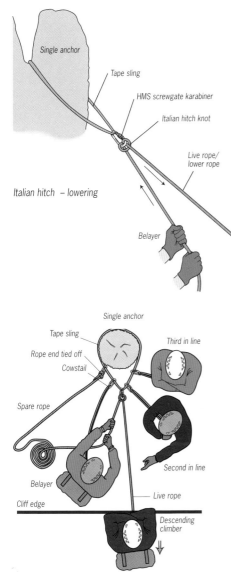

Single anchor

Tape sling

HMS screwgate karabiner

Italian hitch knot

Live rope/
lower rope

Italian hitch – lowering

Belayer

Single anchor

Tape sling

Third in line

Rope end tied off

Cowstail

Spare rope

Second in line

Belayer

Live rope

Cliff edge

Descending
climber

Italian hitch cliff-top management

OBSERVATIONS

1 The integrity of your anchor is critical!
2 It is worthwhile organizing your group in order of descent and ensure that members are either sitting or standing in a safe position back from the edge whilst the system is being prepared.
3 Once the descending climber has been lowered you should ensure that any knot connected to his harness is completely untied so that the rope does not snag when being pulled back up the cliff.
4 Each member of your group should carry their own screwgate karabiner. This prevents the need for gear to be hauled up the cliff, which has the potential to cause snagging problems.
5 It is important to encourage the descending climbers to maintain their weight on to the rope using an abseil position, feet wide apart and leaning back. Their hands will probably be used for balancing themselves away from the rock, although this will depend upon the rock shape and situation of descent.
6 Once the group have descended it is likely that the leader will need to abseil.

It is possible, with a bomb-proof belay and sound lowering rig, to lower two people at a time, particularly down non-technical ground. They can be attached in a number of ways, but we find the following to be the most practical. An isolation loop is tied two metres or so from the end of the rope with an overhand knot on the bight going on to the end of this. One person attaches here with a screwgate, the other person clips or ties on to the end of the rope. The advantage of this method is that you can adjust the position of the people to be either side by side or, more likely, staggered, with the person on the isolation loop a metre or two above their companion, making it less likely that they will get in each other's way during the descent. Alternatively, if maximum rope length is desirable for the lower, use a sling tied as an inverted 'Y-hang', with the central point clipped to a figure of eight on the end of the rope and each person connected to the sling with a screwgate.

TIPS

1 When using an Italian hitch to lower, the thicker the rope the easier it will be to handle and will achieve greater friction.

2 Kinking of the rope can sometimes occur when feeding the dead rope through your hands to the Italian hitch on the HMS. To help avoid this, flake the rope out on to the ground and ensure that the rope feeds from the top of the pile and not from the underside.

As a climber, you will rarely be more vulnerable than when you are abseiling, and there are a great many reasons for needing to do so. Getting to the bottom of a route on a sea cliff, bailing out from a multi-pitch route, descending to help someone, or simply retrieving stuck gear are all common reasons for abseiling. Many factors must be considered when an abseil has to take place: anchor selection, rope length, abseil length, rope retrieval, direction, destination, objective dangers and so on. Anything that you can do to reduce the risk is of value, and protecting yourself with a back-up is one of the most important.

Below we look at a couple of the ways of organizing a personal abseil, as well as a method of looking after a number of novices.

■

APPROPRIATE EQUIPMENT FOR AN APPROPRIATE DESCENT

There are a huge number of devices on the market that are designed for belaying, and an equally large number designed for abseiling. The wise mountaineer will select an item of equipment that does both jobs, negating the need to carry around extra gear. It is common to see climbers sporting both a modern belay device and a figure-of-eight descender on their harness, where either one or the other would suffice. Modern belay devices are excellent for abseiling with, while figures of eight are not particularly efficient when used for belaying. Thus, for the purposes of this section, we will assume that the climber will be carrying a modern multi-purpose belay device.

The mechanics of setting up a group-activity abseil, and techniques using just the rope with no extra equipment, are covered elsewhere.

PERSONAL ABSEIL

The method described here is the best way to organize a personal abseil for the vast majority of cases where descent is either planned or performed in an emergency.

There is no extra equipment needed, other than that normally carried on a route.

■ A 15–20cm extender is equipped with two screwgates, one of which clips into the abseil loop on your harness; the other, which should be an HMS karabiner, has the rope clipped into it via the belay device in the normal manner.

■ Ensure that the dead rope, the side that you will be controlling, is coming out of the lower side of the device. Put a French Prusik onto this, and clip it into your abseil loop below the extender with another screwgate.

■ The Prusik is held loosely open with the controlling hand while abseiling, and released when needing to stop. The controlling rope can pass between the legs, allowing smooth control with either hand.

Protecting a personal abseil

TIP

Abseiling is just one of the many reasons why it makes life easier to have the middle of your rope marked. Some ropes will come with the centre marked but, if not, it is worth doing it yourself. Tape of a contrasting colour to the rope sheath is ideal, or it is possible to buy a specifically designed rope-marking ink from a specialist climbing shop. The use of 'marker' pens should be avoided, as they often contain solvents that can damage the rope fibres.

TIP

A Petzl Shunt is a very good device for protecting an abseil, and it is placed at the same point that a Prusik would otherwise be used. Although we would not recommend carrying a shunt for general mountaineering, you may have one with you in some situations, particularly when running a group climbing and abseiling session. Thus, its use in protecting a personal or rescue abseil in this situation would be completely justified.

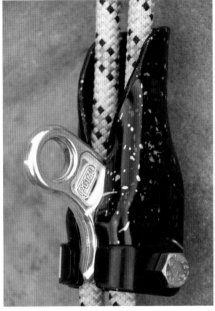

A shunt

OBSERVATION

It is important that a separate screwgate is used for attaching the French Prusik. If the same screwgate as is holding the extender is used, there is a chance that the Prusik will touch the extender with the possibility that it will not lock off effectively.

OBSERVATION

There is a method by which the Prusik loop is clipped into a leg loop for ease of control, with the belay device being clipped directly to the abseil loop on the harness without being extended. Although quick to set up and quite fine in many situations, this has a major drawback in that if the climber is knocked unconscious, he will have his back-up leg loop drawn upwards by the Prusik attachment on the rope, which results in:
- his body twisting in the harness so that he ends up supported simply by the waist section;
- the back-up Prusik having a real chance of touching the top of the device and releasing.

Another concern is that, in some situations, adjustable leg loops with self-locking buckles could end up with the Prusik karabiner under the buckle causing it to undo. Thus if you choose to use this method of protecting an abseil, be aware of the above problems.

MULTI-PITCH ABSEIL RIG

This is a useful way of setting up your abseil, either on a multi-pitch descent or when working near the edge of a crag and needing to be clipped in to the last second before you descend. Lark's foot a 8ft (120cm) sling into your harness strongpoint, either around the abseil loop or linking the leg and waist sections. About a third of the way along tie an overhand

Using an 8ft (120cm) sling as a cowstail and abseil extender

knot and it is in to this smaller section of sling that your abseil device will go. The far end of the sling can be equipped with a screwgate karabiner.

This rig means that you can use the sling as a cowstail to safeguard yourself at the anchor, and can connect your abseil device to the rope whilst still attached. Once the Prusik is in place and you are ready to abseil, unclip the screwgate keeping you at the anchor, clipping on to the side of your harness out of the way, and descend. Once you arrive at the new stance you simply clip the screwgate in to the new anchor and remove the abseil device and Prusik.

TIP
To ensure that you pull on the correct side of the abseil rope when retrieving it, you can clip the screwgate at the end of the sling on to the correct section of rope so that it sits above the abseil device. This will help you remember which side to pull on, as well as show how to undo any twists that occur at the end of the abseil.

OBSERVATION
It is essential, if using a sling lark's-footed around your abseil loop to create a cowstail or abseil connection, to ensure that this is never shock-loaded. Always be positioned below the anchor so that a slip results in as little force as possible being transmitted through the sling to the anchor.

A basic
'Y-hang'
abseil rig

THE 'Y-HANG' ABSEIL

This is used where two people need to abseil at the same time, such as in a rescue situation. An 8ft (120cm) sling is ideal, and the simplest set-up is shown in the photograph.

OBSERVATION
A 'Y-hang' can be set up using the multi-pitch abseil rig detailed above. In that case, however, it is essential that you clip through either side of the knot, otherwise the weight of your companion could pull the sling through the supporting karabiner causing them to drop a short distance, not a good idea at any time, particularly not when dealing with an injury. See the photographs on page 122.

THE ITALIAN HITCH ABSEIL

This is a useful method if, for example, a belay device has been dropped, or in winter if ropes are starting to freeze to the extent that they do not fit through a belay device. It is important that an HMS karabiner is used, to give a smooth descent with little chance of jamming.

■ If doubled ropes are to be used, one large Italian hitch is tied in both ropes together, and clipped into the krab. If two separate knots are tied, they would jam almost immediately. Ensure that there is no chance of the controlling rope ever touching the gate of the karabiner and undoing the sleeve. If you are right handed, clip the HMS onto your abseil loop with the gate opening to the left. This should ensure that the controlling rope runs across the back bar of the krab, staying well away from the gate.

Italian hitch
with free krab
on top

- The maximum braking effect with an Italian hitch is achieved with both ropes parallel, the dead rope held in front of the krab. When abseiling, especially at the start of the descent, it is very difficult to hold the rope in this manner because of its weight, and just holding tight to control descent will suffice.

OBSERVATION
The Italian hitch tends to twist the rope, so care should be taken to remove kinks before any subsequent abseilers descend.

TIP
When retrieving the rope following an Italian-hitch-controlled descent, care must be taken that any twisting in the ropes is removed before pulling them down through the anchor. Before you leave the stance at the start of the abseil, clip a karabiner onto one of the ropes and let it slide down and sit on top of the Italian. As you descend, the ropes will twist slightly, stopping this free-running krab from staying with you. When you reach safe ground, unclip the Italian and start to untwist the ropes by hand. When the free-running krab drops down to you, you know that there are no more twists in the rope, and can start to pull it down.

THE STACKED ABSEIL

This is a method of attaching one or more less-experienced people to the rope, and controlling their descent from below. The main advantage of this method is that, on a multi-pitch route, you, as leader, can abseil first and set up an intermediate stance. For the purposes of this description, we will assume that there are two novices with you, and, for the sake of clarity, will not go into detail about personal and group security at the stances. This should be obvious from the lowering and stance management sections.

- All three abseil devices are attached to the rope, the two for the novices being those closest to the anchor. Connect yourself to your device and back-up as usual. Attach a 4ft (60cm) sling to each of the other devices, and clip these to their respective owners. They can be shortened if need be, either by knotting or doubling them. These slings avoid your second and third being pulled around as you go down, and give them a little space to move. As you will be looking out for their safety, they will not need independent back-up Prusiks. Get them to position themselves near to the rope, possibly sitting on the ground, and ensure that they are fully briefed as to what they must do once you are down. You can then start to abseil.

- As soon as your body weight is on the rope, the two other devices will be locked and unable to move. Once you reach the ground or the next stance and have made yourself safe, the first of the two can start to descend. Hold loosely onto the end of the rope. They should be permitted sufficient rope to control their speed, but you must be attentive at all times, and ready to pull on the rope in order to stop them descending should the need arise. Once they are down, the second can join you in the same manner.

The stacked abseil

It is worth describing here the process of changing from an ascent to descent on a multi-pitch route. Retreat may be considered for a number of reasons: the onset of darkness, foul weather, being off-route, the climb getting too hard for you, illness, etc. The procedure is given in bulleted list form, in the simplest format for a logical progression. The climbers are using a single rope.

- The second arrives at the stance, in this instance belayed from a sling around a spike with an Italian hitch.
- The second is secured by tying off the Italian hitch, while plans for the descent are made.
- An abandonable anchor is rigged, such as a spare sling around the spike.
- Both climbers secure themselves to the new anchor with slings lark's-footed through their harnesses, set up as abseil cowstails as detailed earlier.
- The original belay system is dismantled.
- One climber unties from the rope and threads it through the new anchor until the middle mark on the rope appears.
- The climber who has untied holds the rope secure at the anchor as the other unties from his harness.
- The ends of the rope are knotted, it is flaked and delivered down the crag.
- The first to descend connects up his abseil device plus back-up, collects all spare kit, unclips his safety sling from the anchor, and descends.
- When he arrives at the next stance, he stays connected to the abseil rope while he rigs the anchor.
- When completed, he clips himself onto the new anchor with the sling on his harness, and removes the abseil device and back-up. He can hold the ends of the rope loosely to help field the second.
- The second person can now descend in the same manner, clipping himself into the anchor when he arrives and removing his abseil device and back-up.
- The knots are removed from the ends of the rope.
- One end of the rope is threaded through the anchor. This is then pulled down as far as the middle mark.

- When the middle mark appears at the anchor, it is held secure by one climber, while the other pulls on the second half of the rope.
- When the rope is down, the ends are knotted, it is thrown down the next pitch and the process repeated.

There are two positions where the back-up Prusik knot can be placed, below or above the device. Thought should be given to the mechanics of the system – if the knot is placed below the abseil device, the device itself holds the majority of the climber's weight, and the knot simply keeps the rope held back secure at the 180 degree angle required for maximum braking. However, if the Prusik is placed above the abseil device, all of the climber's weight is suspended by the knot, and the device is not loaded. The problem here is that the climber is now suspended by 6mm cord, and, if knocked, the French Prusik has a chance of releasing and melting through very quickly, possibly within a metre. If a Klemheist is used in this situation to prevent the knot from sliding, and it is loaded, it will be almost impossible to release again.

The only situation where the back-up knot could be positioned above is when using an Italian hitch. If the knot is used below the Italian, it can be argued that the hitch is being held in the open position, with the ropes at 180 degrees to each other, the position of least friction.

At the Anchor

It is worthwhile carrying something with you from which to fashion an anchor, which can then be used in case a descent has to be made. This can be a couple of old slings, some untied tape from a reel, or, in a real emergency, a knife can be used to cut a short section from the end of the climbing rope. Once secured, this does not need to have a karabiner in it, as this is the only occasion on which we can sanction having the climbing rope being connected directly through, and in contact with, another piece of soft-wear. As you abseil, the rope will be static. When you pull it down, it will rub against the sling and generate a lot of heat at the anchor end, but not on the rope itself.

It is for this reason that you should never use slings or bits of tat found in the hills – they may well have been used for retreat with the resulting heat build-up and loss of strength.

Knotting the Rope at the Ends

If the abseil is to anywhere except the ground or a very large ledge, the ends of the rope should be tied in some form of knot, so as to avoid the possibility of abseiling off. The best method is to tie an overhand knot on each piece of rope. This means that any kinks chased down the rope as you abseil can come out of the end, and you will not finish up with a large twist-knot as you might if the ends were tied together.

In extreme cases, where the abseil ends up out of sight over a roof or bulge, you could tie the ends of the rope together with an overhand knot, pull a little slack rope on one side and then tie a second overhand knot about a metre higher. This creates a step into which your foot could go if you reach the end of the rope and need some respite from your harness whilst you transfer to a Prusik ascent.

Knotting the Rope in the Middle

When abseiling with two ropes, or if one has been damaged by rock-fall, you will need to join the ends together. One way is by tying them with a double fisherman's knot. This does tend to tighten when loaded, so an option is to tie a reef knot in the ropes first, then tie the fisherman's. The reef knot stops the fisherman's sliding together and over-tightening. These knots, though, are a little bulky, and have a chance of catching on the rock on the way down.

Another very good method, however, is simpler. Hold the ends of the rope together and simply tie an overhand knot in them, approximately 60cm from the end, and pull it tight at all points. Now tie a second overhand knot, tightened up against the first. The advantage here is that when the rope is pulled down the crag, the overhand knot will automatically roll over to present the flat side of the knot to any obstruction, such as when it runs over a tight edge, with less chance of it catching. It goes without saying that the knot should be on the same side of the anchor as the rope that is to be pulled,

Two ropes joined with a double overhand knot

OBSERVATION

It is absolutely essential that a figure of eight knot is never used here in place of the overhand knot to join two ropes. Although it may appear to be safer, the figure of eight can roll apart when pulled sideways, even with a very low loading.

so it is here that having different coloured ropes helps, or clipping a free running karabiner on the side to be pulled as a reminder, in a similar fashion to that already mentioned for the Italian hitch abseil.

Throwing the Rope

Better described as 'delivering' the rope, this may seem to be a minor point, but it becomes important at times when a wind may be blowing, or when the area through which the rope must go is narrow, such as in a gully. Start from the anchor end of the rope, and allow two or three metres of slack. Instead of coiling the rope, flake it over your hand, doubled, laying it across one way then back the other. Split the rope into two equal sections and, grasping the centre of these flakes, throw the rope with some force at the target area so that the rope runs cleanly out of your hands. Flaking the rope is better than coiling, as it helps to prevent it knotting as it unwraps in flight.

Rope Orientation at Anchor

This is a small detail, but extremely important. When pulling the rope through, the correct rope to pull down on is the one exiting on the inside of the anchor sling. This prevents the sling from being pulled into the rock and creating a lot of friction, and the possibility of you being unable to retrieve the rope.

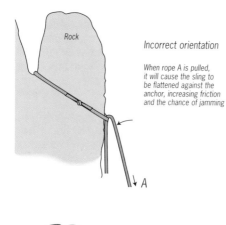

Rock

Incorrect orientation

When rope A is pulled,
it will cause the sling to
be flattened against the
anchor, increasing friction
and the chance of jamming

↙ A

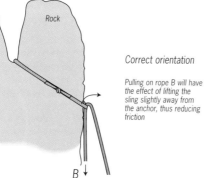

Rock

Correct orientation

Pulling on rope B will have
the effect of lifting the
sling slightly away from
the anchor, thus reducing
friction

B ↓

A B S E I L   S I D E

The set-up for a single rope retrievable rig

Retrieving a Single Rope Abseil

It is possible to abseil with a device, such as a Grigri or similar, that only allows you to abseil on one section of rope, but to still retrieve it.

Using just one rope, this method allows you to abseil half a rope length.

■ Tie a figure of eight on the bight at the half-way point of your rope.

■ Having used the smallest possible screwgate on your anchor, clip the rope in so that it is suspended.

■ Now clip the figure of eight to the rope on the other side of the anchor with another screwgate.

■ You can now abseil on the single strand of rope emerging on the opposite side of the anchor to the figure of eight.

■ Pulling on the figure of eight side of the rope, once you are safe, will pull the rope down to you.

It is possible to set up a similar system with two ropes, with a figure of eight at the end connecting them to each other and the anchor as above. However, if you have two ropes you will be likely to have been belaying with a device that allows two ropes to be used together, thus could use this device for the abseil, or you could use an Italian hitch.

Shortening an Abseil Rope

In some situations, you may need to shorten an abseil rope once it has been deployed. An example here could be at a sea-cliff, where you secure one end of the rope around a large thread and deploy the other end down the crag. However, you would not want the lower end to be in the sea, thus the rope needs to be shortened (we are assuming that using a sling at the anchor is not an option, as this would obviously be the easiest remedy). A short distance from the anchor, tie a figure of eight knot in the abseil rope. Arrange the lower end of it at an appropriate point to suit your descent and tie a second figure of eight at the top end of it. Now connect the two knots with a screwgate karabiner. You have effectively by-passed a length of the rope by doing this.

An abseil rope shortened with two figure of eights and a screwgate karabiner

Short Roping

Short roping is a group of techniques where instructors will plan to safeguard their clients, moving roped together over steep and exposed mountain terrain. Short-roping techniques are among the most misunderstood of mountaineering skills, as well as being the most difficult to deploy and the most dangerous when done so incorrectly.

■

Why does Short Roping Differ from Confidence Roping?
As opposed to confidence roping, short roping is a planned event whereby the instructor may be controlling up to two clients at one time on a rope. If it is not managed correctly, a slip could have severe consequences for the whole party.

Where is Short Roping Used?
In summer conditions it is used on steep narrow ridges and scrambling ground in both ascent and descent. In winter it can be used for the approach and exit slopes of winter climbs, and for descending moderate-angled snow slopes. If there is any concern about the suitability of short-roping as a technique, pitching may be the safer alternative.

What is Moving Together?
Moving together is a technique used to secure one or two persons on the end of a rope, while constantly moving over steep and exposed terrain.

The ability always to maintain control derives from the experience, skill and judgement of the instructor and their ability to constantly read the ground ahead, allied with having appraised the experience and competence of those in his charge.

Tying-on techniques used by the instructor and clients can be varied. However, it is essential that the tie-on is tidy, practical and efficient. Remember, you may be moving on steep exposed ground, so an error in rope-work techniques could contribute to a serious accident for your entire group.

It will not always be possible to find a suitable area to stop and rope-up; this is why you must be constantly planning ahead and always be interpreting the terrain. When moving together, you may also find it necessary to stop and pitch short sections, particularly in descent. Remain flexible.

Method One – Tying off Chest Coils
■ Prior to taking chest coils, tie into your harness. You should be wearing your rucksack at this point.
■ Place your left hand facing out, palm down, at a point near the front of your harness belt. This will act as a guide for the coil size.
■ With your right hand, take the rope from your harness up round your neck from left to right, and round your left hand, maintaining tension. Ensure that the coils are neat. Take in coils until the required length of rope is left.
■ When enough coils have been taken, move your left hand and put your left arm through them. Adjust them so that they sit tidily on your shoulder.

Tying off chest coils method one

■ Standing upright, the coils should not be loose but also they must not restrict breathing.
■ To lock off the coils, take a bight of rope and pass it through your central tie-in loop, up behind all of the coils, through and back down to an HMS karabiner that has been clipped between your harness leg loops and waist belt (NOTE: this should be the only time that a karabiner is ever connected to your harness in this manner). Clip in this loop of rope, do up the gate, and pull on the main rope to tighten the knot. The coils will now be firmly locked off through the friction created by the way it has been threaded.
■ To take hand 'coils', hold the rope and stretch your right arm forward.
■ Using your left hand, hold the main rope and flake the rope backwards and forwards over it.

Starting to lock off hand coils

To lock off the coils, see photograph opposite. With Method One, you can take off the coils if required by simply unclipping the loop in the HMS and pulling the main rope – there are no knots to undo – and coils can very quickly and easily be removed. Note that this method, sometimes called a 'soft-lock', should only be used where there is no chance of the instructor being suspended by the rope, or of being severely shock-loaded in some way. If this is a possibility, Method Two would be the one to choose.

Locked off hand coils. However, many variations exist

TIP

Be prepared with a few items of gear to use as runners, as it will be awkward to get into your rucksack once you start short-roping. A set of wires, two or three 8ft (120cm) slings and a 16ft (240cm) sling, each with an HMS karabiner, will prove useful. A couple of large chocks could also be handy, but watch out for using camming devices. These are sometimes tricky for a client to remove, especially if they have been rotated or 'walked' due to the movement of the rope as you led on ahead.

Method Two – Tying off Chest Coils

■ Take coils around your body as above, but this time ensure that the live rope is exiting forwards from underneath your left arm.

■ To lock off the coils, take a bight of rope from the main rope of approximately 35cm in length. Pass this bight from left to right underneath and back round the rope leading from your harness tie-in to the first chest coil.

■ Holding the bight with your right hand, pinch both the bight and the chest coils with your left hand.

■ Now pass the bight in your right towards the left, then up behind (on your chest side) the coils. Bring it through to the front, then back down through a small half hitch that has been created by the bight.

■ You should now have a small loop of about 10cm; clip this loop into the main tie-in loop using a screwgate karabiner.

■ Pull the main rope, and your coils are locked off.

■ Take hand coils as above if appropriate.

OBSERVATIONS

1 It is vital that the hand coils are locked off, as this will prevent them sliding through your hand and resulting in a complete loss of control.

2 We recommend that gloves always be worn when short roping.

3 It is important to have an arm's length of rope between the chest coils and the hand coils, allowing you to shock-absorb a fall.

4 It is important to practise on a variety of terrain types. Being able to tie off the coils does not mean that you can operate effectively on steep mountaineering terrain; any user of this technique needs to be competent, highly trained and practised.

5 When undoing the chest coils it is important to reverse the way you coiled them, one by one. If you take off all of the coils at once and drop them on the ground, you will most likely end up with a huge knot.

Notes on Maintaining Control in Ascent and Descent

The further apart the instructor is from his second/s, the more difficult it is to hold a slip or a fall. It is obviously important to maintain control when ascending, traversing and descending as you all move together at the same pace. The other option is to move from ledge to ledge, just climbing short steps at a time and belaying your clients up appropriately, possibly with an intermediate runner or two placed for your protection. Alternatively, you may need to protect a longer section of ground by pitching it using runners, bringing your clients up once you have selected a sound anchor.

Tying off chest coils, method two

■ The instructor will tie on and will then take chest coils. The distance that he ties himself off from the second person will vary depending upon the terrain, but will usually be in the region of 6–10m. The spare rope between instructor and client will be carried in locked-off hand coils.

■ Tie on the end client using a rewoven figure of eight.

■ Tie on the second client using an 'isolation loop', an Alpine butterfly or overhand knot with a loop approximately 40cm long, with an overhand knot on the bight tied on the end. Clip a screwgate karabiner into the client's abseil loop. This system of tying on the second with a screwgate is only appropriate on very short sections of scrambling or winter terrain.

■ If you are short roping on graded ground, anywhere of a serious nature or on longer sections of terrain, then the second should be tied in through the harness with a re-threaded overhand knot with the short tail clipped back into the tie-in loop.

■ Distance apart should be as short as possible but this will depend upon the terrain. For example, in summer you may have your two clients spaced 1.5m apart, then you may change that distance when you need to pitch, say 2–3m, to create a safe and comfortable climbing environment. This may be done by adjusting the rope through the overhand knot at the isolation loop or by retying the rope to a suitable length.

■ The instructor should always have the coils held and locked off in the downhill arm; this arm should be at a right angle with the elbow 15–20cm from the side of his waist. This powerful position allows the arm to draw in and out to maintain constant tension in the rope between himself and his second/s, providing reassurance and confidence to the clients and giving the instructor the ability to react quickly to hold a slip or fall.

■ The uphill arm must be free to climb with, and in winter this arm will be holding the ice axe. It is also crucial that his footing is always as solid as possible to be able to resist a downhill pull.

■ The seconds should be briefed as to the position of the rope between them and the instructor, particularly when traversing. The rope leading to the second client and on to the instructor should be positioned on the uphill side of their legs. It is also important that the isolation loop is not too long as the second could easily trip over it.

■ It is important that the client tied on to the isolation loop is independent, which helps to prevent a knock-on effect should the back person slip.

■ The second person should be briefed to stay below the knot that forms his isolation loop, as if he did not this will make a slip longer and will be harder to control from the front.

■ The instructor's belaying technique will vary from a braced stance and just taking in the rope through both hands where only a small slip could or may occur, through to a technical belay system that takes time to set up, with a host of belaying variants between. The skill for the instructor is to know what is appropriate in what situation, and have practised the skills, constantly erring on the side of caution and with the thought in mind that a slip, one day, will happen.

■ Clients waiting at a stance for the instructor to negotiate the next section can be secured by clipping a clove hitch from the rope between them onto an anchor.

■ When traversing with either one or two others

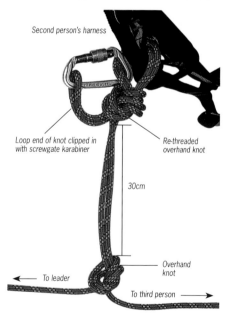

Second person's harness

Loop end of knot clipped in with screwgate karabiner

Re-threaded overhand knot

30cm

To leader

Overhand knot

To third person

Tying on in the middle of the rope using an isolation loop

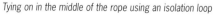

on the rope, it is important that they always remain on the downhill side of the instructor.

- On a traverse section, an appropriate technique is to protect the two seconds by 'en fleche' or 'arrowhead'. To perform this, hold the centre of the rope between the two people, and twist it 180 degrees to form a handle. The instructor now stays up-slope of them, and is able to provide a good deal of support.
- In descent, steep ground can be negotiated by lowering the clients and the instructor then abseiling after them. The clients can be lowered singly or as a pair, with the usual consideration about the solidity of the anchor system and the degree of control that the instructor has over the system being paramount. They can be arranged to travel one next to the other or one above the other, depending upon the terrain and style of lower.
- Clients should always receive a briefing on working together when short roping. This will allow the system to run smoothly and ease any potential frustration when moving closely together.

Changing Direction in Winter

To change direction in the winter, the following procedure should be adopted. This is assuming the ascent of an uncomplicated snow slope.

- The instructor stops, still with his rope arm bent in a powerful position.
- He tells the second/s to kick themselves a ledge, stand in it facing up-slope, and push

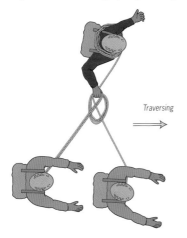

Traversing

Short roping using 'en fleche'

their ice axes into the snow, holding on to the axe heads. The person on the isolation loop can push his axe shaft down through the rope loop for extra security.

- The instructor, having been moving with his right-hand side up-slope, turns to face down-slope.
- He places the ice axe under his left arm, unlocks the coils, swaps the rope to the right hand, relocks the coils, the left hand then retrieves the axe.
- He continues to turn until he is facing the right direction.
- The instructor then tells his second/s to turn to face the right direction one at a time, the person on the isolation loop carefully stepping over the rope.
- The group continues.

The instructor may decide to simply place the axe in the snow and turn round but, as this is possibly on more technical terrain than with confidence roping, it is recommended that a grip be kept on the axe at all times.

OBSERVATIONS

1 It is vital that the instructor be alert at all times and be continuously looking ahead, anticipating any potential problems and looking out for running belays, stances, alternative routes etc.

2 The instructor must remain aware at all times of the comfort of his seconds, and, if there is any indication that either is struggling with the gradient, that section should be pitched or avoided altogether.

3 Should the instructor be uncomfortable or uncertain at any time, then he should stop moving together with the clients and pitch.

4 When moving together it is important to think about your clients' strengths and weaknesses. It is generally best to position the weakest to the front and shortening the distance of rope between instructor and that person.

5 When the seconds are of a different size, the heaviest needs to be closest to the instructor.

6 It is important to move at a continuous and regular pace suited to the clients' ability and fitness; while doing this the instructor will be constantly adjusting the length of rope to maintain tension. Keeping the pace slow and steady is usually the best way of managing the group and giving you time to look and think ahead.

Improvised Rescue Techniques

Much is made of improvised rescue. It is frequently referred to in instructional books, which give a bewildering variety of ways of constructing systems. Below, we deal with major problems that can occur, and give a reasonable response to each one. Practise these and you will find that answers to more complicated scenarios, and indeed far easier ones, will become apparent with ease. Remember that it will often be the simplest procedure that will get the best result. The following techniques are a selection of tools that are designed to be used individually or collectively to solve a variety of problems, most often in a multi-pitch situation.

■

If you get into the habit of bringing all of your anchors down to one point, this simplifies the execution of the hoisting and rescue systems greatly.

Be practical and think ahead. Do you have to spend hours constructing an elaborate anchor system when on a ledge only 10 metres up, or would lowering your second solve the problem simply and effectively?

Ascending the Rope

Scenario: you need to ascend the rope as you have swung away from the rock below an overhang.

■ Clip a Klemheist to your abseil loop with screwgate.
■ A French Prusik for your foot, placed below Klemheist, is connected to a 8ft (120cm) sling to act as a foot loop. A couple of turns can be taken around your foot to shorten the sling if necessary.
■ Clip an HMS karabiner on to your abseil loop and connect a clove hitch to this, tied with the rope from below the French Prusik. This will act as your back-up in case the system slips.
■ To move up the rope, push down on the foot loop.
■ Slide the klemheist up as far as it will go.
■ Sit in your harness and, holding on to the rope below the French Prusik to aid movement, slide it up.
■ Stand up, holding the rope for support, move the klemheist up again and repeat the process.

■ Every few feet, adjust the clove hitch to limit the distance it is possible to slide.

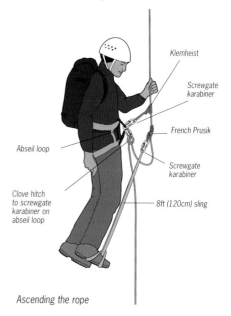

Klemheist
Screwgate karabiner
French Prusik
Abseil loop
Screwgate karabiner
Clove hitch to screwgate karabiner on abseil loop
8ft (120cm) sling

Ascending the rope

OBSERVATION

It is here that a small mechanical device such as a Tibloc or Ropeman might be useful, as they will provide quick connection to the rope and ease of use. Bear in mind, though, that these devices cannot be released under load, so take great care if choosing to use one on any particular system.

Changing from Abseil Descent to Ascent of Rope

Scenario: having made an abseil descent of the rope in poor visibility, you find that you are hanging free and have passed the last safe ledge. Ascending the rope is the only option.

■ Clip a clove hitch, taken from the dead rope below your back-up Prusik, into your abseil loop via an HMS screwgate.
■ Tie a klemheist above your abseil device and connect it to your abseil loop with a screwgate.

- Abseil until the klemheist is taking all of your weight.
- Remove the abseil device.
- Use a long sling to connect to the French Prusik back-up for use as a foot loop.
- Remove the screwgate that originally connected the French Prusik to your harness.
- Ascend in a normal Prusiking manner.

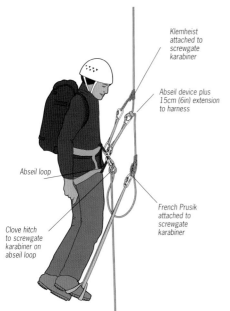

Klemheist attached to screwgate karabiner

Abseil device plus 15cm (6in) extension to harness

Abseil loop

Clove hitch to screwgate karabiner on abseil loop

French Prusik attached to screwgate karabiner

Changing from abseil descent to ascent

Passing a Knot on a Lower

Scenario: you are lowering an injured partner with two ropes tied together, allowing a greater distance to be covered and fewer stances to be taken. You have elected to use an Italian hitch to control the descent.

As for passing a knot on a free abseil, this technique is hopefully rather rare! Things are greatly eased if the person being lowered can get his footing on the rock or snow and take his weight off the rope, which will normally be the case. Remember, though, to be careful of a French Prusik placed on a rope that will be unloaded. There is a chance that the French will release and not sit back in its correct position once the rope is re-weighted.

- Set up an anchor system brought down to a single attachment point if at all possible.

- Clip in two HMS screwgates, and one extra screwgate attached to a Prusik loop via a 4ft (60cm) sling. One of the HMS's has an Italian hitch tied into it, with a French Prusik being placed on its live-rope side.
- Holding the French released, lower the casualty until the rope knot is about 50cm away from the HMS. Allow the French to take the weight.
- Without letting go of the dead rope, tie an Italian hitch on the dead-rope side of the rope knot and clip it into the second HMS, with the knot hard up against the karabiner.
- Unclip the first Italian hitch.
- Holding firm on to the dead rope, pull up on the French Prusik to release it and allow the weight of the casualty to come on to the new HMS.
- Undo the French Prusik and replace it above the rope knot, just below the new HMS, if required. It is extremely important during this process that you do not release your hold on the dead rope, so locking it off would be an option.
- Continue lowering, holding the French Prusik just released.

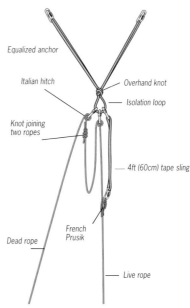

Equalized anchor

Italian hitch

Overhand knot

Isolation loop

Knot joining two ropes

4ft (60cm) tape sling

Dead rope

French Prusik

Live rope

Overview of lower set-up

Improvised Rescue Techniques

In many emergency procedures, when a French Prusik is being used as part of the load-bearing system, there is a slight chance of either the climbing rope creeping through the Prusik, or the Prusik jamming, especially when wet and under full load. An extra back-up may be placed in the system by connecting the Prusik to the anchor using a narrow-diameter sling. This should be attached to the anchor by using an Italian hitch tied off; thus, if the French Prusik now slips or jams, the system can be released by simply undoing the Italian. This consideration is relevant for the majority of the procedures detailed here.

Passing a Knot on a Free Abseil

Scenario: two ropes have been tied together to allow a single abseil on to safe ground to be made. This abseil will be free for part of its length.

It should be mentioned that there are not many times that this is likely to have to be used! It is usually the case that you can get some foot purchase on the rock or snow, which makes the whole process far easier.

■ Abseil to approximately 60–70cm above the knot and stop.
■ Put a French Prusik on to the rope above you, extended for about 50–60cm with a sling, and clip it into your harness.

■ Abseil a little further, stopping 30cm above the knot, with your weight being taken by the extended French Prusik.
■ Clip a clove hitch to your harness via an HMS karabiner as a back-up.
■ Remove your abseil device and abseil-protection French Prusik, and replace them below the rope knot, ensuring that they are placed as close to the underside of the knot as possible.
■ Remove the safety clove hitch.
■ Release the extended French Prusik by pulling it down towards you, and take it off the rope.
■ Continue abseiling.

Second Climbs Past Runner

Scenario: your second is so involved in the climbing that he climbs above a runner that has been extended with a sling, and ends up on desperate ground tight on the rope which is now coming up from below him. It is not possible for him to down-climb or reach down to the placement.

■ Lock off the belay device.
■ Using the dead rope at the point it connects to the anchor, clip a screwgate to a loop of rope and lower it down to the climber. He clips this to his rope tie-in loop or his abseil loop on the harness.

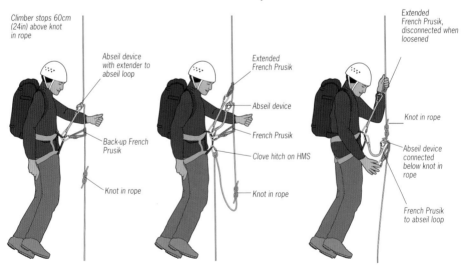

Climber stops 60cm (24in) above knot in rope

Abseil device with extender to abseil loop

Back-up French Prusik

Knot in rope

Extended French Prusik

Abseil device

French Prusik

Clove hitch on HMS

Knot in rope

Extended French Prusik, disconnected when loosened

Knot in rope

Abseil device connected below knot in rope

French Prusik to abseil loop

Passing a knot on an abseil

■ Clip an HMS karabiner on to your rope tie-in loop and clip an Italian hitch on to this, on the side of the loop coming back up from your second.
■ Holding on to the dead rope from the Italian hitch, undo and release the belay device. You can now belay your second down to retrieve the runner.

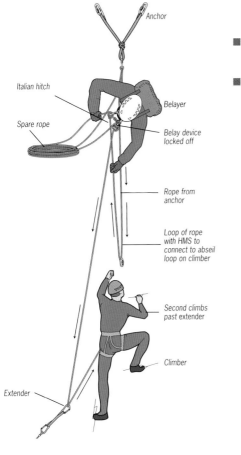

Anchor

Italian hitch

Spare rope

Belayer

Belay device locked off

Rope from anchor

Loop of rope with HMS to connect to abseil loop on climber

Second climbs past extender

Climber

Extender

Assisted Hoist

Scenario: the last few feet of a climb are too hard for your second, and lowering is not an option.

■ Lock off belay device around the back bar of the karabiner.
■ Attach French Prusik on to live section of climbing rope in front of the belay device, ensuring that there are plenty of turns. Clip it directly to the belay-device karabiner with a screwgate, and push it snugly down the rope.
■ Clip a screwgate on to a loop of rope coming from the dead side of the belay device, and lower it down to your second.
■ Instruct him to clip it on to the abseil loop of his harness, making sure the rope is not twisted.

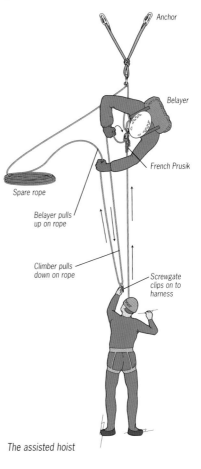

Anchor

Belayer

French Prusik

Spare rope

Belayer pulls up on rope

Climber pulls down on rope

Screwgate clips on to harness

The assisted hoist

OBSERVATION
You will now most likely lower the climber back to retrieve the runner. This means that you could revert to belaying him on the normal climbing rope, having unlocked the belay device and taken the rope in tight before they disconnect the rescue loop and you pull it up out of the way.

- Holding on to the dead rope with a couple of wraps around your wrist, untie the belay device and pull in the slack rope as you go. Be careful not to shock-load the Prusik knot in the process. Clamping your hand around the dead rope coming out from the belay device as you pull the last loop through will help to lessen the shock.
- Instruct your second to pull on the rope coming to him from what was the dead-rope side of the belay device; you pull on the rope feeding up from his recently attached karabiner. Coordinating the pulling helps greatly with the amount of effort needed.
- As you both pull, your second moves up towards you using the mechanical advantage inherent in the system. The French Prusik will slide up to the belay device and release.
- When you need to stop for a rest, or to remove a runner, first slide the French Prusik down the rope as far as it will go. You can then both gently reduce the pull on the rope, and let the Prusik take the weight. DO NOT let go of the rope, as it is still possible for the knot to slide.

Unassisted Hoist

Scenario: your second has slipped off a bulge, and is hanging some distance from you in mid-air. Lowering is not an option either owing to him being injured or insufficient rope being available.

This process is much easier if you have escaped from the system first, although a number of factors will go to determining if this is possible. The following is the basic process if still part of the system.
- Lock off the belay device.
- Attach a French Prusik on to the live section of climbing rope in front of the belay device, ensuring that there are plenty of turns. Clip it directly to the belay-device karabiner with a screwgate, and push it snugly down the rope.
- Reaching as far down the rope towards the victim as is possible, attach a Klemheist to the rope, and clip in a bight of climbing rope from the dead side of the belay device with a screwgate.
- Holding on to the dead rope with a couple of wraps around your wrist, untie the belay device and pull in the slack rope as you go.

Be careful not to shock-load the French Prusik in the process.
- Pulling on the dead rope initiates a pulley system. Pull in the rope until the Klemheist is a short distance from the belay device.
- Holding the dead rope secure, push the French Prusik down the rope as far as it will go.
- Gently release the weight of the victim on to the French Prusik.
- The Klemheist can now be moved back down the rope as far as possible, and the process repeated.

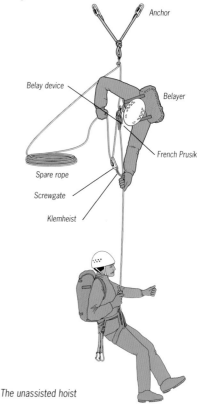

Anchor

Belay device

Belayer

French Prusik

Spare rope

Screwgate

Klemheist

The unassisted hoist

Escaping the System: Anchor Points Within Reach
- Lock off the belay device.
- Attach a sling to the anchor point, adjusted so that the end of the sling is just in front of the belay device. An overhand knot is the simplest way of shortening it if necessary.
- Attach a French Prusik on to the live section

of climbing rope in front of the belay device, ensuring that there are plenty of turns. Clip it into the sling from the anchor with a screwgate.

■ Clip an HMS into the sling and put a locked off Italian hitch on to this, taken from the dead rope coming out of the device lock-off knot. This will act as a safety back-up in case the French slips.

■ Ensuring that the system is as snug as possible from the anchor through the sling to the French Prusik, slowly release the locked-off belay device, making sure that you do not shock-load the French.

■ Take in the slack rope introduced into the system by taking it in through the Italian hitch, which is locked off again.

■ The belay device may now be removed from the rope. This means that the rope between the Italian hitch and the French now has a little slack in it, this is by design and should be left.

■ You are now free to untie from the rope, first ensuring your own safety by the use of a cowstail or similar.

Escaping the System: Anchor Points out of Reach

■ Lock off the belay device.

■ Use a sling and tie a Klemheist around the anchor rope/s (escaping the system is far easier if all anchors have been brought to one point). Organize it so that the end of the sling is just next to the belay device.

■ Continue as for Escaping the System: Anchor Points Within Reach (point two).

■ When untied, tie a knot in any ends of rope left to prevent any chance of the sling sliding off.

TIP
It is worth carrying a small knife with you when on multi-pitch routes. This can perform all sorts of functions, from cutting tape to fashioning anchors to solving hopelessly jammed Prusik knots.

Accompanied Abseil from Stance: System Escaped
Scenario: your partner is feeling unwell enough to cause you concern about his ability to organize and safeguard his own descent.

■ Select the most appropriate position for the casualty – either side by side or suspended just above and in front of you, at 90 degrees across the rock face.

■ Organize your abseil device with an 8ft (120cm) sling tied off to suit the situation – equal lengths for side-by-side descent, or have the casualty suspended from one-third of sling length for assisted descent. If casualty requires evacuation via the assisted-descent method, ensure that he is correctly supported and cannot slip back in his harness. It may be necessary to construct a temporary chest harness for him.

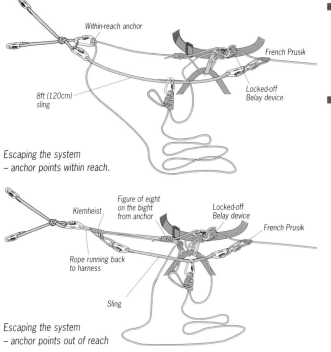

Within-reach anchor

French Prusik

8ft (120cm) sling

Locked-off Belay device

*Escaping the system
– anchor points within reach.*

Figure of eight on the bight from anchor

Klemheist

Locked-off Belay device

French Prusik

Rope running back to harness

Sling

*Escaping the system
– anchor points out of reach*

- Ensure that your abseil backup French Prusik is correctly positioned.
- Release any temporary cowstail system, and descend.
- With the assisted method, it will be necessary for you to carefully select your footing on the way down, and to field the casualty away from the rock and any obstructions.

Converting to Counterbalance Abseil: Anchor in Reach

Scenario: your second has been injured by a rock-fall some distance below you and needs your assistance to descend. It is not possible to safely lower him to a ledge.

- Escape from the system, remembering personal safety.

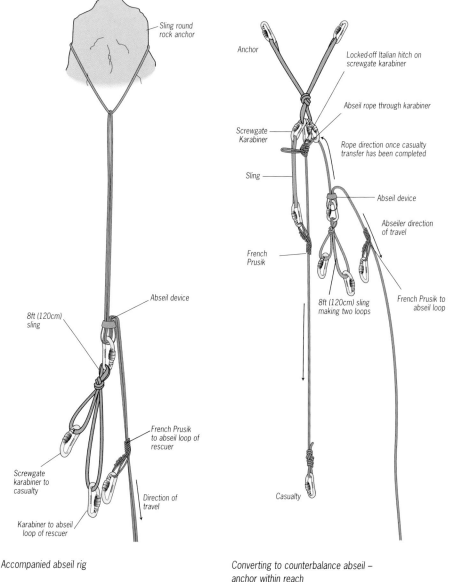

Sling round rock anchor

Anchor

Locked-off Italian hitch on screwgate karabiner

Screwgate Karabiner

Abseil rope through karabiner

Sling

Rope direction once casualty transfer has been completed

Abseil device

Abseiler direction of travel

French Prusik

8ft (120cm) sling

Abseil device

French Prusik to abseil loop of rescuer

8ft (120cm) sling making two loops

French Prusik to abseil loop

Screwgate karabiner to casualty

Direction of travel

Casualty

Karabiner to abseil loop of rescuer

Accompanied abseil rig

Converting to counterbalance abseil – anchor within reach

- Clip a screwgate into the anchor, and run the climbing rope through this, with the end of the rope thrown down the crag (now referred to as the 'dead' rope).
- Put your abseil device on to the dead rope, extended with sling as required, as well as a French Prusik back-up. Move up close to the anchor.
- Undo the locked off Italian hitch and remove the karabiner.
- Take in slack through belay device and French Prusik, moving close to the anchor again.
- Lean out from anchor with all of your weight on the rope, and release the French Prusik placed when escaping the system. Strip Prusik, sling and any spare karabiners from the anchor.
- Remove personal-safety cowstail.
- Abseil to casualty. Remember that, from this moment on, you are counterbalancing the weight of the casualty, so ensure that you do not un-weight the rope at any point.
- Strip any runners from above the casualty if relevant.
- On reaching casualty, connect him to you by using a short sling or extender, and arrange him either next to you or across in the assisted mode. It is important that even a seemingly completely able second is connected to you, as there could be a difference in your respective body weights, which will be amplified by the friction inherent in the system.
- Abseil to next ledge/safety.

Leader Falls on Traverse

Scenario: the leader has climbed a short way above you, then traversed to the right. He has fallen off, and is hanging in an area of unclimbable rock. This technique can be adapted for use with either a conscious or unconscious casualty.

- Lower the leader so that he is on a line just above the height of yourself and the stance.
- Lock off the belay device.
- Pass a loop of rope from the anchor end of the system to the leader. It will often be possible to throw this to him, but if he is incapacitated for some reason or is simply out of reach of a throw, it will mean escaping the system, Prusiking along the rope, attaching, throwing or lowering the loop to him, then regaining the stance.

- The leader connects the loop to himself using a screwgate karabiner.
- Clip an HMS karabiner on to your anchor system and tie an Italian hitch on to it, on the side of the rope loop coming back from the leader.
- Pull the rope in as tight as possible through the Italian and lock it off.
- Release the belay device and lower the leader a metre or two.
- Lock off the belay device, release the Italian, and pull the leader across as much as possible.
- Lock off the Italian, undo the belay device, lower the leader another metre or so.
- Repeat the above processes until the leader has reached climbable ground, or has been hoisted in an arc towards you and is now at the stance. The climb can now be continued, or the ropes pulled through and a retreat made.

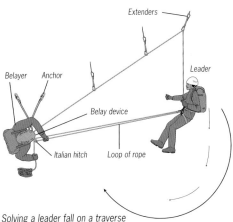

Solving a leader fall on a traverse

OBSERVATION

It is possible that the leader has fallen to a point below the level of the stance. If they are unable to make contact with the rock or are incapacitated in any way, it will be necessary to incorporate a hoisting system on the loop of rope being used for their recovery. This can then be used in conjunction with the method detailed above to help the leader regain the stance.

Leader Falls on Traverse – Unconscious or Incapacitated

Scenario: the leader has fallen at the end of a traverse and become incapacitated. The stance is very high up the route, but there is a safe ledge below the point that the leader has fallen. However, it will not be possible to reach it in one lower.

- Lock off the belay device and escape the system.
- Make your way along the rope to the leader, reinforcing runners along the way if appropriate. When you reach the leader, render any immediate first aid required.
- Directly above the leader, construct a new, sound anchor system.
- Place a French Prusik from the new anchor on to the leader's rope and push it down snug.
- Make your way back to the original stance.
- You will now become the back-up for the French Prusik that will soon be taking the weight of the leader. Use a French Prusik of your own on the dead rope coming from the back of the locked off belay device. Also include a clove hitch onto a screwgate at your harness as extra protection.
- Release the locked off belay device and gently lower the weight of the leader on to the French Prusik at the new anchor.
- Now remove the belay device from the original system and clip it into your harness, replacing the clove hitch. Make sure that there is no slack in the system.
- You will now be in a 'back-roping' situation, where the rope runs from the leader, through the original anchor and back to yourself, so that the rope is running through a karabiner on the anchor like a pulley, with you attached to the dead rope side of it. Using this system, make your way back across to the leader as you did originally, but this time paying out the rope every now and then through your French Prusik as you proceed. It is worth tying a knot below the belay device, which can be moved along the rope at regular intervals, as an extra fail-safe should your French Prusik slip.
- Secure yourself to the new anchor using a cowstail or similar rig.
- Add a locked-off Italian hitch to the leader's French Prusik.

OBSERVATION

There still may not be sufficient rope to make it all the way to the safe ledge, so you will have to make up intermediate stances. This will entail leaving a lot of equipment behind so make sure that you salvage as much as is possible from each stance before leaving it. NEVER, though, compromise on the security of the system.

TIPS

A mechanical ascender is a useful piece of kit to use when traversing the rope to and from the leader.

Crossing along the rope to the leader is hard work, particularly if the ground is difficult or very technical, and you may find it easier to pay out slack at each runner point so that you end up directly below the next one, and Prusik up to it, repeating the process as required.

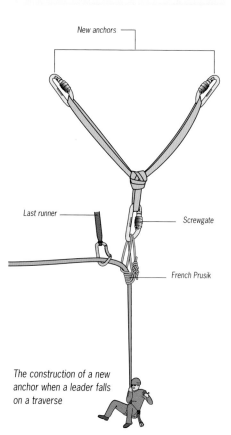

New anchors

Last runner

Screwgate

French Prusik

The construction of a new anchor when a leader falls on a traverse

- Remove your own belay device and French Prusik and pull the rope through from the original anchor.
- You now have a full rope length to allow you to lower, counterbalance abseil or whatever is appropriate.

Stirrup Hoist

Scenario: your second needs help past some blank ground, but there is insufficient rope to set up an assisted hoist.

- A free end of rope, either gained by escaping the system or the spare end of a double rope system is lowered to the second with a loop tied in it.
- At the stance, it is secured to the anchor with a klemheist, and above that is a clove hitch back-up.
- The weighted climbing rope is attached to the anchor in the same manner.
- It would help the second if they clipped a free running extender between the two ropes to keep them close together.
- The second places their foot in the loop of the spare rope and stands up. The belayer takes in the slack thus created on the original rope by pushing the klemheist down.
- The second now sits in their harness and takes their weight off the spare rope. This is moved up a distance, maybe half a metre.
- The second repeats the process by standing up in the foot loop.

This continues as necessary. It is important that the belayer takes in rope through the back-up clove hitches every now and then.

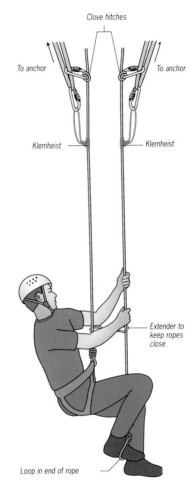

Clove hitches

To anchor

To anchor

Klemheist

Klemheist

Extender to keep ropes close

Loop in end of rope

The stirrup hoist

Improvised Rescue Techniques

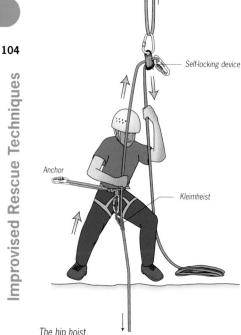

Self-locking device

Anchor

Kleimheist

The hip hoist

Hip Hoist

Scenario: the fallen second is some distance away from the belayer and needs to be lifted a short distance to gain easier ground. They were being belayed with a self-locking belay device on a direct anchor.

■ The belayer connects a klemheist from their abseil loop on to the rope to their second.
■ They bend their knees and slide the klemheist down the rope.
■ They stand up straight, assisted by pulling down on the dead rope coming from the belay device.
■ Bending their knees again, the klemheist is moved down and the process repeated.

Hanging Hoist

Scenario: a climber is hanging free with the rope to their belayer jammed solid in a crack above them. You just happened to be passing!

■ Rig a rope so that you can abseil next to the stuck person. Set it up in a 'Y' hang style.
■ Stop about a metre above the person.
■ Place a Klemheist and screwgate on their rope a short distance above them.

OBSERVATIONS

It is essential that the initial connection is to their abseil loop and not the rope tie-in loop, as this will be removed during the latter stages of the rescue.

Any time that you are hanging on the rope having abseiled to a casualty, or even if you are going up the rope to them, do not just rely on the French Prusik to hold you whilst you are alongside them dealing with the problem. It is important that you either tie a large overhand knot on the dead rope under the device, or better still take a few wraps of the dead rope around your thigh, as a back-up in case the Prusik slips.

■ Through this, thread an 8ft (120cm) sling. One side of this will be clipped to their abseil loop, the other is hanging free.
■ Place your foot on the free end and push down hard whilst at the same time pulling up on their harness. This allows their weight to be taken off their rope.
■ They clip themselves to the correct side of your 'Y hang' system.
■ You can lower their weight onto your rope, disconnect or cut (with great care) theirs and abseil.

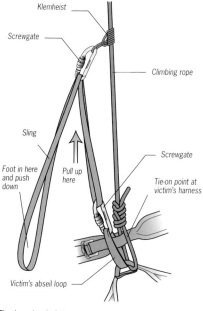

Klemheist

Screwgate

Climbing rope

Sling

Foot in here and push down

Pull up here

Screwgate

Tie-on point at victim's harness

Victim's abseil loop

The hanging hoist

Single-pitch Climbing Sessions

The idea of the following chapter is to help clarify the role of a rock-sports' instructor, involved in providing climbing and abseiling sessions for novices. These may be held for one or more people and could involve either friends or paying clients. The intent here is to look at both the hard and soft skills involved in providing a safe and enjoyable time on the rock.

■

VENUE SELECTION

What Makes a Crag Qualify as 'Single-pitch'?

There is a very convenient description of a cliff or crag which can be designated as suitable for use with novice groups. As safety is paramount, these guidelines should be well considered when choosing an activity venue. A true single-pitch crag will be no more than a rope length in height, and will be described as single pitch in a guide book. It must be climbable without intermediate stances, and must allow a second to be lowered to the ground at all times. It must be non-tidal, and have no navigational nightmares involved in reaching it. There should be little objective danger, and should allow easy access to top and bottom.

What Else Would Make a Crag Good for Single-pitch Activities?

Apart from conforming to the above criteria, an ideal single-pitch crag will have a variety of features that make group management and route choice simpler. A few of the more important features are listed below, together with some elementary considerations.

■ Car parking. It would be very useful if this were off the main road. Having a group, especially younger participants, around your transport on a busy or narrow road could lead to an accident.

■ Short walk in. Not only because there may well be a lot of equipment to carry, but also in case a return has to be made to the transport for any emergency.

■ Safe area at crag. This needs to be a defined safe area, perhaps a flat area of grass

surrounded by rocks or bushes, which is unmistakable to the group members.

It should be easily in view from the activity area, without being in a dangerous position too close to the edge or too near to the bottom of the crag.

■ Toilet area. This could either be properly designed public toilets, or a designated area near the crag. If the local area has to be used for the toilet, EXTREME consideration must be given to environmental impact, line of water courses, etc, and thought given to the carrying out of solid waste.

■ Crag accessible by public or by consent. Consideration should be given to any access agreement and landowner's requirements, as well as to any nesting bird or environmental restrictions.

■ Warm-up area. It would be useful to have an area in which your group could warm up, or be introduced to the different ways of using holds. An area with large holds and a safe landing underfoot would be ideal.

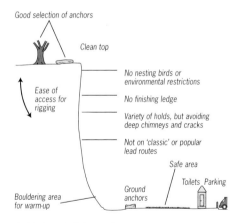

Good selection of anchors

Clean top

Ease of access for rigging

No nesting birds or environmental restrictions

No finishing ledge

Variety of holds, but avoiding deep chimneys and cracks

Not on 'classic' or popular lead routes

Safe area

Toilets Parking

Ground anchors

Bouldering area for warm-up

An ideal single-pitch venue!

> **TIP**
>
> It can prove very useful to have a large plastic bag or bin liner to hand. This can be placed in the centre of the safe area and not only be used as a receptacle for rubbish, but also act as a physical reminder to your group about the location of your designated safe area.

To make your activity session more enjoyable for your group, it will be necessary to consider the weather and its effect on the day. For instance, if the crag is north-facing and the weather is forecast to bring cold winds with blustery showers, would a different venue be more appropriate? Conversely, if the crag is south-facing and you are in the middle of a heat-wave, is it still a sensible choice?

■ Variety. A variety of routes and abseils would be useful. These should allow the novice to achieve early on; to put a beginner on a desperate overhanging prow as a first route would guarantee his failure and subsequent lack of interest in the rest of the day's proceedings.

■ Other users. Consideration must be given to other crag users. Avoid blocking routes that are popular leads, 'classics' or abseiling down those with delicate holds. Avoid covering steep hard slab routes with mud from boots. Talk to other crag users to ensure that you are not getting in their way – remember that a couple leading will always take precedence over a group. Remember group control: noise is also a very anti-social thing to many people.

■ Route choice. Your choice of route can either cause or save you so many problems, it is really worth taking time to select carefully. The steepness of the route should be considered, taking into account the proficiency of your group. A route with no defined finishing ledge is ideal, especially for novices, as it can help to negate the problem of the crag-fast climber. A variety of holds is ideal, but avoid deep chimneys and cracks.

■ Anchors. A good selection of anchors at the top of the climb will obviously be necessary, for either top-rope or bottom-rope sessions, and ground anchors will be extremely useful for direct belays when bottom roping.

■ Access to top. Ease of access to the top is important when rigging, especially if group members are helping to carry equipment for you. Remember that one of the criteria for group use of a single-pitch crag is that access must be simple. That means that if any group member has to use his hands to get up the path, its suitability as a venue should be questioned.

TOP AND BOTTOM-ROPE SYSTEMS

It is necessary to be aware of what is meant by 'top roping' and 'bottom roping'. Top roping simply means that the belayer controlling the rope is at the top of the climb, bottom roping means that the person controlling the rope is at the foot of the climb, with the rope running up and back down to the climber through a pulley-type system.

Both systems have their pros and cons, and there will be many factors to consider when deciding which option to use. Below are listed a number of the main for-and-against points of each method. It will be noticed that the bottom-roping system appears to have more going for it than its counterpart, but it should be remembered that it is only by true top roping that a climber will get to complete a route from bottom to top, surely the reason for climbing in the first place.

A Comparison Between Group Top and Bottom Rope Systems

The Top-Rope System

PROS	CONS
■ Quick to rig.	■ Difficult for belayer to see all the moves on the climb.
■ Allows for traditional topping out and feeling of achievement.	■ Creates maximum distance between belayer and climber at start.
■ Good approach to climbing for those progressing to leading, multi-pitch routes etc.	■ Communication can be difficult and confusing to the novice.
■ Nervous novice is approaching a friendly face, can be encouraged upwards and has something to focus on.	■ Novice feels that they have 'failed' if they do not reach the top of the cliff.
	■ Providing direct assistance by pulling on the rope is hard to do.
	■ Group management at top of cliff requires close attention.
	■ Some group members remain at bottom of crag during part or all of the activity - difficult for management.
	■ Difficulty of checking attachment of climber to rope.
	■ Very difficult for group members to belay other climbers.
	■ Top-roping causes general wear and tear to cliff top.
	■ Group needs managing on descent paths, with resultant wear and tear.

The Bottom Rope System

PROS	CONS
■ Allows an instructor to move around freely and supervise more than one rope at the same time.	■ Each system takes time to rig correctly and the anchors are out of sight.
■ Students are able to belay under supervision, and several can be occupied at the same time.	■ Anchors need to be bomb-proof as loading can be around two times the force exerted by a single climber.
■ It can be easier for a novice to learn how to use a variety of belay techniques correctly.	■ It prevents students from 'topping out' and thus gaining a feeling of real achievement.
■ The instructor is with his group, making group management easier.	■ May encourage the assumption that bottom-roping is the 'normal' way to climb.
■ The instructor is 'right there', and can offer close encouragement and assistance to anxious novices making their first moves on a climb.	■ Care must be taken to not be monopolising a route.
■ Easy to provide direct assistance by belayer sitting back on the rope.	■ A nervous novice ends up a long way from a 'friendly face' and may have trouble committing themselves to a lower.
■ Cliff top and descent path safety concerns are removed.	
■ Students do not feel that they have failed if they fail to reach the top.	
■ It can reduce cliff top erosion and unsightly descent paths.	
■ Correct attachment of the climber to the rope can be guaranteed.	

TOP-ROPE SYSTEMS

Careful thought must go into setting up a top-rope system when dealing with novice climbers. If climbing with peers, the simplest and most popular method would be to belay with a device attached to your tie-in loop. However, in a group there may be more of a chance of having to escape the system and leave the stance, and a direct-belay system will be more appropriate. The diagram below shows a very simple and safe way of organizing the system, and allows a lot of flexibility for the position of the belayer.

Attachment to the Rope

This must be carefully considered for both top and bottom-rope sessions. Our recommendation for either is that the climber is always tied in through the harness, rather than be attached by a screwgate karabiner. Although a krab may be convenient, there is a danger of a sideways loading occurring across the gate, seriously weakening the system. There is also the chance of the gate rubbing on the rock and unscrewing. When using a top-rope system, it would be very convenient, although frequently not practical, if there were a helper at the bottom to assist and check that each of the climbers was tied on before they started.

OBSERVATION

Ensure that all group members are fully briefed as to what is expected of them before you go to the top of the crag – shouted instructions rarely make sense. Once they have climbed up to you, have a safe area designated behind you well away from the cliff edge, to which they can go before taking off the rope.

Also make sure that they will not end up taking the lead as they go past you. This could occur if you have organized the stance a little way down an eroded exit for instance; great care must be taken to prevent this from happening. It is not acceptable for a novice to be leading, as the consequences of a slip on the final moves are dire.

BELAY METHODS

There are various ways of securing a climber, and below are listed some of the most common. The main emphasis of this is on protecting a climber during a group bottom-roping session. Often, the choice will be determined by the experience of the people you are climbing with, the equipment available and the availability of ground anchors.

OBSERVATIONS

If you elect to clip your group in rather than tie them, some harness manufacturers recommend that 2 screwgate karabiners are used for connecting the rope to the harness. This helps to negate the chance of a sideways loading on a single karabiner, as well as any possibility of it opening. Make sure that you know what the manufacturer recommends for any kit that you are using.

Take great care when attaching children as well as adults to the rope. Have them facing their friends or family and, if you are tying them on rather than using karabiners, get them to thread the rope through the appropriate part of the harness before you finish the knot off for them. Be extremely careful about any chance of inappropriate touching and make sure that everyone is aware of what you are doing.

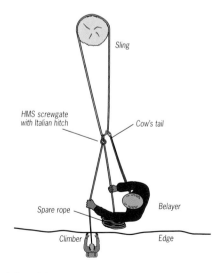

Sling

HMS screwgate with Italian hitch

Cow's tail

Spare rope

Belayer

Climber

Edge

A direct belay system

Method	Pros	Cons
Belay device onto harness.	Easy to operate, good control.	Needs ground anchor or other group member to escape the system.
Italian Hitch onto harness.	Simple, good control.	Twists the rope, needs ground anchor or other group member to escape the system
Belay plate onto direct anchor.	Smooth take-in, belayer out of system.	Awkward to control, 'floppy' action, belayer must be behind plate, relies on availability of ground anchors.
Italian hitch onto direct anchor.	Smooth take in and pay out, easy to control, belayer can be in front of anchor, belayer out of system, easy to lock off.	Twists rope, relies on availability of ground anchors.
Belay plate or Italian hitch controlled by student on their harness.	As above, plus instructor out of system, group members occupied.	Care needed when teaching novices.
Two or three novices clipped together and walking back as climber ascends.	No technical kit needed, keeps group members occupied.	Dependant upon having lots of space and flat ground, anti-social to other crag users, danger of belayers 'larking about'.
'Bell 'ringing', where one group member sits at base of route facing out and pulls rope down into Italian hitch, with one or two other group members pulling out on dead rope.	Group members occupied, instructor out of system.	Demeaning for group member at bottom of climb, chance of them being injured by fall or debris from above, spinal injury possible by being pulled up in event of a fall.

OBSERVATION

Make sure that you are clear about the difference between direct and indirect belays. The best way to remember it is that the direct belay goes directly to the anchor, without being clipped to the belayer in any way, while an indirect belay is controlled by the belayer from his tie-in loop or similar.

BOTTOM-ROPE SYSTEMS

There is a number of ways of rigging a bottom-rope system, but whichever is chosen it should have the same result – total security and ease of operation. Given below is arguably the best of the many possible systems. Here, we will assume that two anchor points are being used.

EQUIPMENT
Low-stretch rigging rope, slings, screwgates, climbing rope, rope protectors.

Method
- Assuming that the anchors are roughly equal distance from the edge of the crag, tie a double figure of eight in the centre of the rigging rope.
- Judge where you want the figure of eight to hang by placing it over the edge as a measure, and tie an overhand knot about a metre back from the cliff edge. This makes protecting the rope easier, as well as directing the forces along one line - 'vectoring'.
- Clip two screwgate karabiners into the figure of eight, Arrange these so that they open in opposite directions and have the gates opening at the bottom to prevent vibration during use from unscrewing them.

Bottom rope rig

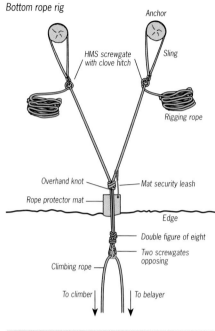

Anchor

HMS screwgate
with clove hitch

Sling

Rigging rope

Overhand knot

Mat security leash

Rope protector mat

Edge

Double figure of eight

Two screwgates
opposing

Climbing rope

To climber | | To belayer

TIP

Rope protectors are very useful, not just to stop your rope from possible damage on edges, but also to save areas of soft rock from eroding. They are available commercially, or can be made very simply. Use a square of carpet, about 30cm x 30cm, such as are commonly used as samples by carpet showrooms. Make a hole about 5cm in from the centre of one side, lark's-foot through an old sling, and attach a Prusik loop to this. The Prusik loop or the sling can be used to secure the protector in the right place.

OBSERVATION

It is usual to use low-stretch rigging ropes for the anchor part of the set-up. Using standard dynamic climbing ropes is OK, but as they tend to stretch they can make the rig feel somewhat springy. However, the main reason to avoid using them is that, if they run over an edge, the weight of climber or abseiler will cause them to stretch and contract many times causing damage to the rock and, as seriously, damage to the rope.

■ Clip the climbing rope in and deploy it down the crag. It is easy to hold on to the rigging rope whilst doing this (but if you are concerned then clip a clove hitch on to an anchor so that you do not drop the whole lot. This would also be an appropriate attachment point for your own security).

■ Let the weight of the climbing rope help you get the figure of eight back into position, then attach the rigging rope to each of the anchors with a clove hitch.

■ Tidy up the rope ends, place any rope protectors, check through everything and that is the rig finished.

TIPS

If you can see the karabiners on the figure of eight from your belay position at the bottom of the crag, this usually means that they are far enough over the edge.

When setting the system up, you may decide to not use the centre of the rigging rope but start closer to one end. This means that you will have some rope left over that may be useful if an emergency procedure has to be put into place.

OBSERVATIONS

1 Be very careful to look after your own safety when rigging a system; it is easy to clip yourself in as you work and it makes a lot of sense to do so.

2 Check your kit after use for wear and tear, particularly karabiners. These have a hard life being used for group sessions, and can become worn and pitted quite quickly. Steel karabiners wear more slowly than alloy, so they could be used as the two top krabs in the rig where the rope runs.

3 If the tail end of the rigging rope coming out of the clove hitches is short (around half a metre), lock them off with a couple of half hitches for extra security.

RIGGING FOR USE BY LESS-ABLE GROUPS

If you are working with, or teaching the supervision of, climbers with special requirements, in particular reduced mobility, there is a method of rigging the bottom rope that allows them to belay each other. Indeed, this system can even be used by someone in a wheelchair who wishes to learn to belay.

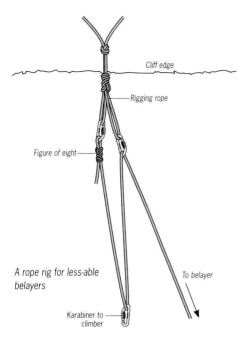

Cliff edge

Rigging rope

Figure of eight

A rope rig for less-able belayers

To belayer

Karabiner to climber

OBSERVATION

Another option, and one that is more suited to indoor climbing, is to arrange the system so that there is an Italian hitch at the top of the climb, so that the rope runs up from the climber, through the hitch and then back down to the belayer. This again is a very good way of reducing the loading on a less-able belayer, but it is a huge judgement-call to state that the Italian hitch will not jam during normal operation. Obviously, if it does, it is out of reach at the top of the route and would be difficult to remedy.

■ With the rigging rope set up as normal, adjust the double figure of eight so that one loop is about 20cm longer than the other.
■ A figure of eight is tied on the end of the climbing rope and clipped into the shorter of the loops.
■ Allowing a long loop of rope to reach the ground, clip the rope back into the lower loop so that it runs freely, with the dead end reaching down to the belay point.
■ The climber is clipped in to the long loop of rope with either one or two screwgate karabiners, depending upon harness instructions.

■ Belaying on the dead end now gives a mechanical advantage to the belayer.

The belayer will have to take in more rope than with a normal up/down rig, but the advantage of not being pulled around when the system is loaded means that even a seated person can take part in the activity. Obviously, if there is any chance of the belayer being pulled from their seat then a ground anchor will be needed to keep them in place.

GROUP-ABSEIL RIGGING

The following is the standard method of organizing a group-abseil rig. It is assumed that there are three excellent anchors available.

Method

■ Ensure that all anchors are sound and equipped with screwgate karabiners. Tie a figure of eight on the bight on one end of the rigging rope. Clip this into the first anchor point and run a loop of rope from here loosely on the ground towards the edge of the crag.
■ Bring the rope up to the second anchor point, clip it in and repeat the loop on the ground, then take it to the third anchor point, clip it in and carry the remainder of the rope back to the end of the loops. The position of the knot on the rig is critical, as everything will be operated from here. It must be near enough to the edge of the crag so that you can reach it at all times, but not so close that someone using the system ends up hanging over the edge before all of the slack is taken up. In practice, this means that the knot will be tied about 2 metres back.
■ Take the rope loop from between the first and second anchors, adjust it so that it is the right length and tension, take the rope from between the second and third anchors and repeat the process. Then lay the rope coming from the final anchor on top and create a loop in that as well.
■ Make one of the loops about 20cm longer than the other two and, holding them together under tension, tie an overhand knot. All of the subsequent pieces of kit will clip into these central loops.

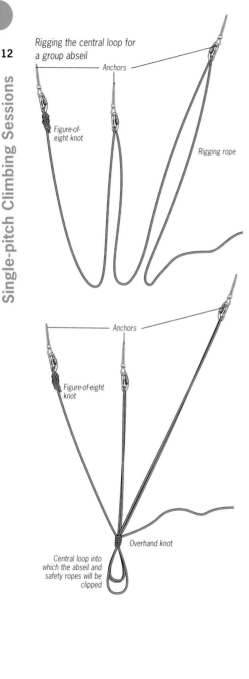

Rigging the central loop for a group abseil

Anchors

Figure-of-eight knot

Rigging rope

Anchors

Figure-of-eight knot

Overhand knot

Central loop into which the abseil and safety ropes will be clipped

RELEASABLE ABSEIL

What is a Releasable Abseil?
A releasable abseil is one that allows the abseil rope to be slackened off whilst under load.

When Would it be Used?
This method of securing the rope should be encouraged as the standard system for all group-abseiling activities, allied with a safety rope.

What is its Advantage Over Other Systems?
If the descender should jam for any reason, this method allows the weight of the abseiler to be taken on the safety rope and for the abseil rope to be loosened. This will let the abseiler release any obstruction jamming the descender, and he can then either be lowered to the ground, or the abseil rope tied off so that he can continue the descent himself.

If a non-releasable system is used, for example a figure of eight on the bight clipped into the anchor krab, and the system is loaded, it will prove extremely difficult, and often impossible, to haul up the abseiler to a degree at which the abseil device can be un-jammed.

Method
The setting up of the releasable system is extremely simple. An HMS karabiner is clipped into the rigging loop, turned gate up with the wide end facing down hill. An Italian hitch is tied in the abseil rope. This can be tied either singly or double, depending on a number of factors but usually decided by the amount of friction required. The Italian hitch is then clipped into the krab, and the gate done up.

■ The knot should be rotated on to the down-hill side of the krab, and it should then be locked off using the standard method of a slippery hitch followed by two half hitches, leaving a bight of rope of at least half a metre in length. This bight should be laid neatly at the side of the set-up, and should not be knotted or clipped back with a krab in any way.

■ The amount of abseil rope used is very important. It should be just above the ground at the bottom of the abseil, and not be allowed to lie on the floor in a heap. To have an excessive amount of rope at the bottom of the crag will almost certainly contribute to problems, and it should be ensured that there will always be plenty of spare rope at the top to allow for lowering procedures to take place, without having to let go of the end. The spare abseil rope at the top of the crag must be carefully flaked into a pile, making sure that there are no knots or twists, with the rope leading neatly from the top of the pile to the Italian hitch.

GROUP-ABSEIL SAFETY ROPE

It is not acceptable, in group activities, to allow participants to abseil without the security of a safety rope. Quite apart from the obvious problem of them hitting the bottom at speed, the safety rope is your insurance that if anything should go wrong, you have the means with which to go about doing something to rectify it.

Method
A dynamic climbing rope will normally be used. One end should have a figure of eight on the bight tied in, with a screwgate clipped through it; the other end can be clipped out of the way on one of the anchors.
■ An HMS screwgate is clipped into the rigging loop, with the gate facing up and the wide end towards the edge of the cliff.
■ An Italian hitch is clipped into this, and the other end of the safety rope is clipped into the group-member's abseil loop before he starts, underneath the descender attachment.
Once he is connected to the abseil device and has started going down, the Italian hitch can be

TIPS
1 Stop a problem before it occurs. Make sure that the knot that you have tied into the end of the safety rope at the abseiler's end has an extremely short tail on the stopper knot, otherwise there is a chance of it catching in the abseil device.
2 Once down, a common problem, especially for younger folk, is caused by them having trouble taking the karabiner off the harness once they have unscrewed it. This is because they get the notch on the nose of the karabiner hooked on their abseil loop. There are screwgates on the market that have been designed with the notch on the inside of the gate, and the nose presents a smooth surface to anything clipped in and out. A karabiner of this type is excellent for using with safety ropes and abseil devices.

OBSERVATIONS
The HMS of the safety rope can often jam up against the HMS of the abseil rope if it is clipped into the same part of the rigging loop and not into an extended loop as detailed above. To prevent this happening, either rig the system as shown or, where this is not possible, such as on a single-anchor system, clip a 15–20cm extender onto the rigging loop, and put the safety-rope's HMS onto this.

1 One of the main causes of nervousness amongst novice (and indeed experienced!) abseilers is a low take-off point. If the rigging rope is high, then the angle at which the abseiler steps over the edge is greater, and he will feel better supported.
2 Take great care with your group management at the top of the abseil. Ensure that they are sitting in a safe area, and know what to do when called forward. It is very tempting for folk to creep forward to see how their mates are getting on.
3 It is important to ensure that your group members have been told to tuck away any 'flappy' bits of clothing or loose hair, and check that helmet straps have been secured and tucked in. Carry out a quick individual check as each person comes forward to abseil.

TIPS
1 It is possible, when exiting over a sharp edge, for the rope to catch and lark's foot over the abseil device, in particular when using the figure-of-eight descender. The remedy for this is simple – instead of threading the rope up the big hole and round the little hole, which puts the rope on the lower side of the device, thread the rope down the big hole and up over the little hole. There is now no rope on the underside that will catch.
2 To help reduce the chance of a group member catching his hair or loose clothing in the abseil device, extend it with a sling. This can be a 20cm extender or a 4ft (60cm) sling doubled, attached to the descender with a small screwgate or maillon, which keeps the sling away from the descender so that it is not damaged through heat. Another advantage is that the abseiler now has somewhere to put the hand that is not controlling the rope; before, there was a danger of him getting his fingers too close to the device.
3 It is worth carrying a few hair ties or elastic bands on a small krab on the back of your harness. These can be given out to the group members who will inevitably have 'forgotten' to bring their own, and will help to keep their hair out of the way of the abseil device.

controlled as normal, but ensure that you are not holding him too tight – pay out slack with your free hand as he descends. In the case of an emergency, the safety rope can be pulled in tight and locked off at the Italian hitch.

PERSONAL SAFETY WHEN RIGGING

Your own safety is extremely important – you are of no use to the group if you are lying at the bottom of the crag in a strange shape. When rigging, running an activity and de-rigging, always look after yourself and don't take risks.

Methods

■ The simplest is an 8ft (120cm) sling lark's-footed onto your abseil loop as a cowstail. Have a screwgate karabiner on it, and it will be ready to use by clipping into an existing anchor or rigging loop. This method is extremely useful if you are moving between a variety of sites. When not being used, the sling can wrap around your waist and the krab can be clipped in to stop it flapping about.

■ A Petzl 'Shunt' provides an excellent method of safeguarding yourself whilst rigging, as long as it is connected to a rope from a bomb-proof anchor. The shunt allows you to move backwards and forwards along the rope easily, but provides a secure 'stop' should it be needed. Ensure that you are always on the down-slope side of the shunt so that you do not shock-load it, and in some circumstances it may be appropriate to tie an overhand knot below it as an extra back-up.

■ A Klemheist tied on a sling around a rigging rope will suffice for a short period of time, but be aware that these will not always lock off, and they should never be shock loaded.

■ Use a length of the rigging rope that you are setting up, once the first bomb-proof anchor has been connected.

■ Use a rope from an anchor that will not be used during the session. For instance, it may be appropriate to rig a safety line for yourself from a convenient tree and to clip into this whilst you rig the main anchor system.

■ If you are running the abseil session, another method is to use the length of rigging rope you had coming in from the third anchor then out from the central knot, the end of

which is not attached to anything. You can connect yourself to this by using either a clove hitch or a figure of eight on the bight.

Using a shunt as personal protection when rigging from a bomb-proof anchor. The rigger is tying an overhand knot as an extra back-up

LEADING NOVICES

There will come a time when you find yourself in the position of leading novices; often this will be when introducing a friend or friends to the art of climbing. It may be that you have been coaching them on a climbing wall for two or three sessions, and now the time has come for them to sample outdoor rock for the first time. Running through the basics with a couple of visits to a wall is very worthwhile, not only because they can pick up the mechanics of moving on rock, but because they can become familiar with belaying a leader in an atmosphere with few distractions. After practice, this will then allow them to belay you on outdoor routes. The decision as to whether you can trust someone enough to belay you is yours. It must be remembered that being belayed by someone who is not proficient is the same as soloing, with the added worry of injury to your second if something goes wrong.

Climbing with Two Novices

Attaching a second to your climbing rope is a simple process, and this allows him to learn quickly through individual contact. If you are in a situation of having two novices to follow you, then a bit of thought must go into their attachment point and method on the rope. There are five practical methods, any of which may be used.

■ The first is the least efficient, in which one rope is used. When the second reaches the top of the climb, he unties and the end is thrown down to the third, who ties on and climbs. This method can only be recommended for shorter routes with more experienced novices because of the following points:

1 you are unable to check whether the third person has connected himself to the rope correctly

2 there is a chance of the rope snagging when it is thrown down. The habit of throwing down the rope with a knot and a karabiner in the end, and getting the second to clip in to his abseil loop, is to be discouraged.

■ Two more methods, using just one rope, rely on the certainty that half a rope length will be more than ample to reach the top and belay, for instance on a shorter route with good anchors near the edge at the stance. The leader ties on to one end, with the second in the middle and the third at the other end; this is known as 'climbing in series'. Alternatively, the leader could place himself in the middle, with this system being known as 'climbing in parallel'. Whoever ends up as the middleman must be attached by tying into the harness, as opposed to clipping in with a karabiner. The knot can be a standard figure of eight rewoven on a bight with a stopper, although this does end up as being rather bulky and some may find it feeling a little restrictive. The other method is to tie a rewoven overhand knot on the bight, and clip the loop

end back into the harness with a karabiner to prevent the knot from unravelling, the same as is used for short-roping but without the isolation loop.

■ The fourth and fifth methods use two ropes, and are recommended as the best way of organizing things. Rope handling and stance-management dynamics are greatly eased if these ropes are of different colours. The leader ties on at one end of a rope, with the second attached at the other end. The second is then connected to the other rope, with the third climber tied on at the far end (in series). Alternatively, the leader could tie both ropes into his harness, and have one climber on each (in parallel).

One of the pros of the first method, in series, is that when the second reaches the top his rope can be connected to the belay system and he can then belay up the third person. The rope between the leader and second is then free to be used for another purpose, such as rigging an abseil, to be coiled up ready for the descent, or it can be deployed in case of an emergency.

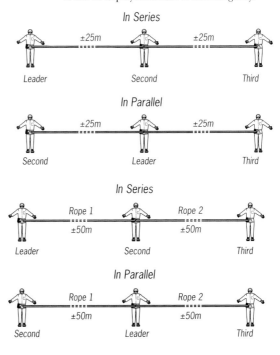

In Series

±25m   ±25m

Leader   Second   Third

In Parallel

±25m   ±25m

Second   Leader   Third

In Series

Rope 1   Rope 2
±50m   ±50m

Leader   Second   Third

In Parallel

Rope 1   Rope 2
±50m   ±50m

Second   Leader   Third

The pros of the second system, with the climbers in parallel, is that both can belay the leader, gaining valuable belay practice as well increasing the leader's safety. They can also both remove protection as they ascend, as the leader will have placed runners on each of the ropes. We would usually recommend this as the best method, but of course the final decision is up to you given each individual situation.

A QUICK AND SIMPLE DIRECT BELAY SYSTEM

You may wish to use a direct belay at the top of the route, as this has a variety of advantages over a semi-direct system, such as the ability to escape easily. However, it is not worth spending a lot of time untying from the rope or making things complicated. The following two methods are very quick and simple and will be appropriate for the majority of situations.

Single Anchor Direct Belay
Having selected a suitable single anchor, or after bringing two or more to a single point using a

sling, clip the rope in and get yourself to the stance. Pull a bit of extra rope through and, folding back both sections of rope coming from the anchor so as to make two identical loops, tie an overhand knot on the bight. This will be the attachment point for the Italian hitch, you are made safe by being on the end of the rope and secured by the overhand knot.

Double Anchor Point Direct Belay
Clip the rope into both anchors and pull the rope from between them towards you. At the stance, feed a bit of extra rope through so that you are to one side of the system and fold all the sections of rope back so that there are, unavoidably, three loops. Tie an overhand knot on the bight around these loops and use either one or all of them for the Italian hitch.

Clipping into Runners
If climbing with one other person who is going to follow you, clipping into runners while leading should present no problems. When climbing with a second and a third, though, some thought must go into the process. When leading in series, the simplest solution is to

A single anchor point direct belay

A double anchor point direct belay

have one person belaying you and clip the runners as normal, with the other person just observing. If climbing in parallel, it is possible to have either one or both people belaying. If both are involved, this will allow you to clip each rope into a variety of runners, and lets both the second and third remove gear thus learning about placements. This method also has the advantage that you are being belayed by two people, with a consequentially increased margin of safety.

An extremely important consideration, whichever method is used, is the run of the rope if the route necessitates a traverse of any kind. If you have placed gear to protect yourself and the second while traversing, and the gear is removed, the third person may not be protected. It is important to bear this in mind, and to ensure that any briefings contain concise information on what the second is required to do when unclipping a runner – clipping it back on behind him to the rope trailing to the third is often the answer.

TIP

Before leading novices on routes where you are going to place gear, it would be worth spending a little time showing them how to efficiently remove runners. When to take them out (almost exclusively from below – don't let them climb past), using a nut key and attaching the runner to their harness should be covered. Pay particular attention to camming device removal, something that is often very difficult for a novice to do if they have not had a practise beforehand.

It should be realised that the chances of a problem arising during a single-pitch climbing or abseiling session are greatly reduced if there has been proper planning, preparation and briefings. For instance, the common problem of a helmet strap caught in a descender is prevented, not by running into a full-blown releasable-abseil scenario, but by checking that the strap was properly tucked away in the first place. Below are given a few of the commonest problems that may occur during a session, the cause and the remedy. This list is non-exhaustive, and is designed to demonstrate that the simplest solutions are normally the best. It will be noted that addressing and understanding the cause should become the remedy for the following sessions, with the lesson having been learnt.

It cannot be emphasised enough that briefings and preparation are the key to a successful and trouble-free session. All of the scenarios in the table could have been easily avoided by a little thought beforehand, and by paying attention to the activity involved. If practical action is needed, then the simplest remedy and course of action will normally be the best. Massively complicated rope systems, hoists and pulleys are fine in their place, but there will always be a simpler alternative. Safety, efficiency and speed are what are required, in that order.

Example

You are running an abseiling session for a group of twelve- to fourteen-year-olds. Even after your best attentions, one of the girls gets halfway down the slab and a tuft of her hair blows forward and gets trapped in the abseil device.

OBSERVATIONS

1 As far as this abseiling incident is concerned, it is worth thinking about the instructions that you give. Keep any verbal instructions simple, loud and clear, and remember that if someone is in distress hanging from her hair on a scary piece of rock in a gale in the pouring rain, the last thing that she wants to hear is you calling down, 'Right, I'm now going to undo the abseil rope …'!

2 It may be noticed that some instructors working on single-pitch crags carry a pocket knife with them, hanging from the back of their harness. It can only be hoped that these implements are to be used in the event of personal attack, and are not for use during a group session. It cannot be emphasised enough that EXTREME caution should be shown when wielding a knife, as climbing rope under tension cuts very easily indeed.

She is crying out in pain, gripping the abseil rope for all she's worth. Do you:

1 call out to her not to worry; bend down and tie off the safety rope with a slippery hitch and two half-hitches while keeping her informed of what you are doing; untie the locked-off Italian on the abseil rope, at the same time as letting her know you are untying it; slowly release her weight on to the safety rope, then call down to see if she is able to free her hair from the device?

Or:

2 pull hard on the safety rope as soon as it is apparent that something is wrong, lifting her weight off the abseil rope, and call down for her to free her hair?

The point is that, although there may be a textbook way of doing things, a simpler remedy is often available given just a little thought.

Thoughts on Route Choice

The four diagrams show very simply how important route choice is, and how a problem can be avoided. In the first example, the top karabiner of the bottom-rope system has been situated above a large ledge at the finish of the route. This allows a nervous climber to stand on the ledge and feel safer there rather than committing his weight to the rope for a lower, even though one should have been practised at the bottom. To avoid this problem ensure that, when rigging, the karabiner has been lowered down on the rigging rope to just below the ledge, ensuring that the climber is unable to climb on to it in the first place.

Here, a problem has occurred as the top karabiner has been rigged above a ledge. The climber feels secure and is unhappy about committing his weight to the rope for a lower

The top karabiner has been rigged below the ledge, thus preventing the climber from becoming 'crag-fast'. The climber stays under the ledge

Problem	Cause	Remedy
Helmet strap/hair caught in abseil device.	Inefficient checks.	Pulling on safety rope, release of abseil rope.
Refusing to commit weight to rope on bottom-rope lower	Did not brief and practise lower before allowing climb to start.	Verbal encouragement; assistance from above; assistance from below; rope tricks.
Freezes on ledge.	Poor route choice, reading of clients' ability	Verbal encouragement; assistance from above; assistance from below; rope tricks.
Climbing up rope hand-over-hand	Inefficient briefing, inattentive belaying.	Verbal instruction.
Climbing off route.	Inefficient briefing, poor route choice, inattentive belaying.	Verbal instruction; tight rope.
Climbing past runner when following led climb	Inefficient briefing, inattentive belaying.	Verbal instruction, downclimb, rope loop passed down with krab.
Climbing beyond top krab on bottom roped climb	Inefficient briefing, inattentive belaying.	Tight rope; careful verbal instructions.

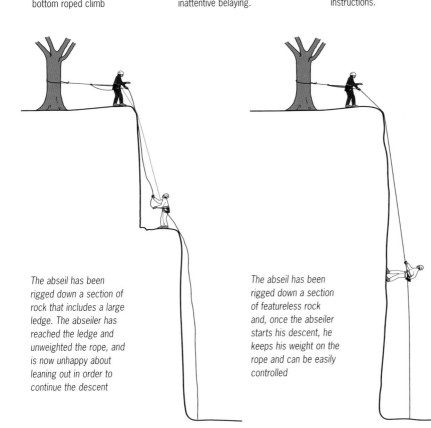

The abseil has been rigged down a section of rock that includes a large ledge. The abseiler has reached the ledge and unweighted the rope, and is now unhappy about leaning out in order to continue the descent

The abseil has been rigged down a section of featureless rock and, once the abseiler starts his descent, he keeps his weight on the rope and can be easily controlled

In the second example, an abseil has been set up over a route that has a ledge part way down. This is asking for trouble, as a nervous abseiler will automatically stand up when he reaches the ledge, un-weight the system, and be very wary about leaning back out again. As it is not possible to lower the top of the abseil down the crag, a different route should be selected if possible, one which allows for a straight descent with no obstacles to be negotiated.

TECHNICAL EMERGENCY PROCEDURES

As we have said, proper planning before and throughout the session should negate all of the problems. There should be no call for a large amount of 'rope tricks' to be used to solve a situation. For instance, knowing how to lock off a belay device under load may not be relevant. If a device is loaded with a person's body weight, then he can simply be lowered to the ground, from either a top- or bottom-rope set-up, and there should be no occasion on which a person is left locked off and suspended in mid-air while climbing. However, it may well be relevant to know how to secure a device and pass it over to another group member when the device is not fully loaded, for instance when the climber has become 'crag-fast' and refuses to move either up or down from a ledge.

All of the following procedures should be practised until they become second nature, and they are in the technical rope-tricks category. The final procedure, the solution of the stuck screwgate, has been included to indicate the many ways there are to solve a simple problem.

Releasing an Abseil Rope Under Load
The classic case is someone has their hair caught in the descender. The first thing to do is to take in the safety rope tight and, making sure that you do not let go of the dead end, get both hands on the live rope and pull upwards. In many cases this will lift the abseiler up far enough for them to release their hair. If this does not work, hold the safety rope in the maximum braking position and release the abseil rope with your other hand. This is easy to with one hand if a low-stretch rope has been used. If there is difficulty with this, you may

need to lock off the safety rope to give you both hands to work with. Once the abseil rope has been released, pull plenty through so that the abseiler is hanging on the safety rope and can sort out the problem.

Locking Off and Escaping from a Belay Device on a Bottom-rope System
Scenario: the climber has become crag-fast, and refuses to move up or down. You have been unable to find a suitable ground anchor, and did not wish for your group members to belay, hence controlling the device yourself.

- Call over one or two of the other group members. Clip an HMS karabiner onto the abseil loop of one of them. Tie a clove hitch in the dead rope close to the belay device and clip it into the krab, doing up the gate.
- If the group members are young or very inexperienced, or if there is a large weight difference between the new belayer and the stuck climber, clip a sling between the abseil loops of your two helpers.
- With little slack between the climber and new belayer, undo your belay device screwgate and take it off your harness. The device can be removed in case it is needed later. The new belayer/s could now sit on the ground if appropriate.
- Brief them to stay put until told otherwise, and remember to keep talking to the stuck climber while all of this is going on. You are now free from the system.

TIP
Remember that another option for releasing yourself from an indirect belay system, particularly in a top-rope situation, will be to lock off the belay device and step out of your harness.

Taking Control of a Belay Device From a Novice
Scenario: you have a novice belaying their companion (whilst you control the dead end of the rope of course), and the climber becomes stuck on a slab a short way up. You realise that ascending the rope will be by far the quickest remedy (see opposite for this method).

- Either keeping tight control of the dead rope or after using the clove-hitch system escape method to another person, attach a screwgate karabiner to your abseil loop.
- Get in close to the belayer and, with a little slack in the system (which will be there anyway as the climber is not loading the rope), clip your screwgate into the correct section of the rope emerging from the back of the belay device, right next to the novice's karabiner.
- Having done yours up, you can unscrew theirs and release them from the system.
- You are now hands-free to set up the ascent.

Retrieving a Stuck Climber from the Top of a Route on a Bottom-rope System

Scenario: despite your best efforts and after having practised lowering at the start of the climb, a climber reaches the top karabiner and refuses to commit his weight to the rope. You are not part of the system, having either selected a ground anchor, allowed group members to belay each other, or have escaped the system as above.

- Remember that the climber may not have to be lowered to the ground – he may be able to climb up and over the top. This will avoid you having to rig a complicated abseil system.
- Get to the top of the route quickly (most likely via the path!), and gain eye contact with the stuck climber, and continue reassurance. Look after your own personal safety by attaching yourself to a suitable part of the system.
- Select an appropriate anchor, clip in an HMS krab and, using either a spare rope or the end of the rigging rope, tie a figure of eight on the bight and clip in a second karabiner. This is then passed down to the climber, who clips it into his abseil loop and screws up the gate.
- Be very attentive at this point, and ensure that the screwgate has been correctly done up by both visual inspection and by getting him to perform a squeeze test, where the climber squeezes the krab across the back bar and gate with one hand. An Italian hitch on the new climbing rope is now clipped into the HMS on the anchor.
- The belayers on the ground are at this stage able to undo the clove hitch and let the rope go, as you have the climber held safely from above. The climber can now climb over the top and be fielded well back from danger.

Abseiling to Retrieve a Marooned Climber

Often known as a 'crag-snatch', the following is a technique that is amongst the most advanced of the skills needed for running a single-pitch session, and should be seen as being more relevant to the skills required by the multi-pitch climber and instructor. However, it could be useful during group-climbing sessions as a remedy for one or two awkward scenarios, hence its inclusion in this section.

Scenario: the climber has become stuck on a ledge part way up the route, and is unable to move for whatever reason. You are not part of the belay system, or have escaped from it as above.

- From the top of the crag, drop down a spare rope and attach it to a solid anchor (this rope could either be a spare of yours, the tail-end of a top-rope system, be a length from the rigging rope or even 'scrounged' from other crag users). Prepare to abseil to the climber. This is organized by using a 8ft (120cm) sling doubled, with an overhand knot on the bight tied at the centre, known as a 'Y hang'. The karabiner and abseil device will clip into this knot. You will be clipped on to your abseil loop with one half of the sling; the other half will be left hanging free so that you can clip the stuck climber to it. This sling may have been already clipped to your harness as a cowstail, perhaps with an overhand knot tied half way along it.
- Tie an overhand knot halfway up the spare sling side, so that you have some flexibility when deciding where to attach the climber.
- Protect the abseil in the usual manner. Descend to the stuck climber. Attach him to the spare sling loop with a screwgate karabiner: at the end of it if he is going to walk down next to you, above the middle knot if you need to assist him down, such as with an unconscious casualty. This is accomplished by you swinging him horizontally across in front of you so that he is suspended from the abseil device, you keeping your feet out in front of you and flat on the rock so that he does not swing into you.
- For multi-pitch assisted abseils, there may be a need to improvise some form of chest support, but for use on a single-pitch crag, it is much better to get him straight down to the ground.

■ Once he is securely clipped to the sling, the original climbing rope can be released. This can be done either by untying the knot to his harness, or by getting a helper on the ground to release the belay device. Proceed to the ground.

OBSERVATIONS

If using a system similar to the cowstail/abseil rig, it is absolutely essential that the abseil device is clipped into the correct sections of the sling, in other words through both sections either side of the overhand knot. If this is not done and the device is simply clipped to one side of the knot, as would be appropriate for a personal abseil, when the weight of the stuck climber is taken the sling will slide through the abseil karabiner, dropping the casualty down by your side.

If needing to 'crag snatch' from an abseil rig, you have a number of options as to which rope to use, depending upon the situation. There is the spare abseil rope, the back end of the safety rope, a length of left-over rigging rope or even the rope that the abseiler is hanging on, as it may be possible to pull up a little slack for connecting to your abseil device.

OBSERVATIONS

1 There are a couple of scenarios where you could abseil from the back-end of a locked-off Italian hitch, such as when using the safety rope on an abseil or the climbing rope on a top-rope system. Although it is possible to abseil directly on the dead rope coming from the Italian, it will be better to take a bight of the rope and clip it into the anchor with a figure of eight, and abseil from that.

2 Be aware that the rope that you are using for the crag-snatch may be thin and slippery, especially if new. Thus, bear in mind that a) you need to have compete control over the rate of your descent by using a French Prusik or similar, and b) that when you clip the stuck person to you and lean back, there will very likely be a good deal of rope stretch and you will both drop a distance. Taking as much rope as possible in nice and tight before leaning back will help reduce the distance you travel, but it will be difficult to do much about it.

A cowstail clipped correctly for a crag-snatch abseil

A cowstail clipped incorrectly for a crag-snatch abseil

Safeguarding Yourself on an Easy Slab Climb

Scenario: you need to ascend for some reason to assist a climber who is having difficulty on an easy slab route.

■ Assuming you are belaying through a standard device, place a French Prusik on the live rope immediately above it, clipped into your abseil loop. If your Prusik is too short, clip it into the belay device's HMS with a separate screwgate as shown. It is essential that the distance between the front of the device and the Prusik is minimal to avoid any potential shock loading. When the dead rope is pulled through, the Prusik acts as a back-up, and you can make your way up the ground to the climber, pulling through the slack rope as you go.
■ It is essential that every few feet you tie an overhand knot in the dead rope to act as a stopper in the event of a slide and the Prusik failing to hold you.
■ When you reach the climber, attach him to you with a short sling, then abseil to the ground, a method known as the 'counterbalance abseil'. You can hold the Prusik against the device so that the rope slides through, but bear in mind that this is above the device, not below as would be the norm for protecting an abseil.

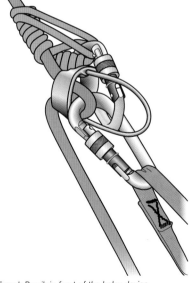

A French Prusik in front of the belay device

Although a handy technique to be familiar with, this method of ascent has two severe limitations. First, if the ground is anything more than very easy it is extremely hard to make any headway. Second, remember that you are relying on the weight of the stuck climber as a counterbalance. Therefore, if he is lighter than you and you keep slipping off or committing your weight to the rope, he will have an uncomfortable time!

OBSERVATIONS
If a Prusik loop is being used for anything more than a back-up for a personal abseil, it is probably an inappropriate technique and outside the usual remit of skills associated with running a single-pitch group session. If rope tricks are to be employed, they should be simple, quick, effective and safe, and employed only after all other possibilities have been considered.

As for any emergency system, we must re-iterate that any time that you are hanging on the rope having abseiled to a casualty, or even if you are going up the rope to them, do not just rely on the French Prusik to hold you whilst you are alongside them dealing with the problem. It is important that you either tie a large overhand knot on the dead rope under the device, or take a few wraps of the dead rope around your thigh, as a back-up in case the Prusik slips.

Undoing a Stuck Screwgate

Scenario: a person has abseiled to the ground, but is unable to undo the screwgate connecting the safety rope to himself. This is either because it has some grit stuck in the sleeve, or because it has been over-tightened.

There are a number of remedies; these are in a logical order:
■ check he is unscrewing it the right way
■ get him to hold the screw sleeve with a piece of material to improve grip
■ see if there is someone else close by who could help
■ get him to tap the gate with another karabiner – this often helps to dislodge debris
■ have him sit on the ground, then you pull hard on the safety rope. This can stretch the karabiner shape sufficiently to allow the sleeve to turn
■ tell him to undo the knot on the rope
■ get him to take off his harness
■ go down to him.

PART THREE

Avalanche Awareness

This section presents a number of considerations for safe travel in the hills under winter conditions, as well as some practical methods of appraising snow stability.

The Snow-pack

Safe-travel Tips

Searching Techniques

The Snow-pack

Snow falls, it's a fact of life. What we are interested in as mountaineers is how anchored each layer is to its partners throughout the snow-pack. Weak cohesion between adjoining layers or between the snow-pack and the ground could very well lead to ideal avalanche conditions. There are three ways in which the snow-pack will consolidate.

■

Isothermal Metamorphism

Also known as settling, it is the natural conversion of the crystal structure within the pack to a single compact layer; the whole process is speeded up as the snow temperature rises towards melting point.

Melt/Freeze Metamorphism

This is, as the name suggests, a process during which the temperature within the snow-pack alternates between below and above freezing point. A continued MF Met cycle gives fine hard snow, when it is frozen, that is good to travel over and climb on. But care must be taken

during the melt process that moisture has not invaded the pack to such a degree – this could be to its full depth – that it may avalanche.

Kinetic-growth Metamorphism

This is the effect of the temperature gradient between the base layers and surface layers of the pack. Where a large gradient exists, water vapour migrates through the pack and forms extremely fragile cup-crystals, also known as depth hoar.

FACTORS DETERMINING SNOW STABILITY/INSTABILITY

Surface Hoar

Crystals are formed on cold, clear nights when the surface temperature of the snow-pack becomes colder than that of the air surrounding it. The danger from surface hoar becomes real after subsequent snowfall covers the crystals and leaves a fragile layer within the pack which may exist for some time.

Winter ridge walking   ■

Snowfall

This has a large effect on pack stability with most avalanches occurring during or immediately after a heavy fall of snow. For the purposes of clarity, heavy snowfall is defined as being at a rate of 2cm per hour. This also covers wind-blown snow, as it doesn't have to be snowing for there to be a rapid build-up of deposits.

Angle of Slope

Obviously a factor, and it is not often realised that a slope with an angle of as little as 15 degrees can avalanche. The most prone to avalanche are those between 30 and 45 degrees, with slopes of more than 60 degrees rarely accumulating enough snow, except as cornices.

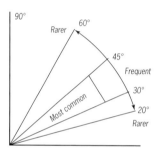

Avalanche frequency in relation to slope angle

Shape of Slope

This can affect stability: at the back of a concave slope the snow is compressed and so reasonably stable; however on a convex slope, such as at the top where it reaches a plateau, the snow is stretched within the pack and on the outer surface, and cohesion can fail.

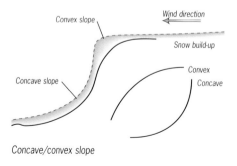

Concave/convex slope

Air Temperature and Wind

The snow-pack is profoundly affected by this. Cold temperatures allow the snow to remain in an almost-unchanged state for long periods, warmer temperatures allow crystal change and conversion of the crystals to a different state. The presence of wind, or lack of it, is a major factor.

TYPES OF AVALANCHE

Loose Dry-snow Avalanches

May be quite large and form from a single point, and occur when cohesion is lost due to isothermal met. The avalanche will flow at speeds of up to 40mph, and if it exceeds this speed it may become airborne.

Airborne Powder

Such avalanches are extremely destructive, and in the Alpine regions can be immense. They may start as a loose dry-snow avalanche or slab, but become airborne after around 40mph is reached. Other types of avalanche such as hard or soft slabs may be pulverized by their own motion and may turn into airborne powder. The destructive power is immense as the speed of the avalanche can be around 175mph.

Slab Avalanches

There will be a marked lack of cohesion under the layer, sometimes with the slab being completely unsupported over a large area. Soft slabs are associated with accumulation of snow on lee slopes owing to wind action, with winds of up to 30mph. Most soft-slab avalanches are released by their victims, so all slopes, not just those in the lee of the wind, should be treated with suspicion until the snow settles, remembering that this may take some time in cold conditions. Straight-edged angular blocks breaking away under your boot are a sure sign of soft-slab danger. Bear in mind that it need not have been snowing for the snow to have accumulated; wind transportation will do the job on its own.

Hard slabs are one of the greatest hazards in the mountains. Wind speeds of over 30mph help hard-slab formation on lee slopes, and the slab will feel underfoot as hard as concrete. Release is usually accompanied by a loud cracking noise, and the slab breaks up into huge angular blocks which remain intact during their descent. Hard slab has a dull chalky appearance and does not easily reflect light, often squeaking, sometimes booming, underfoot. This 'booming' sound will come from the inherent weakness underneath. If you are using trekking poles you may be aware of a squeaking under the tips, as if someone were rubbing polystyrene along them.

Wet Avalanches

Common in spring, and at any time following a thaw. They are caused by water weakening the bonds between layers or between the bottom layer and the ground. The danger is greatest when there is a heavy snow storm which starts cold and finishes warm. Wet avalanches can be loose or in slab form, and move either fast of slow. They will set like concrete immediately upon stopping, so the survival time for a buried victim is extremely short. They can be expected at the start of rainfall, and for 24 hours thereafter, as well as during a period of thaw.

Ice Avalanches

In their purest form these are uncommon in the UK. However the danger is from a thaw when an icefall attached to a crag peels off and crashes down the hillside.

Cornice Collapse

Often associated with thaw conditions, although cornices may well collapse under their own weight given extra snowfall. As with slab formation, there need not be any snowfall to form a cornice; wind action alone will do the job.

To Sum up

- Lee slopes are very prone to slab build-up.
- Low temperatures prolong avalanche risk.
- A sudden increase in temperature increases danger.
- High-danger slopes are between 30 and 45 degrees.
- The convex section of the slope will often be the fracture point.
- A reliable indicator of unstable conditions is evidence of recent avalanche activity.
- Snowballs rolling down-slope indicate rising temperature.

- Angular blocks breaking away underfoot indicate slab conditions, as does a chalky appearance and squeaking underfoot and below trekking poles.
- Danger period is up to 48 hours after snowfall, longer in cold conditions.
- Accumulation rate of more than 2cm per hour of falling or windblown snow can lead to a heightened avalanche risk.

AVALANCHE AWARENESS

It is a fact that mountaineers and skiers sometimes get caught in avalanches. Statistics show that many either had no knowledge of avalanches or safe-route-travel skills, or they simply ignored all the signs of instability and convinced themselves that everything would be all right and it wouldn't happen to them.

If you were caught in an avalanche what would be the consequences? Statistically, the more time you spend walking and climbing in winter, the greater the chance you have of being caught-out in an avalanche, or of observing others trying to survive one. Victims of avalanches often trigger the slide themselves, with the same mistakes repeated time and time again.

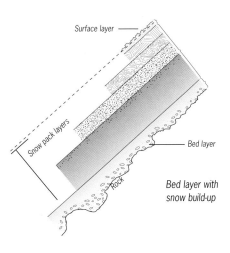

Surface layer

Snow pack layers

Rock

Bed layer

Bed layer with snow build-up

Avalanches often occur during heavy snowfall, during windy periods that re-deposit snow, and up to 48 hours thereafter. To minimize risk when travelling in the mountains where a moderate- to high-risk condition may prevail, two courses of action are open to you:
1 improve your overall understanding of avalanches and practise safe travel
OR
2 don't go.
It is very important to be objective according to weather conditions and not to let personal goals and ambitions cloud your judgement.

Warning Signs: Snowpack

- Avalanche activity.
- Fresh avalanche debris.
- Snow cracking or easily breaking away in blocks underfoot.
- 'Whumphing' noises underfoot.
- Signs of snow-pack instability at test sites.
- Rollerballs/sunwheels.
- Squeaking underfoot or under trekking poles/ice axe.

Warning Signs: Terrain

- Slopes, in particular those between 30 degrees and 45 degrees.
- Lee slopes and wind-sheltered gullies.
- Slope aspects.
- Cornice build-up.
- Previous avalanche paths and debris.
- Natural terrain traps.

Warning Signs: Weather

- Heavy snowfall.
- Wind loading on lee slopes.
- Sudden rise in temperature; rain and warm winds soon after snowfall.
- Prolonged periods of very warm and very cold weather.
- Solar warming.
- There can often be sudden and dramatic temperature changes throughout the winter period, so it is very important that you monitor the weather conditions before and during your trip.

Fact Finding

It is best to always base your avalanche-hazard evaluation on solid facts, and never rely solely on feelings, assumptions or guesses.

The first things that you should be thinking of when faced with uncertainty are: is it safe or is it unsafe? You must begin to fact-find and identify meaningful information upon which you can establish your evaluation. This is called the fact-find approach:

- does a hazard exist?
- is the weather contributing to instability?
- can you recognise avalanche terrain?
- could the snow-pack slide?
- what are the alternatives and any consequences?

Remember, you have lots of ways of gathering information to form your hazard evaluation. For instance, weather reports, local avalanche forecasts and the ability to identify suspect slopes all help to build the bigger picture.

The Fact-find Approach
WEATHER WARNING SIGNS
TERRAIN WARNING SIGNS
SNOW-PACK WARNING SIGNS
THE HUMAN FACTOR

Safe-travel Tips

1 Always ensure that you are carrying essential safety equipment and prepare for the worst.
2 Spend some time with your companion, partner or clients discussing safe route travel options and procedures if caught in a avalanche.

A lightweight 3-piece extendable shovel

Planning Your Trip
1 Check the current weather and local avalanche forecasts.
2 Ensure that you have appropriate emergency equipment.
3 Check that all group members are capable of the proposed trip.
4 Consider alternative route options should conditions not be in your favour.
5 Leave information about your intended route, and time due back, with a responsible person.
6 Check that you have appropriate map and guide-book information.
7 Be aware of natural-terrain traps and known avalanche-producing slopes.
8 Never presume that the summer path will be safe in winter.
9 Be aware of the slope aspects in relation to the weather, as well as possible changes in the weather during the day.

1 Always consider where the stress point of a slope may be.
2 Be aware of travelling over cornices or underneath them.
3 When travelling through potential avalanche terrain, use natural islands of safety such as ridges and exposed high points.
4 Minimize your exposure time on a suspect slope.
5 Only allow one person to cross a suspect slope at any one time. Always consider the run out should someone be swept away.
6 It is an idea to favour one or other side of the slope, rather than the middle, as this will give you a better chance of escaping should an avalanche be triggered.
7 Always consider the slope angles, aspect and altitude.
8 Look out for stress points and fracture lines.
9 Stability tests should be carried out at relevant points along the route.
10 Never assume that others know better. Footprints ahead of you do not mean that the slope is necessarily safe to cross.

A collapsible avalanche probe, marked off in 50cm sections

PREPARE FOR THE WORST

1 Choose your line of travel carefully.
2 Never stop in the middle or at the bottom of an avalanche-prone slope.
3 Ensure that clothing is fastened, gloves are on, hood up and goggles worn.
4 Remove ski-pole safety leashes from wrists, undo rucksack hip belts and loosen shoulder straps.

OBSERVATION

An excellent resource in the UK is www.sais.gov.uk. This is the Scottish Avalanche Information Service, and they produce forecasts during the season of avalanche predictions for the main mountain regions of Scotland. If you ally this with www.mwis.org. uk, a weather forecasting site for British mountain areas, you can come up with a good idea of current conditions in the mountains.

5 Protect with a rope if appropriate.
6 Think of the consequences if caught. Have a rescue plan and be prepared for the worst.

THE INTERNATIONAL AVALANCHE GRADING SYSTEM

This is a system used in a number of countries across the world where avalanche prediction and monitoring takes place, and the results are posted up on notice boards and the Internet on a daily basis for walkers, climbers and skiers to refer to. The predictions should always be used in conjunction with your personal observations of the snow as well as weather patterns, but they do provide a good source of important information, useful when planning a journey or climb.

Degree of Hazard	Snowpack stability	Avalanche probability
1 (low)	The snowpack is generally well bonded and stable.	Triggering is possible only with high additional loads on a few very steep extreme slopes. Only a few small natural avalanches (sloughs) possible.
2 (moderate)	The snowpack is moderately well bonded on some steep slopes, otherwise generally well bonded.	Triggering is possible with high additional loads, particularly on the steep slopes indicated in the bulletin. Large natural avalanches not likely.
3 (considerable)	The snowpack is moderately to weakly bonded on many steep slopes.	Triggering is possible, sometimes even with low additional loads. The bulletin may indicate many slopes that are particularly affected. In certain conditions, medium and occasionally large sized natural avalanches may occur.
4 (high)	The snowpack is weakly bonded in most places.	Triggering is probable even with low additional loads on many steep slopes with an incline of more than 30 degrees. In some conditions, frequent medium or large sized natural avalanches are likely.
5 (very high)	The snowpack is generally weakly bonded and largely unstable.	Numerous large natural avalanches are likely, even on moderately steep terrain.

THE RUTSCHBLOCK TEST

This form of the Rutschblock test, or walking-shear test, is based on a ski-shear test using a similar scale of stability. The following sequence will provide you with guidance as to the stability of the snow-pack.

The first step will be to select a safe test slope that is representative of the slope aspect, altitude and angle that your intended route will take. This site could be located down and to one side of the line you wish to take, perhaps under a small outcrop of rock or an island of safety.

Method

When preparing your test block, it is important not to disturb the snow-pack on the up-slope side of your test site. Mark out a 1m square on the snow. Using the axe pick and adze, or far better your shovel, carefully excavate the front and sides of your block, ensuring that the front face remains vertical. Excavate down to just past the first stable layer. Load the test block in the following sequence, noting which stage produces a failure, and identify what this means in the scale of instability.

Step 1

Fails while isolating the test block.
Category: Extremely Unstable

Step 2

Fails while approaching the block from above.
Category: Highly Unstable
In order to approach the block from above, it is an idea to first ascend 3–4m clear of the test area, walk across the slope until above the test block, then walk directly down towards it.

Should a companion be available, he can assist by observing any movement at the test block.

Step 3

Fails while shuffling feet heel-to-toe on the block and standing up straight.
Category: Very Unstable
Before shuffling your feet heel-to-toe on to the top edge of the block, it is best to sit down above the block. This will ensure that the block is not shock-loaded with your body weight, which would then give a false result. It is important to maintain balance while standing. The stability result from a slide will be 'Very Unstable'.

Step 4

Block fails with a downsink.
Category: Unstable
Maintain your feet in the heel-to-toe position to create the downsink effect. Simply bend your knees slightly, then straighten them, followed by relaxing your body weight back to the knees-bent position, all done in quick succession. Your feet should not leave the snow.

Step 5

Fails with a soft jump.
Category: Potentially Unstable/Marginally Stable
Maintain your feet in the heel-to-toe position and jump softly on to the top edge of the block.

Step 6

Fails with a hard jump.
Category: Relatively Stable

Step 7

No failure after several hard jumps.
Category: Stable

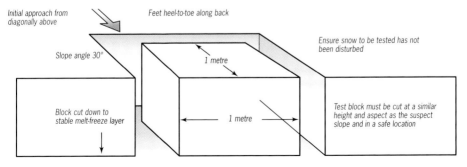

Initial approach from diagonally above

Feet heel-to-toe along back

Slope angle 30°

1 metre

Ensure snow to be tested has not been disturbed

Block cut down to stable melt-freeze layer

1 metre

Test block must be cut at a similar height and aspect as the suspect slope and in a safe location

The Rutschblock or walking shear test

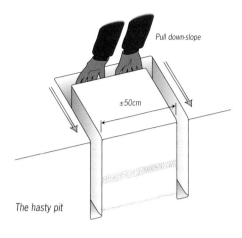

Pull down-slope

±50cm

The hasty pit

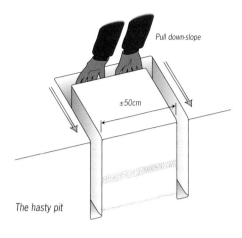

What is a Hasty Pit?

A hasty pit is a very quick and practical test to evaluate snow stability. This could be described as a mini-Rutschblock but, as the name suggests, it takes only a fraction of the time to construct. Because of this, it is a very practical test to carry out at a number of points during the day.

When and Where is it Used?

The hasty pit can be used at a number of places along your route, in order to evaluate the stability of the layers nearest the surface.

TIP

Remember that conditions and locations change, one test in a day is not enough. Combine shear tests with frequent hasty pits and on-going observations of the weather and terrain.

Method

■ Use your axe to lightly mark out the sides and bottom of a 50cm-square test area. Be careful not to disturb the snow inside the test site.

■ Using the pick, cut around the sides and bottom of the square that you have marked out and remove the snow using the adze. Excavate down to the first stable layer.

■ Cut along the top line of the square with the pick to the first suspect layer, ensuring that you do not disturb the central block, and carefully remove the snow from here, again with the adze. You should now have a free-standing block, separated from the snow-pack on all sides.

■ Place both hands, with your fingers spread wide, a few inches down the slot at the back of the block, and pull down-slope with gently increasing pressure. If no sliding layers are detected, cut the back slot a little deeper, move your hands further down, and repeat the process. Continue until your hands are at the bottom of the slot, or until a failure has occured.

Results

By applying progressive pressure to this column of snow at varying heights, unstable layers may shear off along a clean surface. If the test is incorrectly conducted by pulling hard at the bottom of the slot, weakly bonded layers further up the block may be missed.

1 If a layer slides as the block is being isolated from the up-slope side, or if a failure occurs when the snow is lightly touched with the hands, the result shows that the snow-pack within that area is extremely unstable, and potentially a high avalanche hazard exists.

2 If the test reveals no obvious sliding layers, and sections of the block only break away in lumps after some effort, this indicates a stable and well-bonded snow-pack in that immediate area. Remember that this does not mean that nearby surrounding areas are safe as well.

The ease with which a column of snow shears is rated as:

5 Very easy	Extremely Unstable
4 Easy	Highly Unstable
3 Moderate	Unstable
2 Hard	Relatively Stable
1 Very hard	Stable

SURVIVAL TIPS

If You Get Caught
- Shout out.
- Escape to the side.
- Discard gear, such as ice axe, trekking poles etc.
- Attempt to stay on the surface by rolling or 'swimming'.
- As the avalanche stops, try to thrust your hand, foot, body to the surface, fighting with all your effort.
- Try to create a breathing space around your face as the avalanche slows.
- Once all movement has stopped, try to relax and conserve energy.

If Someone Else is Caught
- Keep him in sight and note his last position.
- Check for further danger.
- If possible, attract the attention of other people to assist with a search.
- Appoint a look-out for further danger and decide on evasive action if necessary.
- If you have one, conduct a transceiver search.
- Mark where the victim was last seen.
- Search for surface clues.
- Probe likely burial areas with ice axe, etc, followed by a systematic probe line search.
- Only if numbers allow, send for help.
- Remember you are the victims only real chance of a live recovery – keep searching.

CHANCE OF SURVIVAL

In most cases people recovered from a burial within fifteen minutes will have a fair chance of survival. This is dependent upon them finishing with a sufficient air pocket around their face, as well as their final resting position within the snow-pack. Those that have sustained serious injuries as a consequence of the avalanche will have a lesser chance of survival.

Should their body be facing downhill, then there is a possibility that the snow will not have blocked their airway. If the victim is facing uphill, then snow may have got into the mouth and nose, and asphyxiation may result.

Up to one hour and beyond, the chance of survival is considerably reduced. However, victims have been known to survive burial for periods of up to 24 hours or more. KEEP SEARCHING.

Searching Techniques

WHAT TO DO

■ Having assessed that there is little further immediate danger, the first to arrive at the scene of an avalanche should spread out across the debris and search the entire deposition zone. The aim of this initial search is to find any clues as to the possible whereabouts of a buried victim. You should spot-probe where clues are found, and in any obvious catchment areas.

■ When you find clues, such as gloves, trekking poles, ice axe, rucksack, etc, you should leave them in their exact position, as this will help to identify a pattern that may lead to a more defined search area.

■ If the victim is not located after a very thorough initial search of the entire deposition zone, then begin a course probe in the obvious catchment area.

■ Course probe: use either avalanche probes, trekking poles with baskets off or ice axes, spread out in a horizontal line with rescuers 1 metre apart. Mark the two ends of the line with snow mounds or clothing to verify the start point, and continue to do so as the line progresses.

If using avalanche probes, this tactic has an approximate 70 per cent chance of finding your victim on the first pass.

COMMON PROBLEMS

■ No leadership.
■ No rescue plan.
■ No rescue equipment.
■ Not probing in likely spots.
■ Inadequate search patterns.
■ Not searching the entire deposition zone.
■ Not possessing, or knowing how to use, a transceiver beacon.

ELEMENTS OF A SUCCESSFUL RESCUE

■ Self-reliance.
■ Continuing to search until you have found the victim.
■ Having a plan.
■ Speed with safety.
■ Leadership.
■ Efficient allocation of resources.
■ Appropriate equipment (shovel, probe, transceiver).
■ First aid knowledge and equipment.
■ Evacuation.

OTHER CONSIDERATIONS

When searching, it must be thorough and fast for buried victims to have any chance of survival. In most circumstances you will not have the luxury of several extra people to assist you with the digging so you will need to shovel fast but carefully.

Once you have located the victim, immediately clear the snow from his head, airway and chest, observing whether his nose and mouth were blocked or not (this will have important implications for his treatment and evacuation), and administer first aid if appropriate. It is worth noting that when the victim is exposed to the weather elements his body will be cooling rapidly so you will need to react quickly and insulate him.

AVALANCHE TRANSCEIVERS

What is a Transceiver?
It is a small compact electronic device that is designed to transmit and receive a signal, helping with the location of a buried avalanche victim.

How do you Carry it?
Transceivers should be worn underneath your shell garment, switched on 'transmit' mode.

How do They Work?

Working on a generic frequency, most transceivers emit a bleep sound when switched to search mode and will have a direction indicator. The bleep will get louder as you get closer to your target. An experienced searcher can usually find a buried transceiver in around 2 to 4 minutes, depending upon the size of the search area.

OBSERVATIONS

1 Even when wearing transceivers, mountaineers have been killed in avalanches. Transceivers are simply victim locators, and offer a better chance of recovering a completely buried victim alive. However, they are no substitute for proper planning and preparation.

2 It is worth noting that should you be wearing a transceiver and do not know how to operate it, then there is not much point in wearing one in the first place.

3 When leaving your route information with someone responsible, remember to specify if transceivers are being worn.

4 Full information on transceiver usage, battery testing and search techniques is available from the manufacturers – practise is essential in order to be able to carry out a search in a proper and efficient manner. Remember that transceivers are of little practical use if shovels and avalanche probes are not carried as well. Most of all, remember: transceivers are no substitute for safe-travel skills!

5 Take time to find out more about transceivers and their use. They are becoming more available and are a really useful addition to your arsenal in winter.

Avalanche probes and line searches are usually the preserve of the professionally equipped rescue team, but it is interesting to understand how they are deployed. The notes below give an indication of this.

Line Searches

■ **Coarse probe.** When using a long avalanche probe, hold it vertically and lean it against your shoulder. Place the probe point directly in front of you with your feet either side of it, then push the probe into the snow as far as possible and then retrieve it. Step forward approximately 1 metre and repeat the process. If at any time you detect something soft that could conceivably be a body, it should be investigated.

■ **Fine probe.** Should you not have any success, the next option is a fine probe, First position your feet shoulder-width apart, angled slightly outwards. Begin to probe first at the toe of your left boot, then probe in between the feet, then probe at the toe of the right boot. Move one step forward and repeat the process.

OBSERVATION

In any line search there are a number of difficulties that can arise. The main one is maintaining a straight line. You should designate a leader who will organize the rescuers and give commands, eg: 'Probes in... probes out...probes forward... step forward...probes in' and so on.

PART FOUR

Snowcraft Skills

Snowcraft is the name given to the ability to progress swiftly and safely over snow-covered terrain using axe, crampon and boot skills.

The Ice Axe

Self-belay

Self-arrest

The Boot as a Tool

Step Cutting

Crampons

The Teaching of Crampon Techniques

Snow and Ice Anchors

Snow Shelters

The Ice Axe

No other piece of equipment, possibly throughout climbing in all its forms over both summer and winter seasons, is as essential as an ice axe. It is a tool with which to make progress, and, more importantly, it is the key to arresting a slip or fall on steep ground where, without its help, injury or death would be a distinct possibility. Your ice axe should be chosen wisely.

■

AXE LENGTH

The question of axe length has for many years been accepted as being judged by one method – that when you stand with the axe head in your hand and your arm down by your side, the point of the axe should be approximately 5cm off the ground. This method of selection is somewhat outdated, however, and unfortunately those purchasing an axe of this length will only find out its drawbacks when it is first used in anger, if indeed it is capable of being used at all. The days have gone of an axe being used as a walking stick, with its secondary purpose being as a practical tool.

Axes have got shorter over a number of years, and they have now settled at a length of around 50 to 60cm, possibly up to 65cm – the choice is personal preference – measured from the tip of the spike to the top of the axe head. There is no difference in length between 'walking' axes and 'climbing' axes these days, the only noticeable contrast being the shape of the head section, notably the pick, as well as technical axes often having a bent shaft. Axes longer than 65cm are unwieldy, difficult to carry, lack precision and balance when swung, and are difficult to cut steps with; they give little support on steep ground and make it very difficult to perform an efficient self-arrest.

A short axe performs all of the above tasks with ease. As an indicator that personal height is no longer a factor when choosing a tool, both authors use 50cm axes for all winter mountaineering: Stuart is 5ft 10in, Pete is 6ft 6in. This is, of course, personal preference, and many instructors will use a 55 or even 60cm long tool.

Comparison of axe lengths

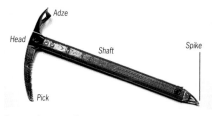

A general purpose ice axe

Why Choose a Shorter Axe?

It may be necessary to explain exactly how a shorter axe is more efficient at self-arrest – this is rather tricky without demonstrating on snow, but the following simple test could help in understanding.

Stand upright, make a fist and bend your right arm to just below hip level by your right-hand side. Then get someone to push down on your arm as you push up and try to resist, and remember how it feels. Then bend your right arm to just above hip height and repeat the experiment. It should be felt that in the second position, you could resist far more effectively, as all the muscles in the upper arm were able to work together. This is the key to efficient self-arrest.

One hand holds the head of the axe, the other must completely cover the spike. If the axe is too long, the hand that covers the spike is almost completely ineffective, and it is extremely difficult to remain in control of the axe during a slide. With a shorter tool, both arms are able to work together, multiplying many times the efficiency of the arrest position.

WHAT MAKES A GOOD AXE FOR GENERAL USE?

There are a variety of considerations governing what makes a good axe. Most axes these days are made from composite materials that are extremely strong. Wooden axes, although warm to the touch, should be avoided as their strength is often in question. An axe intended for general walking and mountaineering use should not be of an ultra-light design, as it will have trouble penetrating hard ground, especially with the adze when cutting steps. It should have a spike that is not too long, as the longer the spike the harder it is to hold on to in the event of a slip.

It is important that the spike is not too sharp either, as this will simply result in the ripping of expensive clothing. There should be some form of grip, but this must not be too pronounced from the shaft as it will impede the axe when placed into snow. The head of the axe should be a one-piece construction, with a gentle curve to it. If the head is too flat, it will be very unstable when performing self-arrest and climbing techniques; if it is too steep a curve, then it will tend to snatch when placed in the snow and be wrenched out of the hand.

There should be a good-sized, slightly scooped adze, at an angle that continues the curve from the pick. A hole in line with the shaft through the head is important for the attachment of an axe safety loop. Do not be tempted to purchase an axe with the intention of using it for walking and general purpose mountaineering if it has a reverse-curve shape to the pick and a bent shaft, as such axes are designed for technical climbing.

Finally, the feel of the axe is all-important; if it is not a comfortable fit in the hand then there will be little incentive to have it ready to use.

A classic and a technical axe

AXE RATING

Modern axes will be seen to have a 'B' or 'T' rating. These stand for 'basic' and 'technical' respectively. A 'B' rated tool is not as strong as a 'T' rated one, so if you envisage using your axe for climbing, where it may be used as part of a belay system, a 'T' rated axe would be the one to go for. The rating is designated by the UIAA and 50cm axes are tested, with the shaft being loaded cross-ways. A 'B' rated axe will have withstood a loading of 2.5kN, a 'T' rated axe will have survived a 3.5kN load.

TIP

When purchasing an axe, it is important how it feels in your hand. It is worth, from the very outset, learning the correct way to carry the axe. The axe should be picked up with the adze facing forwards, the pick pointing back. This is extremely important as far as self-arrest is concerned, and holding an axe in this way in the shop will tell you a lot about how it will feel on the hill.

Axes with a welded adze, and those with bolt arrangements at the head, can sometimes be uncomfortable. Remember to take a pair of winter gloves with you to the shop, as some material can be remarkably slippery on axe-shaft grips.

Axes and Hammers

If you are looking at taking part in technical climbing, you will most likely want to purchase a matched set of tools, one with an adze and the other with a hammer head. Exactly what style, grade and frequency of climbing you want to pursue will dictate the type of tool that you buy. For instance, radically curved shaft and head tools would be next to useless for working with groups on easy ground, as they would limit your ability to perform techniques such as stomper belays (see below). Conversely, using axes with a gently rounded classic curve to the head would be perfect for general and low-grade climbing, but be very tiring to use on higher grade technical climbs. The photographs below show some variations in styles of matched tools.

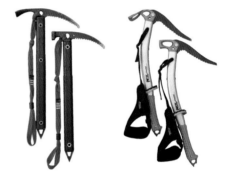

Tools suitable for general mountaineering and low grade climbing

General purpose climbing tools, appropriate for most mountaineering and climbing techniques

High specification technical tools for steep ice

Tools designed for the steepest of ice routes and dry tooling

Axe Loops and Leashes

There is a bewildering variety of ways of attaching your axe to yourself. It has been said that you should not use an axe leash of any sort, suggesting that to do so is in some way 'cheating'. Don't you believe it, get a wrist loop on! There may be an argument on lesser-angled ground for not using one, and certainly for self-arrest practice the loop should be left off, but for all other occasions one should be available if not actually used.

One type of loop attaches the axe to the body by a long piece of cord or sling, either tied around the waist or clipped on to a rucksack shoulder strap. This is often used by winter climbers on steep technical ground. The advantage for the walker is that the hands are free when zigzagging up a slope, the main disadvantage being that in the event of a fall there is a possibility that the leash would wrap itself around the body, making axe recovery and self arrest almost impossible. Another method uses a sliding-ring system up the shaft of the axe. The main drawback here is that in very cold weather the shaft of the axe ices up and the ring is unable to slide.

The simplest and recommended way is to attach a plain purpose-made axe loop to the hole in the head of the axe, with an overhand knot on the bight tied onto the sling, it being fixed onto the axe with a lark's foot, ensuring that the knot ends up under but not too close to the adze. The length should be carefully measured so that your gloved hand can grip the end of the shaft covering the spike. The advantage of the lark's foot connection is that it makes it very simple to remove and replace the sling quickly if necessary, without having to battle with frozen knots.

A leash lark's-footed onto an axe

Leashes for technical tools vary greatly. Support is needed, but so is the ability to move your hands away from the tools to make a move or to place gear. For this reason, some high specification tools come with 'clipper' leashes, which clip on and off the axe shaft in an instant. The other option is to not use a leash at all when on technical terrain, and this is popular with those climbing the hardest of routes and when dry tooling. Although dropping a tool would be disastrous, it allows far more complicated manoeuvres to be undertaken, axes to be easily swapped from hand to hand, gear placed etc.

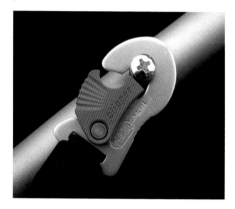

A clipper leash connection to the shaft of a technical axe, easily released when needed, even with gloved hands

When Should I Have an Axe in my Hand and not on my Rucksack?

The correct time to get out an ice axe will always be early on, well before it is needed. This may be as early as leaving the car park, or at some point low along the trail. Standing in the middle of a snowfield, teetering in balance as you try to get off your rucksack to release your axe, is somewhat too late. As a general guide, the time to stop and get the axe ready is just before your foot hits a patch of snow, even a small dinner plate-sized patch on the flat. Always be prepared and think ahead.

Carrying the Ice Axe

There is a number of ways of conveniently carrying the ice axe so that it may be efficiently deployed.

■ Firstly, to carry your axe on a rucksack, it is best to ignore the purpose-designed ice-axe carrying loops. Axes carried on the back of a rucksack can be a great hazard to others, particularly when walking in a group. You may indeed wish to cut off the loops to prevent the sack from snagging when on awkward scrambles.  The best position for the axe is to slide it down the compression straps which are found on the sides of most modern rucksacks. The axe should be arranged with the pick pointing backwards. Carried this way, the axe presents little opportunity for snagging, and is easy to lift out when required.

■ A second method of carrying sees the axe positioned between the body and rucksack. Holding the head of the axe, lift it up behind you so that the spike is placed between the shoulder straps, the shaft at a slight angle, with the pick pointing upwards. Slide it down between the  straps, so that the spike emerges just above the shoulder-strap lower attachment point at your side. The head of the axe should be nestling comfortably on the top of the shoulder straps, and the shaft should at no point be digging into your spine. This method allows the axe to be ready in an instant, one hand able to push up on the spike while the other reaches back to hold the axe head. It is an ideal way to carry an axe when, for instance, navigating on a piece of flat terrain or when crossing snowfields intermittently.

■ The third way of carrying the axe is the most important, as it ensures that the tool is ready to use in an instant for a self-arrest. The axe is picked up by the head, with the adze facing forward, the pick behind. Thumb and forefinger grip around the adze at the point nearest to the shaft, the middle finger runs down the line of the shaft, the last two fingers grip the pick near the shaft. This grip should be quite loose, as a tight grip will not allow the axe to be used effectively. Only by holding the axe in this manner can the correct arrest position be attained. Walking with the axe held as above should be practised until it becomes second nature.

TIP

Rubber spike and point protectors can be purchased to fit onto your axe, protecting others from its sharp point. These are an excellent idea for use when travelling on public transport, and indeed are a requirement in some countries. However, as soon as you set out for your day they can be safely removed and left behind.

Axes should not be stored at home with the protectors fitted, as they tend to trap moisture and can cause certain parts of the axe to corrode.

Self Belay

A self belay is the first line of defence when walking on snow-covered ground, and is designed to stop a slip from becoming a slide. It is an essential skill and its mechanics should be thoroughly understood.

■

When do I use it?
You should be prepared to use the self-belay technique at any time when walking in the mountains.

Method
When walking up, down or across any slope, it is important that the axe is always carried on the uphill side of the body. This allows the axe to be positioned correctly for support, and also allows a self belay to be used to prevent a slide occurring.

- For this description, we shall assume that you are travelling across a moderately steep slope from right to left, thus the axe is held in your right hand. The axe is also being presented to the slope so that it is vertical, the spike being placed firmly into the snow each time it is moved. The progression would be: kick step – kick step – place axe – kick step – kick step – place axe, etc.

Correct stance for the self belay

- The axe shaft needs to be placed vertically for maximum efficiency. If your feet slip, your left hand should move quickly to firmly grasp the axe shaft at the point where it meets the snow surface – keeping the hand as low as possible reduces leverage. Your right hand still holds the head of the axe, but it can be allowed to push the head uphill slightly to counter any chance of the axe shaft pulling out.

- You will end up in a lying position suspended by the axe, and should not be sliding at all. You can now scuff a hole into the snow with your feet to help you back upright again. If for some reason the axe shaft pulls through the snow, you are in the correct position to perform self-arrest, remembering to slide your left hand down the shaft to cover the spike properly.

Incorrect stance for the self belay

■

Self-arrest

Self-arrest, or ice-axe braking, is the basic discipline of winter mountaincraft. It is easy to learn and is an essential skill when travelling in the hills and mountains under winter conditions. There is a variety of positions from which an arrest can be effected, and these should be practised until they become second nature. We have opted to write this section as if we were teaching an instructor, who would in turn be imparting the skills to his students. In this way, a logical progression can be gone through, and the skills learned in the best way possible.

◼

SLOPE SELECTION

The area in which self-arrest is to be taught must be carefully selected. It should be a concave slope that allows a safe run-out if the arrest is not made, be steep enough to allow a slide to be made but not so steep as to be terrifying and difficult to negotiate for novices, and it should be free from boulders. Take care in popular areas as there may be holes in the snow, dug by other groups. Although a hard surface will be ideal for sliding, it may be painfully bumpy and deter the participant from using good style while practising. Conversely, a soft surface means that the knees will dig in and cause the arrest, rather than the axe. A deep trench will also soon be forged by sliding down the slope, and this will inhibit the amount of positions possible. An ideal surface will be a couple of centimetres of fresh snow on a base of older hard snow.

Also, pay attention to what is above you. The slope that you have selected may well be perfect on first inspection, but it may be below a large crag or buttress which could shed rocks and boulders as the temperature rises and the day's sun warms it. A further cause of accidents can be created by others, either by traversing or climbing above you and knocking down debris.

Correct hand position and ice-axe angle for a self belay

Incorrect hand position and ice-axe angle for a self belay

◼

PREPARATION

There are a number of factors other than the practice-slope angle and condition. All participants should be wearing waterproof trousers and jacket, tucking the jacket into the trousers for the first part of the session if possible. An extra fleece underneath will not only help to keep you warm, but will also help to reduce the amount of bumping that you get while practising. Gloves should be worn, but there is a high probability that these will become very wet during practice so a spare pair should be available for breaks and the walk out. Helmets should be worn at all times, unless lunch is being taken in an area free from objective dangers. Also, make sure that everyone has taken anything sharp or breakable, such as a compass, out of their pockets

It must be emphasised that crampons should never be worn when practising self-arrest. The consequences of catching the front points of a crampon when sliding down a slope are severe, with severe upper- and lower-leg injury a possibility. Rucksacks may be worn, but only after a good deal of practice without them. In bad visibility, ensure that the rucksacks are stored in an area easy to locate, otherwise you may have difficulty finding them again after a session. Place them near a prominent rock, or arrange trekking poles in an X to help make their position more obvious.

COACHING NOTE

There is now strong evidence in the coaching world that the early encouragement of students to practise techniques equally on either side of the body leads to a faster acquisition of skills. This is called 'bi-lateral transfer'. Thus, novices should be encouraged to practise self-arrest equally on both the left- and right-hand sides of their bodies.

OBSERVATIONS

1 Some of the starting positions of a few of the techniques are best practised by digging starting pits in the snow. Consider subsequent users of the slope, and fill in any holes at the end of the session.

2 For most novices, ice-axe braking is winter mountaineering; it is what they have heard most about and are the keenest to learn. Thus, there is a very real risk of your group members sliding into each other when starting to practise, caused partly by slipping on the slope, but mainly by enthusiasm. Keep a good eye on proceedings at the start of the session until all of the group have settled down and understand what is expected of them.

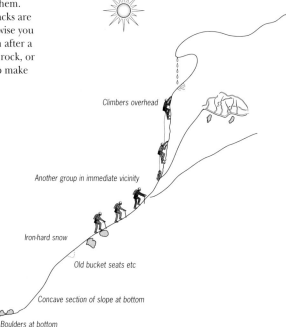

Climbers overhead

Another group in immediate vicinity

Iron-hard snow

Old bucket seats etc

Concave section of slope at bottom

Lochan at bottom

Boulders at bottom

Poor slope for practising self arrest

TEACHING SELF-ARREST: PROGRESSION

The progression of arrest skills can be understood by the novice far more easily if a logical series of steps is taken. This also ensures that those imparting the information have less chance of neglecting to pass on to the participants something vital. In the following sequence, instructions are being given to someone who is holding the axe in his left hand, although it is essential to be equally proficient at arrest skills with both hands.

Step 1

The novice should be allowed to experience sliding on snow with no hindrance. Start the session by having him slide down from a short distance up the slope with no axe. This does two things:
- firstly, it lets him experience sliding, possibly for the first time, and allows him to see what it feels like. Permit him to slide on his back, side, front and headfirst
- secondly, this allows you, as the person running the session, to assess how the slope is as regards slipperiness and speed, and to see how the participant's clothing works – some waterproof fabrics are extremely slippery, some need a steeper slope to get them sliding.

Step 2

This step allows you to talk and demonstrate the correct way to hold an ice axe when walking, with reference to using it to arrest a slide. It is also worthwhile demonstrating the incorrect method of holding it, so that the group can see how injury can occur, especially if the pick is fallen on to.

Step 3

At this point, the group is shown the correct arrest position for the axe, still while standing at the bottom of the slope.
- The left hand should be allowed to rotate on the head of the axe when bringing it up to the body from the walking ready position, so that the hand ends up pulling down on the axe head, the wrist ending up next to the attachment point of the head to the shaft.
- The adze should slot into the recess

immediately under the collar-bone at the front of the shoulder, with the shaft of the axe running across the chest at approximately 60 degrees to the opposite-side hip. The right hand covers the spike to ensure that it does not dig into the snow, and to stop it from puncturing you. Both elbows are tucked into the side of the body, and the user must look away from the head of the axe; in this case he will be looking to the right.

- It is important to look in the opposite direction to the axe head – if you look towards the axe head and it catches on a section of hard ice or a rock, facial injury is a real possibility. Looking away from the head of the axe also transfers weight onto your shoulder, helping the axe to dig in to the snow.

- Once the position has been tried and understood, have your group members raise and lower their axes from the walking to arrest position a number of times, so that they may familiarize themselves with the process. It is important that they are equally proficient with either hand, and you must decide when to get them practising with both. People will naturally favour one hand or the other, and if they are quite able to swing up into the arrest position with their stronger hand, let them try with the other. Be careful, though, of making someone swap hands who is still struggling with his stronger side, as this may confuse him.

Step 4

Once the correct position for the axe has been demonstrated, this must now be combined with an effective body position. This should be practised while still on the flat.
- Get the group members to place their axes in the snow and lie on them face down. Each person's arms should hold the axe in the correct manner, one hand on the head, the other covering the spike. Start at the feet, getting them to raise them in the air. This is for two reasons – if crampons are being worn

when a fall is made, it is imperative that the crampon points do not dig into the snow. But even if crampons are not worn, there is still a chance of the front of the boot digging into the snow. Either of these scenarios could cause injury or cart-wheeling. The knees must be apart, approximately one-and-a-half times shoulder width. This is to ensure stability when sliding in other than a straight line. The backside and stomach must be raised, and the chest and shoulders lowered. This allows the maximum amount of body weight to be transferred onto the axe shaft, imperative when sliding at speed. On very hard snow, it may be relevant to leave the stomach on the snow surface, in order to avoid the knees being injured. The head should also be kept low, to help the weight transfer onto the shoulders.

The correct body position

Step 5

It is now relevant to introduce some motion to the session.

■ With your group a short distance up the slope, have people position themselves correctly as regards axe and body, then get them to lift out the axe by arching the back and let them slide to the bottom, arresting every few feet. Slowly increase the height as their confidence builds, and increase the distance that they can slide before placing the axe in the snow. The pick should be placed positively and with firm pressure, never jabbed in, as the axe may be snatched from them in harder snow conditions.

■ Be vigilant about correcting any wrong positions, as mistakes at this stage could be carried through to the rest of the session.

Step 6

When you are quite happy that all of the group can arrest in the 'normal' position, it is time to introduce a variation. Sliding down the slope in a sitting position is quite common, often the result of a slip while walking downhill facing out. This position is sometimes best practised on the flat at the bottom of the slope.

■ Have someone sitting upright on the ground, legs out straight and together, axe held in the usual way, one hand on the head, the other on the spike. The important part of this arrest is to roll onto the chest, turning in a direction towards the head of the axe – for instance, if the axe head is held in the left hand, you would roll over to the left-hand side. Have the person roll over to the correct side, and assume the basic arrest position.

■ It is important to brief your group to keep their heads clear of the adze as the axe goes into the snow, as the tip of the pick contacts the snow surface before the body has finished rotating. Also, brief them to bend their knees slightly as they rotate – this has the effect of keeping the feet away from the snow. Once all members of the group have practised the rolling on the flat ground, they can start to slide down the slope, starting from near the bottom and progressing slightly higher each time.

Step 7

Consideration must be given to the technique for arresting from a head-first downhill position; in this instance we will be starting face-down on the snow. The starting position of this technique is far easier to attain if a slot is cut across the fall line, for the boots to hook into while practising.

■ Start by lying face-down head-first on the slope, feet hooked into the slot to prevent a slide starting too early. The axe is held in exactly the same way as for all the other techniques, one hand on the head, the other on the spike. If the axe head is in the left hand, the axe pick is placed in the snow as far out to the left as is possible, in line with the shoulders, with the right arm now across in front of the face. You should be looking across at the axe, and not down the slope.

- The manner in which the pick is placed into the snow is important – if it is plunged in, it may be snatched out of your hands; if it is not placed firmly enough then the arrest will not be performed efficiently. The best way will be to allow the pick to drag, firmly, at a slight angle on the snow, and increase the downward pressure until you feel yourself starting to rotate.
- Lift your feet from the slot, allow yourself to slide down the slope, place the axe in the correct manner and, with the pick placed in the snow on the left-hand side, your feet will swing round to the right. Keep the knees slightly bent during this manoeuvre, as it keeps the feet clear of the surface. When your feet reach approximately 90 degrees across the slope, lift your axe out and the momentum created should keep you rotating. Arch the back, place the axe into the shoulder and the normal braking posture is adopted.
- It is extremely important to remove the axe from the snow and to keep this technique divided into two definite parts – the rotation and the arrest. If the axe is left in the snow for the whole time, it will be impossible to apply the correct amount of body weight to the axe, neither would it be possible to pull your body weight up slope onto it when sliding down.
- Take great care when teaching this technique that your group keeps the initial axe placement as far out to the side as possible – the consequences of your body sliding over an adze at speed would be very sore indeed.

Step 8

This arrest assumes that the walker or climber has tripped and ended up sliding down the slope head-first on his back.

- To start this demonstration, enlarge the boot slot from the previous technique so that it turns into a ledge large enough to sit on. Sit on it and run your feet round so that they are up-slope and you are lying on your back. It is a good idea to pull the hood of your jacket up and over your helmet before starting, as it may otherwise act as a brake or get damaged.
- The axe is held, as ever, in the normal manner ready to arrest. If the axe is held in the left hand, it is placed out in the snow on the left-hand side in line with the hips, arm straight, with the right hand now over the left hip. This means that the pick will be placed into the snow approximately 40–50cm from your body.
- When the slide starts, the pick is placed in the snow in a similar manner to before, not too fast, not too slow, and slightly back from vertical. This creates a pivot, and your legs will swing round to the right. As they swing round, you must rotate the down-slope hip, in this case the right one, up-slope. This is similar to performing a sit-up towards the head of the axe. Your feet should be together and knees slightly bent; this facilitates the turn and helps to keep your boots clear of the snow surface. The object is to pivot your body through 180 degrees, both from down- to up-slope and from back to front. As your body rotates, the axe is taken out of the snow and an arrest is made in the normal manner.

Head first face down starting position

Head first face down, starting to turn

Head first face up placing the axe

Head first face up starting the turn

■ Once again, it is imperative that the axe is removed between manoeuvres and the whole procedure is treated as two separate parts, the pivot and the arrest. One of the commonest mistakes is for the person arresting to end up rotating the wrong way when pivoting, and performing a log roll down the slope. This is extremely dangerous, as speed will soon be picked up and all control lost.

Step 9

This is the next logical progression once the above skills have been practised. The aim is to perform an efficient arrest without the aid of an ice axe.

■ Part-way up the slope, have your group stand all of their axes in the snow to keep them out of the way. Lie on the snow, head up-slope and face down, arms out to the side. Lift your feet to allow the slide to start. The finishing position will be similar to that of a press-up, except with arms and legs wider.

■ As you slide, carefully place your feet on the snow with the inside edges of the soles in contact, at the same time as pushing your upper-body weight up with your hands. These should be placed at just over shoulder-width apart, and ending up with arms straight.

■ There are a number of important factors with this type of arrest – the first is that it is a last-ditch effort to stop, and is not a replacement for an axe-assisted arrest. The second is to make sure that the edges of the boots are used, not the toes. If a toe is caught, injury may occur to the lower leg. Thirdly, it is not a suitable skill for use with crampons. Lastly, it can be seen that if the upper body is forced upright too quickly on a fast-moving slide, there is a chance that the person arresting

The axe-less arrest

OBSERVATION

In some snow conditions it may be preferable to stay on your elbows and link your fingers, making a type of snow-plough shape with your forearms. This has the effect of gathering lots of snow, thus helping you slow down, and also will not cause you to flick over backwards as your upper body is being held low to the ground.

will flick over backwards and end up in a somewhat worse predicament.

Step 10

This step is simply to let your group members spend time practising what they have just learnt. They may need to go through the full range of arrests, one at a time, or they may have one in particular that is causing them problems.

■ Make sure that they can use the opposite hand to the one they have been using the most for the rest of the session – they are very likely to have been favouring either their left or right hand. With a strong group and good snow conditions, you can demonstrate a method of disorientation – walk across the slope, place one boot toe behind the other's heel, trip, slide and perform an appropriate arrest. There is a method of performing a rolling arrest – two or three forward rolls followed by a stop – but this should be used with extreme caution owing to the chance of back injury caused by jarring on harder snow, hidden rocks etc.

■ Most importantly, let your group relax. A person who is holding on to his axe like grim death is unlikely to perform as efficient an arrest as someone who is slightly more laid back.

COACHING NOTE

As your group progresses through the series of arrests, it is worth introducing the locating of the axe at each stage. This entails the group member holding the head of the axe, but not the spike, and pointing the axe shaft away from his body. He then slides down the snow, locating the axe shaft as he goes, and then performing the appropriate arrest technique. It should be noted that this locating technique should NOT be used for the head-first face-down arrest as there is a chance of the axe spike digging in the snow and being run over by a sliding body.

OBSERVATION

It is very easy, if dealing with a group of people, to lose track of what one person is doing when dealing with another, especially if abilities differ greatly. Keep to best practice as far as group control is concerned, and take into account the needs of the entire group. Be aware that someone sliding at speed into another person is likely to cause a great deal of damage, so be constantly alert to that danger. Specifying a side of the slope reserved for walking up will go a long way to alleviating the problem.

The Boot as a Tool

REMEMBER THE WINTER PROGRESSION:

walking on snow, kicking steps, cutting steps, crampons.

■

Along with an ice axe, your boots are the most important pieces of winter kit that you will use. To skimp on footwear because of cost is false economy, as your feet are your only contact with the ground and they should be looked after. They need to be comfortable, well supported, kept warm and provided with a base with which to walk without slipping. For the purposes of serious winter walking and mountaineering, boots of a fabric or similar construction should be avoided, with leather, plastic, kevlar and composite materials acceptable. The boots should be very stiff along the soles with little or no give, fully rigid boots being the best for technical ground.

Boots whose soles can be bent more than 10 degrees at the toe sections are too bendy. The soles should have a deep tread, with good square edges all round. There are a number of designs on the market with cut-away and stepped heels; these should be rejected as they are not suitable for use under winter conditions. Indeed, boots of this type should rarely be used in summer either, as the chances of a slip owing to reduced grip, particularly in descent, is extremely high.

PREPARATION

The self-arrest slope may also be used for step-kicking practice, or an altogether different area could be selected. Wherever is chosen, care should be taken to reduce risk from any objective dangers. Helmets should be worn while practising, as should gloves. If axes are carried, wrist loops should be left off. However, if the slope allows, it may be better to practise without having to carry axes, as novices will tend to find better balance and fluidity of movement without them.

The Slice Step

■ This is the most basic and frequently used of all steps created by the boot. It relies on the sawing action of the edge of the sole to create a platform, hence the need to ensure that your soles are in good order. We will assume here that you are going up vertically, facing to the right of the slope.

■ From a ledge, or the flat ground at the bottom, stand with both feet facing across the slope, kick your left leg in and across the snow a few inches directly above your right foot, in order to create a ledge cut with the front outer section of the sole. Do not use your heel as part of the cutting tool, as it will jar. You are looking to form a ledge wide enough to place your foot on, thus it will be about half-a-boot width and long enough to support the sole.

■ Place your left foot on the ledge, move your right foot up to the place vacated by the left, and repeat the process. To help keep your feet from sliding off the ledges in harder snow, try to form the step so that it tilts slightly back into the hillside. Also, as with all steps, keep the knee a little further towards the snow than the ankle. This will present the sole of your boot to gravity and keep the placement more secure.

■ Safety is the prime consideration with step kicking; thus if you can create an adequate step with one kick then that is fine, but if you need five kicks to ensure security, then that is also fine. However, if you are on a surface that is requiring more than five kicks, it may be time to start thinking about cutting steps or using crampons.

■ Once you have travelled up-slope a little way, try to progress horizontally across. The steps created here will be staggered, that is, one forward and slightly above or below the other. After a few metres, make your way directly downwards, with the uphill foot being placed into the step left by the downhill foot.

■ The next logical direction is diagonally up, at an angle of about 45 degrees. Experiment a little to see how easy it is to kick steps by crossing your feet; it will come with practice.

■ When the time comes to change direction, first plunge the ice-axe shaft into the snow to give you extra balance and security. Use the toe of the outside foot to kick a good-sized

ledge to step up into, known as a bucket step; step into it, swivel the axe shaft round in the snow so that the head is pointing in the correct direction, move your feet round and continue up.

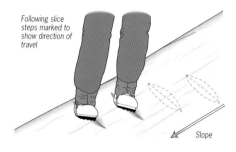

Following slice steps marked to show direction of travel

Slope

Kicking a slice step

Pigeon-hole Steps

This type of step is excellent for use on steeper terrain for progression up, down or across the slope. It is created by kicking in with the toe of the boot, swinging the leg from the knee down. Do not kick in with a full swing from the hips, as this is extremely tiring. Once a step has been formed, the heel is kept a little higher than the toe which helps to keep the step in one piece. The ice axe can be held either to one side or the other, or, on steeper ground, it can be held out in front away from your body in the arrest position, with the pick being used for stability.

Pigeon hole steps

Step Cutting

The art of step cutting has gone through something of a revival in recent years. From being an essential skill in the pioneering days of mountaineering, its use faded somewhat as crampons took over the role of aiding progress on steep ground. These days, step cutting is back and firmly established as one of the most essential tools in a mountaineer's arsenal. Step cutting is extremely relevant to today's winter-mountain leader, as it is a method of speeding up and safeguarding the progress of your group on short sections of snow-covered terrain, where stopping to put on crampons, and the time involved in doing so, may be neither necessary nor relevant. As with all things, practice makes perfect, and a little time spent trying out the various techniques will be a sound investment.

■

OBSERVATION

Whenever walking on snow, be firm when placing the feet. The temptation when on icy ground is to treat it like a slippery pavement on the way to the shops, lightly placing the feet and relying on balance for progress. Although balance is a large part of it, nothing can compensate for a well-directed series of kicked steps for security, both when ascending and descending.

Heel-plunge Steps

These are very effective for use in descent, but care must be taken that the snow is not too hard to allow the heel to dig in. Facing downhill, lock off your hip, knee and ankle, lifting the toes of your boots up slightly. The step is created by dropping your body weight down through your leg onto your heel, which punches a ledge into the snow. Do not swing your leg back into the slope; the movement needed is more akin to a hop than a step. A slight bend at the knee may reduce jarring in harder snow.

PREPARATION

Slope considerations are the same as those for self-arrest and step kicking. Helmets and gloves should be worn. Wrist loops should be used, as there is a chance of letting an ice axe slip from your grasp as it is being swung. An important consideration, and something which must be pointed out at the beginning to those whom you may be coaching, is what happens in case of a slip. It must be noted that when being used in the correct manner for cutting steps, the axe head will not be in the correct orientation for the adze to sit into the shoulder and an arrest to be performed. The axe head will have to be turned through 180 degrees for this to happen.

Slash Steps

The basic step is known as a slash step. These steps can be used in ascent or descent, with a variation being used for traversing. The best way to practise is to start by cutting steps in descent, as this allows you to understand the swing of the axe.

■ Make your way a short distance up the slope (by whatever means!) and turn to face to the right across it. Kick yourself a couple of slice

Heel-plunge steps

steps, one above the other and approximately 15cm apart. Stand upright, and, with your right hand holding the bottom of the axe shaft and the adze pointing behind you, start to swing the axe. This should be a pendulum motion, with the arm and axe in a straight line when next to the down-slope leg, the axe at 90 degrees to the snow. Continue swinging in this arc, the top of which should be no more than shoulder height. Be extremely careful that there is no one behind or in front of you, as they could get badly injured if hit by the axe.

■ When you feel comfortable with the movement, start to bend both of your knees, axe still swinging, and lower your right shoulder until the adze is just scraping the ground about 15cm directly down hill from you. Use six or eight cuts to form a step. This step should be longer than your boot sole, horizontal to the fall line, and angled very slightly into the slope to stop your foot from sliding off it. This angle is created by having your hand on the shaft very slightly up-slope of the adze.

■ Once this step is completed, stand up, put your right foot into it, move your left foot down to the step just used by your right, and repeat the process. This time, reduce the number of swings needed to make the step: maybe three or four slashes will do. If, after some practice, you are managing to cut a step with one cut, then all well and good, but security is the prime consideration here, and if you need five swings, take five swings. Also consider your security as you step down; it may be necessary to place your axe in the slope above you for extra balance and security before you move. Continue cutting steps down until you reach safe ground.

■ A progression of this technique, after some practice, is to incorporate a slight swing from the wrist and elbow as the axe nears the snow, this allowing a little more force to be used for the cut. Start the swing with the axe slightly higher than the elbow, and ensure that arm and axe are in line when the snow is contacted. If the angle of the axe is too steep, the adze will dig into the snow and not follow through, so adjust the height accordingly so that all of the cut debris is carried away on the back-swing.

Cutting slash steps in descent

COACHING NOTE

When leading a party, it should be remembered that the size of the steps that you cut should be determined by the level of security required by the least-confident member of the group.

Slash Steps in Ascent

Slash steps may be created travelling either directly up the slope, or, more commonly, when zigzagging at an angle of between 45 and 60 degrees.

■ To practise travelling diagonally, face across the slope to the right, that is, your left shoulder closest to the snow. Your left foot should be no more than 15cm higher up than the right and it should be in advance of the right foot so that the toe of the right is in line with the heel of the left.

■ Lean your upper body forward, hold your axe in the uphill hand and, swinging from the shoulder as before, cut yourself a step on the up-slope side, the same distance up and in advance of your left foot as your right is behind it. The right foot is then moved up and into this step, crossing over the left, and the process repeated.

■ A couple of errors can occur when practising this method. Firstly, there is a tendency to reach too far away when cutting, which causes the step to be cut at an angle across the slope, instead of horizontally. Secondly, care must be taken to ensure the axe swing is smooth and followed through, otherwise a chopping action will result which will cause a hole to be dug instead of a step. Cut a series of ten or twelve steps diagonally, then change direction. To accomplish this, cut yourself a larger step, place the axe in above it for security and support, step into it, turn the axe round, turn yourself round, change the axe loop onto the uphill hand, drop one leg down to the last step cut in the previous series, and continue up.

Uphill boot edges are used for balance

Slash steps in ascent

Pigeon-hole Steps

These steps are the preserve of steeper ground, such as negotiating the steep side of a frozen stream gully. Once cut, they should appear as a ladder-type series of holds, and can be used for both hands and feet.

■ The easiest method in softer snow is simply to use the adze to fashion a series of holds, each being approximately 10cm wide and flat-based. It may be found better to work two or three holds in advance. For instance, your foot would be on the third hold while you work on fashioning the sixth. If they are to be used for the hands as well as feet, a small lip can be created on the front edge to aid purchase.

■ In harder snow or ice, it will be necessary first to cut an inverted 'V' shape in the surface to aid its removal. If you tried to cut the step simply using the adze, there would be a lot of resistance and energy would be wasted pulling off large chunks of snow or ice. To avoid this, make two cuts with the pick in a teepee shape, then chop out the centre with the adze.

Pigeon-hole steps

OBSERVATION

There is a tendency, when learning, for the novice to lift the down-slope foot off the snow surface before a step has been cut for it. This is often caused by him trying to cut too far away and over-reaching. Reduce the distance between steps, and the problem should stop.

CUTTING PROGRESSION FOR ALL STEPS AND EXCAVATIONS

The cutting of snow, for whatever reason, be it for letterbox steps or bucket seats, is much easier if a logical sequence is followed. In the diagram above, section A is cut first, then B, C and D. If you started cutting at D and proceeded forwards to A, there would be lot of resistance from continuously pulling up against the snow and a lot of effort would be needed.

The cutting progression

A / B / C / D

Letterbox Steps

These are excellent for group use on short sections of steep ground.

■ Face across the slope to the right. Your left hand can be leaning on to the snow for balance, and the axe is held in the right hand. Present the head of the axe to the snow so that the shaft is at 90 degrees to the surface and just in front of your body at around thigh height.

■ Cut a slot in the snow with four or five swings using the usual cutting progression. The axe should not follow through, but should be chopping into the slope. It may be easier to work two slots ahead of yourself, so cut a second approximately 30cm above and about half a slot's length in advance of the first. Kick your boot into the bottom slot, then repeat the process.

■ The finished steps should look like their name, a series of letterboxes, and they provide good support for both hands and feet.

with the axe swing; stop the adze after it has made its cut. It will take five or six swings to achieve a good step. Remember to ensure that it is longer than the sole of your boot, and that you have not left any bumps on the surface. The final swing of the axe can be used to drag the debris from the step to leave it tidy.

■ Repeat the process for the upper foot, starting the first cut in line with the toe end of the step that has just been prepared. You can now move your feet, first the right then the left, and cut the next two steps. The temptation may be to reach too far ahead. This is to be discouraged as it will cause the axe to tap on the surface without efficiently cutting it, and it will also cause you to become out of balance.

Traversing steps

Letterbox steps

Traversing Steps

These end up looking like slash steps, but are cut in a slightly different manner. If starting by facing right of the slope, have your left foot about 10cm above and heel-to-toe distance in advance of your right foot. The axe will normally be held in the up-slope hand, but in practice it can be held in either.

■ Start by cutting the lower step, the one that your right foot will go into. The first cut with the adze should be in line with the toe of the uphill boot, and the cutting progression then followed. It is not possible to follow through

Master-blaster Steps

Apart from the slightly odd, but very descriptive, name, this style of step is very relevant for those leading groups over short sections of steep ground. The technique is rather more akin to open-cast mining than delicate step cutting, and as such is a favourite method of the authors!

The axe shaft is held in both hands, and the ground in front is pounded into submission with a number of blows from the adze. The object of the exercise is to create a large scooped step, big enough to make nervous party members feel secure when standing on it with either one or both feet. A series of these steps can be cut, and they do provide excellent security. As you can imagine, the process is quite tiring and, if a reasonable distance is to be covered, reverting to one of the more energy-efficient techniques such as slash steps may be more relevant.

COACHING NOTES

1 It is valuable for your group to practise step cutting on snow, and then to move them on to ice, as there is quite a difference in how the axe reacts when swung.

2 When practising any technique that requires the swinging of an axe, it should go without saying that you must ensure that there is a large gap between people. Keep your eyes open as the session progresses, as people will be moving at different speeds and may get rather close to each other.

3 Goggles may be a good idea when step cutting on ice, as shards are sent up at each cut.

4 Bear in mind that you are probably the most experienced in your group. Be aware all of the time that some members of your party may not be as happy as you on cut steps, and consideration must be given to stopping and fitting crampons. Remember that safety should always be paramount.

TIP

If leading a group who are finding the going a little tricky underfoot, it is quite possible that you could cut a series of steps for them, but not actually use the steps yourself. For instance, if traversing a slope, you might be completely happy walking along underneath the set of steps that you are cutting, which may allow an easier swing to be adopted.

Crampons

This section will help you to understand a little more about crampons and their usage. It will talk a little about types, strapping systems and the learning and teaching progressions that are important if they are to be used effectively and safely.

Different crampon types

CRAMPON TYPES – WHICH TO USE?

Crampons tend to fit conveniently into three categories: flexible, articulated and rigid. Great care must be put into creating a proper boot/crampon combination as, if this is wrong, your safety or the safety of those in your care will be compromised. A B/C rating has been adopted over the years, showing the compatibility between boots and crampons. This rating is shown below.

Boot Rating	Compatible Crampons
B1 Flexible boots, trekking and hill walking only	C1 Flexible
B2 Semi-rigid, for general mountaineering and mid-grade climbing	C1, C2 C2 = semi-rigid
B3 Fully rigid, for front pointing on steep ground	C1, C2, C3 C3 = rigid

A Note on Boots

It is extremely important that you are happy with your boots and that they perform well. Having stiff boots is not, as may be thought, primarily to do with them being used with crampons, but is in fact to allow you to kick steps efficiently in hard snow before crampons are even put on.

The section on step kicking has a few more details about what makes a boot good for winter use but, when talking about boot/crampon compatibility, there is one golden rule: it is essential that your crampon flexes more than the sole of your boot. If it is the other way round, with your boot flexing more than the crampon, there is a danger of crampon breakage occurring, or of the strapping system loosening and the crampon falling off.

Strapping Systems

There are almost as many strapping systems as there are crampons. The most basic is a one- or two-piece neoprene strap with a buckle-fastening system; the next up is the so-called French-style O-ring strapping system. This has an O-ring linking the two straps from the toe section of the boot, this being threaded by a strap which then goes back to a buckle. Step-in bindings are by far the most popular. These are divided into two main types: those with a bucket-type arrangement at the toe section and those with a curved-wire toe bail. The bucket arrangement is the more secure system, with the design enabling the front section of the crampon to withstand a fair amount of torsional twisting. The majority of the wire-bail designs have an extra strap linking the toe section to the safety strap around the ankle, greatly reducing the chance of a crampon being twisted or knocked off when on a route.

TIP
If you have a pair of step-in crampons that do not have a safety strap linking the front toe bail to the ankle strap, it is worth considering getting hold of one. They are sold in many shops and are easily and quickly fitted. The extra security that they give is well worth the small outlay involved.

Front Points

There are many front-point arrangements available, each designed for a slightly different purpose. General-purpose points will have a gentle downward curve to them. Those with steeply angled straight points are excellent for buttress climbs, where they provide good support but minimal leverage. Vertically aligned front points are generally reserved for crampons designed for steep ice climbing, and they may tend to cut down through steep snow. A design using a single vertical front point is a specialist steep-ice tool, but they have been used with success on buttress routes where the ascent of thin cracks is the key to their success. They are also used extensively in dry-tooling. Crampon designs that have no front points at all are to be avoided.

A variety of front point configurations

OBSERVATIONS
1 It is very important, when choosing articulated crampons, that the crampon articulates at the same point as that at which your boot bends. If you choose a crampon which articulates 5cm from the front points, and the boot to which it is to be fitted flexes further back, there is a good chance of the crampon breaking with extended use.

2 It is vital that the toe sections of crampons using the single- or double-strapping system are threaded correctly. If this is not done, there is a chance that the crampon could be forced off to one side or the other of the boot toe when being used.

Fitting

Step-in crampons need to fit snugly to the sole of the boot, with the rear handle giving a healthy 'thwack' as it locks up into place. Make sure that the toe of the boot is right down against the crampon before locking it in place, taking care to have removed any snow from the sole and bail slots.

Strap-on crampons should stick to the sole of the boot by the pressure of the side posts alone, without the straps being done up. This is a standard test that they have been correctly adjusted. Pull the straps snug as you lace them through, and if they run through two posts at the toe, ensure that they are folded correctly as shown in the photograph.

The correct method for folding back strap-on systems

TIP

There is no such thing as an ideal set of crampons. However, our recommendation for a pair of crampons that will deal with the majority of situations is as follows: twelve-point articulated with curved, not steeply inclined, front points, fitted with a step-in binding and front toe-bucket. These crampons will perform well for both walking and climbing up to the middle grades, and should give many years of service.

Carrying Crampons

The majority of rucksacks designed for winter use come with crampon patches, designated reinforced carrying positions furnished with straps, often positioned on the top of the lid. If these are to be used, first place the crampons inside a purpose-made crampon bag made from a strong fabric. This stops the chance of you snagging yourself and other people on the

points as they are carried. Better still, put the crampons in a bag and carry them inside the rucksack, well out of harm's way.

Putting on Crampons

This may seem simple, and indeed is, but there are a few points to remember. Crampons have a left and a right, with the buckles always being on the outside of the foot. Assuming strap-ons, lay the crampon on a firm piece of snow or an even-surfaced rock and move all of the straps and rings out of the way. Ensure that there is no snow adhering to the sole of the first foot to be placed in and, from a standing position (or kneeling in windy weather), put the foot into the crampon heel first, with the heel tight up against the rear posts. With a hand either side of the boot, pull up the front section of the crampon so that it fits correctly and snugly.

Now use the ground to enable you to put pressure on the foot, so that the crampon is forced into its final position. Do up the straps, starting with the heel, and make sure that they are snug. Tuck away the spare ends of the straps, then repeat the process for the other foot. After a few minutes of use, stop and check the straps again to make sure that they are still tight.

When fitting step-ins, run a crampon point along both the toe and the heel bail positions, if relevant, to dislodge any snow and ice that may have lodged there. Ensure that there is no snow sticking to the sole of the boot. Fit the toe section first, engaging the front bail, if one is used, into the correct position. Place the heel into the crampon, and clip up the rear arm. Care must be taken that this fits into the correct position on the heel welt, and that it does up with a healthy click. Finally, fit the ankle safety strap to the front bail strap and pull it tight.

OBSERVATION

It makes good sense to fit crampons on a flat area before reaching the slope to be climbed or descended. It is also a good idea to fit crampons after putting on anything else that may be needed, such as waterproof trousers or a harness.

1 Crampons come ready with extremely sharp points which are, unless you intend to use them purely for hard-ice climbing, too sharp for general use. There is a chance of catching crampons on skin and clothing, and sharp points will tear either with equal ease. Let your points dull down with use, or, indeed, take off the worst of the point with a file soon after purchase. It is rare to need to sharpen your points to a fine edge. However, do not let them become rounded off as they will be useless on icy ground. Checking the points should be part of general maintenance, which will also include checking straps for wear and tear, and the adjustment mechanism for any give. The rubber point protectors which are commercially available for crampons should not be left on during storage, as they tend to trap moisture next to the metal and cause corrosion.

2 When purchasing crampons, ensure that you take your winter boots with you and that they are fitted correctly in the shop. Bear in mind all of the relevant information in this chapter, and you will avoid buying crampons unsuitable for your needs.

BALLING UP

This very dangerous process happens when moist or sticky snow, as is often encountered during a thaw, wedges itself between the framework of the crampons and the sole of your boot so that you end up on a snow 'stilt'. This means that the crampon points do not grip the ground and thus will very easily result in a slip.

Balling up can happen after even just one step in poor conditions, and it is very noticeable on descent.

The simplest remedy is to use crampons with 'anti-balling plates' fitted to them. This is a piece of plastic or neoprene that forms a slippery surface below the sole of your boot, making it harder for the snow to stick.

However, even crampons with anti-balling plates can still have snow wedged under them, so you may need to use your ice axe to dislodge it. A sharp whack on the side of your boot is normally enough to make the snow drop off, perhaps two or three bangs in poor conditions. Make sure that you use the shaft end of the axe, not the head, as it easy to get this caught under the crampon points and trip you up. For the same reason, make sure that the wrist loop is out of the way, as this could flick underneath your raised boot, catch and cause you to fall.

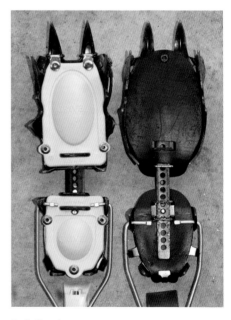

Anti-balling plates

The Teaching of Crampon Techniques

The efficient teaching of crampon techniques is only possible with perseverance and experience. Below we give a logical progression through the skills necessary and, if this is adhered to, progress may be quickly made. We are assuming that all group members have had their crampons fitted and checked, and that they are using a standard twelve-point crampon.

■

SLOPE SELECTION

It may well be that the same slope that has been used for self-arrest now doubles as the slope for practising cramponning. However, an ideal slope will be slightly different. Hard snow throughout, running from flat up to an angle of approximately 45 degrees would be perfect, still with few objective dangers, such as boulders at the bottom or crags overhead. This slope should not be too high, however, as there is the chance of a slip occurring. Areas such as the edge of moraine deposits make excellent crampon-practice sites.

PREPARATION

Firstly, ice axes should be put to one side and not used, as initial balance is important. Explain that the group members are now armed and dangerous, with twenty-four more ways to hurt themselves if they have poor technique. Discuss the progression section that they are now in, the progression being: 'walking on snow; kicking steps on snow; cutting steps on snow; crampons'.

Instil a realisation that if they catch a point on a gaiter or baggy clothing, they will be over in a split second, and get them to imagine a no-go area around each boot, that the other boot cannot get near. The image of a Star Trek-type impenetrable shield around each boot usually gets a good understanding. Helmets should be worn, as should gloves.

Depending upon snow conditions, it may be necessary at this stage to introduce the problem of balling up, and its remedy.

Step 1

Crampons on, walking on the flat. This is the basic movement and is useful as a confidence builder. Walk for a few metres in a straight line, lifting each foot and placing it with purpose in front of, and slightly to the side of, the other. The foot should be placed to the ground with the majority of the sole contacting at the same time, not with the heel touching and the boot rolling forward as we might do with normal walking. A turn is made by a series of small steps in a clockwise or anti-clockwise direction, stepping round on the spot, not crossing the feet at all.

Step 2

This time, use a gently angled slope and progress in the same manner as in Step 1. The only difference this time is that you must flex your ankles a little more and bend the knees slightly, and that when you come to turn round, do so by facing down-slope. Ensure that all downward-facing points on your crampons contact the snow at each step.

Step 3

Once a little height has been gained, step-turn so that you are facing down the slope. The descent is carried out using exactly the same technique, knees slightly bent, ankles flexed, almost a shallow squatting position adopted, sometimes called the 'wet nappy' position. Remember to place the crampon as squarely as possible on the snow, and to avoid rolling the foot down over the heel.

Step 4

Practise the two techniques together on the slope a number of times, zigzag up, turn to face downhill and walk down to the bottom. Make sure that your feet are not getting too close together as your confidence grows.

■

Step 5

It is now possible to progress on to walking uphill in a slightly more natural manner. Still zigzagging, walk up the slope but this time lift your feet high so that you may cross them over each other. Ensure that plenty of space is given between the crampon on one foot and the boot on the other, as there is a chance of catching a point if care is not taken. Pay attention to keeping the sole flat on the snow as you move. As the angle of the slope increases, you may find that the direction that you are facing changes to being up to 45 degrees across the slope, even though you are zigzagging at an angle of around 60 degrees. This is fine, but do not allow your feet to turn more than 45 degrees, as this then makes ascent very awkward and tiring. Let your ankles flex outwards to keep the presentation of the sole to the snow correct, ie flat. When turning, you can now do it facing upslope as you move, carefully placing each boot.

Step 6

On slightly steeper slopes, we can introduce another way of using the crampons. This is called the American technique, and is a very logical method of ascent. One foot, for the sake of description we shall assume the left foot, is placed into the snow horizontally, using the front two, four or six crampon points for purchase. The right foot is placed in the flat-foot position, as we have been practising above. This foot could be turned out to the side at an angle of up to 45 degrees depending upon the gradient of the slope, but once again ensuring that all downward points are in contact.

Progress can be made in a line directly up the slope or at a slight angle to it. The front-pointing foot will be the easier of the two on which to balance body weight, the flat-footing one providing stability. When the leg that is front-pointing tires, you can swap techniques for each foot and continue. This method is only suitable for ascent, not descent, so after practice turn round, face downhill and flat-foot down.

Step 7

Steeper ground requires the use of front-pointing. This is a technique that uses the front two, four or six points of each crampon in turn. The crampon is presented horizontally to the slope, and it is important that the boot is kept at this angle once the points have been placed. If the heel is dropped, there is a chance that the front points will be levered out of the placement. If it is raised, the points may still be dislodged because of the toe of the boot pushing against the surface and, once again, causing them to be levered out. Keeping your foot level when on ice is essential. On steeper ground, front-point up a short way, then descend by the same technique. Pure front-pointing is very tiring on the calf muscles, so, if travelling any distance, make the most of any irregularities on the surface of the snow or ice to give the crampon more purchase and the leg muscles a rest. Cutting a resting step at intervals is a good idea.

The American technique

Front pointing

Step 8

Walking directly across the slope needs to be practised, and this can be done by either flat-footing or front-pointing.

On easier-angled terrain, face across the slope and flex the ankles so that all downward-facing points are in contact with the snow. The down-slope foot should be allowed to swing out and round the uphill leg, the uphill foot then being picked up high and brought through in front again, in order to avoid snagging a point.

On steeper ground, it may be necessary to crab-crawl. This is done by facing into the slope in the front-point position, and by stepping across the slope but not by crossing legs. For instance, if crossing a slope from left to right move the right leg first then bring the left across to meet it, stopping a few centimetres away from it to avoid snagging.

Step 9

As confidence builds, you can introduce one or two more learning methods when operating on an easy-angled patch of ice with little danger if a slip occurs. For instance, bunny hops, hopping down-slope, follow the leader and balance competitions can all be used as aids.

OBSERVATION

There are two important factors to consider when teaching novices the art of cramponning, both of which should be pointed out to students. First, it is not uncommon for a person to sit down on a snow or ice slope, in order to adjust their straps for example, only to find themselves suddenly sliding down the hill at a rapid rate of knots. A ledge, tilting back into the hillside, should be dug and an axe kept to hand if adjustments need to be made.

The second occurs at the end of any session, walk or climb when packing away kit. You are so used to placing your foot on the ground and it staying there that, when you finally take off your crampons, it takes a couple of minutes for your body to adjust to the difference underfoot. Be aware of this, and ensure that crampons are removed in a safe area where a slip will not be dangerous.

Step 10

Now it will be relevant to introduce the axe to the session. The carrying of the axe should make no difference to the way that the crampons are used. It may, however, be tempting to lean forwards onto it and alter the body weight over the feet; this must be avoided. Another common mistake is when the axe is used to aid progress over a small ice step. It is common to place the axe above the step and use it for support, forgetting about the angle of the sole of the boot. As the climber moves up, the crampons then have a real chance of ending up placed almost vertically to the ice, an angle of little purchase. It should also go without saying that the use of knees when surmounting a snow or ice bulge must never be contemplated.

Snow and Ice Anchors

This section is an introduction to the skills of belaying on snow and ice. There are many ways of achieving this successfully, but all of the methods shown rely on two major points: your assessment of the state of snow-pack and your choice of the most appropriate technique.

In winter, keeping your rope work tidy and simple is the key to success. Pay attention to detail, such as providing ledges for the rope to be coiled onto in order to prevent it from sliding down the hill. A rope draped down the slope not only has the chance of getting in the way of your second, but it also has a very real chance of snagging or freezing to the snow surface.

■

THINGS TO THINK ABOUT!

Bear the following in mind when deciding whether or not to use a certain type of snow anchor.
■ The easier the digging the poorer the anchor, the harder the digging the better the anchor.
■ Poor snow-pack = poor anchor, good snow-pack = good anchor.
■ Poor snowpack = direct belays dangerous, thus use indirect instead.

THE STOMPER BELAY

What is a Stomper Belay?
The stomper belay is an excellent way of safeguarding progress on moderate ground, and ideal for lowering. It is also quick and simple to set up.

When and Where do we Use it?
The stomper is ideal for situations such as when speed is important in ascent or descent, for inspecting a corniced descent gully, safeguarding a second over an awkward icy step, or even as an anchor at the finish of a simple route.

It must only be used from above, never to protect a leader, and the most important consideration is your own safety, as you are not anchored in any way if using the standard method. For this reason, it can only be

recommended for use on terrain upon which you are entirely happy with your own safety, without the effect of external forces such as the wind, etc.

Method
■ If not on level ground, either cut or stamp a ledge into the snow, inclined slightly back into the slope. This ledge will ideally be of a wedge shape, just wide enough for you to stand with your feet together. The depth of this ledge can be fashioned so that you will have support from the snow at both the back of the legs from the up-slope side, and from the side walls which will help your stability.
■ The exact placement of the axe shaft can be ascertained by standing in position on the ledge with your boots flush against the back wall, thus marking the snow with your heels, stepping out again and placing the axe shaft in at just in front of the heel mark. Push the axe half way into the snow, just back from vertical, to create a hole into which it will finally be placed.
■ Clip the rope into the krab, and do up the gate. Ensure that the rope is at the narrow end of the krab and emerging from the bottom side of it, and slide the krab up the shaft of the axe to rest just below the head.
■ The axe is then placed into the hole with the head of the axe pointing across the slope, and then pressed into place with your feet. Ensure that the axe head is flush with the snow surface, and that the rope can run smoothly.
■ Place both feet close together on the head of the axe, one either side of the rope. The rope is taken in the left hand, passed behind

Placing the axe through the karabiner for a stomper belay

the left shoulder and down the front over the right shoulder (reversed for left-handed belayers).

- The rope is then managed as a shoulder belay, with sufficient friction being created by the system to remove the need for a twist around the dead-rope arm. (It is important that the rope is not taken up in front of the left shoulder, as any loading could cause the belayer to be pulled forwards at the waist.)
- When the climber arrives at the stance, it is important that he stops below the level of the axe so that he does not exert an upward pull on it, and so that, in the event of him slipping, he does not shock-load the system. It would be advantageous to have a ledge or bucket seat prepared for him just below the level of the ledge.

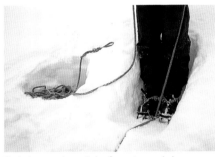

Foot stance and rope ledge for a stomper belay

Progressing slowly downward, protected by a stomper belay

COACHING NOTES

It is important to point out both the advantages and failings of this belay system. The main advantage over the boot–axe belay is the ability to take in the rope. The main failings are the fact that the belayer is unattached to the anchor, and that he may feel unstable in high winds.

It should be made clear that the stomper and boot–axe belays are complementary methods, and skill is required in deciding when one is preferable to the other.

OBSERVATION

There are alternative appropriate methods of controlling the rope with a stomper. Belaying directly from your harness is one option, though we feel that under load you get the sensation of your harness being slowly dragged down past your knees! It is also difficult to get a 'feel' of the rope with this method. The other way is to run the rope up and directly over your rucksack straps, to alleviate any load on your shoulders.

Our choice, though, is the shoulder-belay method given above, with the live rope being gripped snugly – if this is done, you are hardly aware of the load on your shoulder. Also, the method of arranging the krab mentioned above is better than the other option of clipping it through the eye of the axe head. This has the effect of twisting the rope, of loading the axe-head/shaft rivets incorrectly and of exerting a lot of leverage on the placement.

TIP

It is useful to have a ledge prepared for the rope to run into or out of, in order to avoid any chance of it running down the slope and snagging or getting in the way of your second.

Snow and Ice Anchors

OBSERVATION

It is very important to have the rope end secure, to stop any chance of it sliding through your hands and disappearing down the hill. Tying on round the waist or at your harness is the best and recommended way of ensuring this does not happen, although a large knot tied on to the end of the rope is acceptable. Also, consider the attachment of the person being lowered. As for the boot-axe method, if he is to be brought down steep ground a simple waist tie may not be sufficient, and consideration should be given to using a harness for his safety and security.

THE BOOT–AXE BELAY

What is a Boot–Axe Belay?

The boot–axe belay, very much like the stomper, is a way of safeguarding descent on awkward ground, and is an excellent method of lowering.

When and Where do we Use it?

On windy sections, for the security of another on awkward descents, and when speed is a factor. It must only be used from above, never to protect a leader. In windy conditions it may well be chosen over the stomper, as the body position of the belayer is low to the ground and thus more stable. The main drawback is the difficulty of bringing a climber up to the stance, and for this reason we recommend that this system is used in descent only.

Method

■ If not on level ground, either cut or stamp a ledge into the snow, inclined slightly back into the slope. This ledge should be large enough to easily accommodate a boot sideways. Place your right foot on the ledge, with the sole braced against a 3–5cm lip fashioned on the down-slope side. A second ledge for the left foot can be cut a short distance below if required.

■ Place the axe shaft vertically into the snow next to your right boot, running in a line with the side of your shin and with the shaft inclined slightly uphill. The axe should be pushed into the snow as far as possible, leaving a boot-height between the surface and the head of the axe. The pick should be pointing behind you across the slope.

■ The rope is run from behind the belayer, between the legs, in front of the ankle of the right foot, around the head of the axe from the right-hand side (looking up-slope) and down to the climber. The belayer takes a stance allowing him to lean onto the axe with his right hand, his left hand gripping the rope between his legs and low down by the right ankle. When load is applied, the rope pulls the axe onto the boot, and the friction created is enough to hold a climber's weight. This friction can be varied by moving the left hand forwards or back as necessary.

■ The end of the rope needs to be secured in some way so that there is no danger of the end running through your hands – the safest method is to tie on to the rope before starting the lower.

Running the rope around the ankle for a boot-axe belay

The body position for a boot-axe belay

COACHING NOTES

When demonstrating the boot–axe belay, ensure that any loading on the system is below the level of the belayer – if the loading is upwards on the axe, it has a high chance of failing in spectacular style. When running a session, ensure that anyone trying out the system is aware of this.

Also ensure, if using this system for real, that you brief those being lowered before starting, so that they are in no doubt as to what to do when reaching the end of the pitch, such as digging in, cutting a ledge, untying, and so on.

OBSERVATION

In very hard snow where the shaft of the axe cannot be pushed far into the ground, this method can still be used. Care must be taken that the pick is braced securely behind the knee, and is securely gripped by the uphill hand. It is important that the controlling hand is low down next to the snow surface in order to minimise any leverage. A corkscrewing motion with the axe spike can be used to make a hole as deep as possible for the shaft.

TIP

Like most things, preparation makes life a lot simpler. Run the rope through and make sure it ends up in the right place – in a neat pile at the back of the belayer. A shallow ledge can be dug to contain the rope and prevent it slipping off down the slope.

THE BUCKET SEAT

What is a Bucket Seat?

The bucket seat is not only one of the simplest belays to construct, but also one of the most effective.

When and Where do we Use it?

The bucket seat can be used for most snow belay situations, such as climbing and lowering. Used in conjunction with a second anchor system, such as a buried axe, it forms one of the strongest snow anchors available.

Method

The simplest way to construct a bucket seat is simply to dig a pit in the snow with either the axe, gloved hands, or a combination of both.

■ Scribe a semi-circle on the snow with your ice-axe, the straight edge on the downhill side, and excavate the snow inside. The pit needs to be large enough for you to sit in, usually while wearing a rucksack, and have sufficient room on either side of your body so that your arms can move freely.

■ The important details are to have the front face perpendicular to the angle of slope, and the depth of the seat sufficient so that when you sit in it your thighs are supported up to the knees. A ledge should be formed on the dead-rope side of the seat to prevent the rope sliding down-slope while belaying. When sitting in the seat, kick your heels in for a little extra support.

The bucket seat

COACHING NOTES

This seat can be practically tested by having a person sit in the seat attached to the rope by his harness. It is not necessary for him to put on a waist belay. Test the bucket seat by pulling on the rope, but be careful not to shock-load the rope as back injury could occur. Start with a gentle pull and increase the pressure – it is quite possible to have two people pulling at once – and make sure that the belayer knows to say 'stop' if he starts to experience any back discomfort at all. If the seat has been made correctly, he will be unmovable. If not.....!

TIP

Don't skimp on the depth or shape of the front wall. It is worth constructing a bucket seat and then testing it by having someone pull on the rope – if the seat is too shallow, you will pop out of it like a cork!

OBSERVATIONS

1 A similar method has been taught for years, that of a saddle stance which looks like a horseshoe in design. This works well, but great care must be taken that the snow-pack, and the layers within it, are not weakened by the excavation process. There is a chance, in a varying snow-pack, of layers shearing off when loaded. This does not occur with the bucket seat, as it is a simple hole in the ground and the layers are disturbed minimally during construction.
2 Although the bucket seat is primarily for use with a second system, such as a buried axe or dead-man anchor, it is possible to use the seat on its own, for instance when safeguarding group members over an awkward step, either in ascent or descent. This should only be attempted in solid snow conditions, and only for safeguarding a group member lower down the slope than yourself. An indirect belay should be adopted (although with experience and good conditions a belay device at the harness could also be considered), as this will lessen the loading on you should the person ascending slip. As always, there should be no slack rope between you and him and, if in any doubt as to the properties of the snow, a second anchor should be used to ensure complete security.
3 Care must be taken to ensure the security of your group if using the bucket for negotiating an awkward step. There must be a safe place for them to stand or sit when arriving.
4 When linking a buried axe, deadman or similar anchor to a bucket seat and you are tied on with a harness, the slot that connects the seat to the anchor should be cut slightly to one side or other of the centre at its back, depending upon the correct ABC, see diagram on page 169. For instance, if the live rope is in the belayer's left hand, the rope from the anchor should run to the left-hand side of the bucket seat.

Snow and Ice Bollards

These two anchors may differ in size, but their shape remains essentially the same. The snow bollard especially is very useful for retreat leaving no gear behind and is excellent for linking with a bucket seat, or being used as a direct belay in both ascent and descent. The ice bollard, or mushroom as it is often called, is hard work to construct and relies upon the integrity of the ice. It may have its place on descent when gear is at a premium, although many will choose to use an Abalakov thread in its place.

EQUIPMENT

One ice axe, with the addition of an 8ft (120cm) or 16ft (240cm) sling with screwgate for the ice bollard.

Snow Bollard

The size of the bollard is dependent upon the quality of the snow, from 1 to 2 metres across will be average. Cut a horseshoe shape with the pick of the axe, taking care not to disturb the snow in the body of the bollard. When the outline is formed, cut around the outside of the line with the pick, then cut around the outside edge of this with the adze. The depth of the trench created will vary with the snow-pack, but should be no less than 15cm. The bollard is finished off, as its name would imply, by running either the adze or a gloved hand around under the rim to create a lip for the rope to seat into.

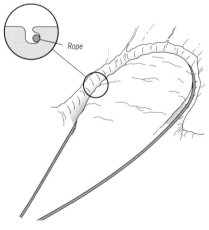

Rope

The snow bollard

COACHING NOTE

To scribe out a symmetrical shape for a bollard in good-quality snow, rest your elbow gently at the centre of the snow and mark out the shape with the pick of the axe in a semi-circle. Make it clear that the snow should be disturbed as little as possible in the process. It is often a good idea to arrange a simple abseil demonstration from the bollard, even on a moderate slope, to show the strength of the snow.

OBSERVATION

Constructing an ice bollard is extremely hard work and very wearing on the wrists. It is possible to use icicles as threads, but, as they are often not physically connected to the rest of the ice, you must be extremely careful about their strength.

TIP

Although the snow bollard is often constructed on open slopes, it is quite possible to make use of the gap between a gully wall and the shrinking snow to help make one. In this case, you often end up with something more akin to a spike belay, but which is still very strong.

It is possible to use a snow bollard as a direct belay. It must never be shock-loaded, thus should only be used for a climber who is below the level of the belayer. It can be used in ascent or descent, but the solidity of the snow is paramount. The rope should NEVER be moving around it, as this will cut through it causing it to fail.

Ice Bollard

The ice bollard will only be as strong as the material it is made from – careful selection of solid ice is important. The size will be about 30 to 40cm across, with the lip being about 5 to 10cm deep.

A rough outline can be scraped onto the ice and the pick then used to chisel out a rough shape. This can be refined using a combination of both pick and adze and great care must be taken not to chip off too large a lump of the bollard, compromising its strength. The finished article should be able to comfortably take an 8ft (120cm) sling, which should sit securely under the lip.

Ice bollard shape

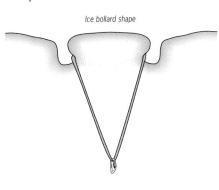

The ice bollard

BURIED-AXE ANCHORS

What is a Buried-axe Anchor?

The buried-axe anchor is the basic belay on snow, and is taught almost from the outset on many a winter-skills' course. There are a variety of ways of organising either one or two axes into a solid anchor; here we will concentrate on the buried axe and the reinforced buried axe. Other systems such as the T-axe and vertical axe are worth experimenting with, but you will find that the system below deals with the majority of situations perfectly.

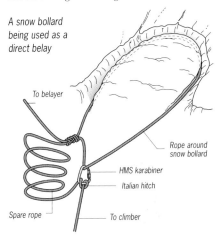

A snow bollard being used as a direct belay

To belayer

Rope around snow bollard

HMS karabiner

Italian hitch

Spare rope

To climber

When and Where do we Use it?

This anchor can be used for most belaying, climbing and lowering situations, on both moderate and steep snow slopes, and is particularly appropriate for linking to a bucket seat when belaying a leader.

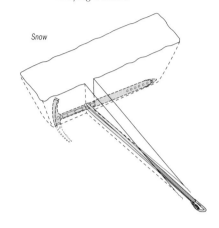

Snow

Buried axe cross section

EQUIPMENT

One or two ice axes, an 8ft (120cm) sling and a screwgate.

Method

■ Select a relevant area of undisturbed snow and try, while constructing the anchor, not to disturb the snow-pack on the down-slope side any more than is necessary. Cut across the slope at right angles to the fall line with the pick of the axe, with the pick vertical, to a length slightly longer than the axe shaft. About 15cm above this, cut another line parallel to it. Using the adze, remove the snow between the two lines, taking care to avoid disturbing the down-slope internal face. The depth of this slot is dependent on the snow type, but will be between 30–45cm for the majority of cases. Care must be taken to ensure that the full length of the axe shaft is flush with the down-slope face of the slot. This face should be either vertical or slightly undercut which can be achieved by running the adze along the bottom of the slot on the down-slope side.

■ A second slot then needs to be cut running down-slope from approximately two-thirds of the way along. This should be only wide enough to allow the sling to run along it (start with the pick and make it sling-width by using the shaft of the axe to clear it out; the adze of the axe is too wide and may compromise the strength of the snow), starting at the same depth as the main slot. If using a bucket seat, this should emerge from the snow at its back, so that the axe is pulling against the bulk of the snow pack.

■ A clove hitch is tied in the sling and placed around the axe shaft at the central point of the surface area, which is normally nearer the head at about two-thirds distance up the shaft. The clove hitch needs to be inverted onto the up-slope side of the axe by taking one loop of the sling around the axe shaft. The axe is then placed in the slot with the pick facing vertically down, and bedded in firmly. The sling is run down the narrow slot, taking care that no debris has fallen into it, and the rope is clipped into the krab. A downward pull on the sling will ensure that the axe has embedded itself into the correct position. The stance should be taken around 2m below the axe, with a bucket seat being the most secure.

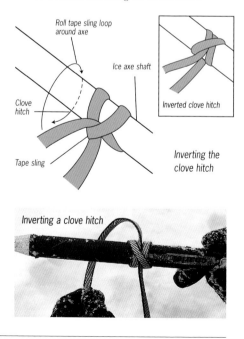

Roll tape sling loop around axe

Ice axe shaft

Clove hitch

Inverted clove hitch

Tape sling

Inverting the clove hitch

Inverting a clove hitch

■ To improve the holding power of the system, insert another ice tool vertically through the sling at the top of the vertical slot, making sure that you do not disturb the horizontal axe. Push the second ice tool down into the snow as far as it will go, with the pick and adze running horizontally across the fall line.

■ Once the axe/s have been placed, in soft snow conditions you may decide to fill the slot back in to help bed the axe/s down. This should be firmed down by foot, with care being taken to not disturb the axe placement or the down-slope face of the slot.

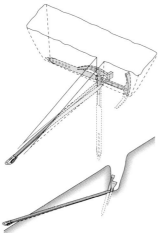

The reinforced buried axe anchor

When using a waist belay, which would usually be adopted when dealing with any snow or ice anchor, and you are wearing a front point attachment harness, it is essential that the rope from the anchor runs under the same arm that is dealing with the live rope to the climber. For instance, if you are right handed, you may well have the live rope on your left-hand side – the rope to the anchor should be arranged on this side of the body as well. If the ropes enter and exit on different sides of your body, a dangerous twisting motion will be exerted on you in the event of a falling climber loading the system, which could result in loss of control of the rope, and in spinal injury for the belayer.

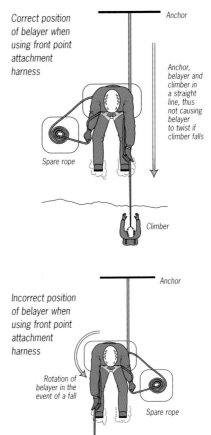

Correct position of belayer when using front point attachment harness

Anchor

Anchor, belayer and climber in a straight line, thus not causing belayer to twist if climber falls

Spare rope

Climber

Incorrect position of belayer when using front point attachment harness

Anchor

Rotation of belayer in the event of a fall

Spare rope

Climber

COACHING NOTES

1 It may be worth demonstrating the strength of the anchor by having a couple of people pull on a rope clove-hitched to the sling; novices are often surprised by its holding power. You should be holding tight to the end of a 4m rope tail, just up-slope of the anchor, in case it does fail.

2 When showing the axe anchor together with the bucket seat, explain how important the correct alignment of the rope is (ABC), from the climber, through the belayer, to the anchor. A simple demonstration can be made by having someone wearing a harness sitting just down-slope of the seat using a classic waist belay with the live rope on the side opposite to the anchor. The twisting motion can be created by pulling gently on the rope – the effect is remarkable! (See diagram).

It is important to think ahead as to the direction the new leader will be taking. This is covered under the general belaying section, but is worth re-emphasising here. Take care that your leader will not be a) unwrapping themselves from your waist belay, or b) wrapping you up tight in it, giving potential for injury should they slip.

It is possible to use a buried axe anchor as a direct belay for use in ascent or descent. It must never be shock-loaded, thus should only be used for a climber who is below the level of the belayer. The solidity of the snow is paramount.

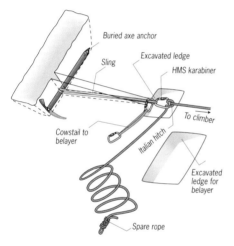

A buried axe being used as a direct belay

TIP
Dig your bucket seat before burying your axe!

THE DEADMAN ANCHOR

What is a Deadman Anchor?
A flat metal device with a 2m wire attached, the deadman anchor is an efficient way of belaying on snow. It has one main advantage over other methods in that you do not use your axe as part of the system, so you still have it to hand for your own security.

When and Where do we Use it?
This anchor can be used in most belaying, climbing and lowering situations, on flat, moderate and reasonably steep slopes.

EQUIPMENT
Deadman, one screwgate, ice axe and hammer.

Method
■ It is essential that the deadman is placed at the correct angle to the slope; – 40 degrees on the uphill side. Place your ice axe into the snow at 90 degrees to the slope, using the sides of the deadman as a square to check the angle.

■ Ensuring that you are working across the fall-line, place the point of the deadman on the snow level with but a little distance from the axe. Look along the line from the side and bisect the angle between the axe and the slope – that will give you 45 degrees. Set the deadman back a few degrees from there to give you 40 degrees, and push it into the snow a little way.

■ Remove your axe, and, using the deadman as a guide, cut a narrow slot with the pick to the side of the deadman and at exactly the same angle. This slot will be used to guide it in at the correct angle, so be careful not to disturb the down-slope face or snow-pack.

■ Remove snow from the uphill side of this line creating a shallow trough and remove any debris.

■ Again using the pick, now create a narrow slot running down-slope and at 90 degrees to the deadman's slot for the wire to run through.

■ Place the deadman flush against the horizontal slot you have cut and, while holding it in place by keeping the wire in tension, hammer it down to below the surface, ensuring that it follows your guide slot, thus ending up at the correct angle. The wire must run in a straight line from its attachment point on the deadman down the slot towards the stance; be careful to ensure that no debris has fallen in and clogged it.

■ Use the shaft of the axe or hammer through the loop of the wire to give it a tug, in line with the snow surface, which helps the device bed in. Keep tugging the wire until there is no more creepage of the device. It should then be well seated in the snow pack.

■ The climbing rope is connected to the wire with a screwgate, and the stance is taken around 2m below.

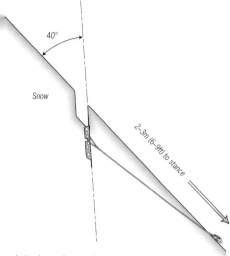

A deadman placement

COACHING NOTES

It is worth discussing the relative merits of buried axes against the deadman; would a lot of steep snow be encountered, in which case burying the axe may not be satisfactory?

Alternatively, would there be little steep snow, with mainly rock and ice being encountered, making the carrying of a deadman unnecessary? It is important to put across both points, with the final yardstick being the safety of the climbing party in any given situation. For the novice, carrying a deadman would be a sensible thing to do; he could then make his own choice after climbing a number of routes.

OBSERVATIONS

1 Some mountaineers never use the deadman, as they feel it is too awkward to place, and that it is a piece of equipment that only does one job, a shame for such a useful piece of kit.

2 Great care must be taken to avoid placing it against snow layers of a different hardness, which could cause it to pivot when loaded.

TIP

Notoriously awkward to carry, the deadman is best clipped on to your rucksack loops well away from the front of your body. Care and time should be taken to ensure that the wire remains firmly wrapped around the deadman, clipped into the carrying krab to help prevent it from unwrapping.

Although the placement angle is correct, pulling on the wire will cause the plate to slide out

Incorrect angles of placement for a deadman

ICE SCREWS AND DRIVE-INS

What are Ice Screws and Drive-ins?

Modern ice screws have evolved a long way in the last few years. They have progressed from requiring both hands to place, one to turn and the other to hammer, to a single-handed operation with the screw turning in with great ease. Drive-ins come as three basic types: the warthog, which is solid in section, a tubular drive-in, and an ice-axe-pick-shaped drive-in. The tubular drive-in is little-used in modern climbing.

When and Where do we Use Them?

It used to be that drive-ins were placed on the lead for speed, with screws being reserved for stances, but modern screws are so efficient that it is rare to see drive-ins on ice routes any more. Thus, screws are ideal for ice, and warthogs are excellent for turf placements on mixed routes.

Ice Screw

Ice screw placements will only be as good as the ice in which they are placed, so select the area carefully and reject sections of ice that are mushy or otherwise obviously soft and non-homogenous. The best angle for a screw placement is at 90 degrees to the slope, so it is necessary to first prepare the ice surface to allow the eye of the screw to rotate when fully screwed home. It may be that you need to make a small hole with the pick of your axe to start the teeth cutting, after that the screw is simply wound in by hand.

If the ice starts to go opaque or 'dinnerplate', cut away the bad ice and continue the placement. The eye should end up lying flush with the surface and facing downhill. To remove a good quality placement, simply unscrew it.

As a guideline, use the longest screw possible for the job, in particular at anchors and directly after leaving stances.

A screw placement, extended and clipped correctly

TIP

Look after your ice screws, in particular the threads and teeth. Specially designed carrying tubes are available, which keep all of the cutting threads sharp and free from damage.

OBSERVATIONS

Tests have shown that 90 degrees, and even as far down as 75 degrees (thus with the shaft pointing slightly towards the direction of loading) gives the greatest holding power for ice screws in good quality ice with external high-relief threads. From a practical point of view, 90 degrees is the easiest to judge when balanced on front points, so we recommend you go with that. Interestingly, similar testing has found that if the screw is placed further back than 90 degrees, around 100 to 120 degrees, the effect here is to weaken the placement as any load shatters the ice below the screw, which can then bend and pull out.

1 Dinner-plating is the process by which ice shatters from around a screw placement, often in large pieces. If placing screws on the lead, ensure that any sections of ice from dinner-plating that you are chopping away do not drop and hit your second.
2 Ice screws should not be used in isolation as a main belay anchor, they should always be placed in pairs. The correct position for the second screw will be 60cm to the side and 60cm above the first placement, making them about a metre diagonally apart. This helps to ensure that the strength of the ice is not compromised, and that any internal lines of stress within it caused by the screw placement will have a minimal chance of running into each other.
3 When using two ice screws as part of an anchor system, great care should be taken to ensure that the loading on each is the same. Bringing the two down to one point using a sling is the most effective way of achieving this.
4 It is important to remove the core of ice from the ice screw before it can be used again. The larger-bore screws are the ideal size to permit a standard warthog to fit inside, so check that you have a compatible screw/hog set-up. Some screws are manufactured with a cleaning slot along one side, which allows for ice removal with an axe.

TIPS

1 If a screw cannot be placed to its full depth, it needs to be tied off to reduce leverage. Leave the eye facing uppermost, and either clove hitch a tape around the tube next to the ice, or use an extender and slip it over the eye ring and down to the surface. Tests have shown that if a screw is up to 5cm away from the ice, the hanger can still be safely clipped, but if the gap is more than 5cm, either tie it off or remove it and use a shorter screw.
2 When clipping ice screws on the lead, it is worth using extenders, as a single krab tends to exert a lot of leverage on the eye and shaft. There is also a danger of the krab levering the screw to the extent that it unscrews it from its original position.

A screw tied off with the eye uppermost

Take care to reduce the impact force on any ice screw set-up. Slings that are designed to absorb energy by their stitching ripping in a controlled manner are a good idea for key placements, and these can reduce the impact force by around 50 per cent.

A shock-absorbing extender, opened out for clarity

Drive-ins

The ideal warthog placement will be made with the stem at 90 degrees to the frozen turf. Hold the eye at about four o'clock, as the threads of the hog will usually cause it to rotate as it is

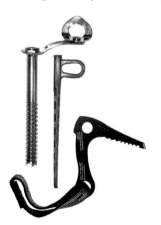

Ice screw, warthog and ice hook protection

driven. Drive the hog fully in so that the eye is flush with the turf and pointing downhill. Solid-section hogs tend to shatter ice, but in frozen turf they tend to sit without compromising the strength of the placement. It is important to consider removal and to ensure that you do not place the eye too close to rock which will stop the hog turning when being retrieved.

Ice Hooks

This type of protection is shaped like a reverse-curve axe pick. These are designed to be placed (either by hand or tapped) into ice axe marks on steep ice, or driven into iced-up cracks on mixed routes. Their holding power is low when used on ice, so they offer only marginal or 'psychological' protection at best. Sometimes used to hold body-weight when resting on a route, it is far preferable to use an ice screw wherever possible as they will offer a much higher degree of protection in the event of a fall, particularly when allied with a shock-absorbing sling. Carrying ice hooks can also be problematic, as they present a sharp point and teeth which can catch on clothing or other equipment.

THE ABALAKOV THREAD

What is an Abalakov thread?

The Abalakov thread, sometimes called the 'V' thread, is exactly as it sounds – a length of cord or tape threaded through the ice. It appears to be one of those tricks that people show you but never gets used. However, a well-constructed Abalakov in good quality ice is extremely strong, leaves no gear behind except for a length of cord or tape and is quick to construct.

When and Where do we Use it?

The thread is useful when ice screws are becoming scarce, or if you do not wish to leave any gear behind, such as on an abseil. They are made from the available ice, so are a very practical alternative to a bollard.

EQUIPMENT

One long ice screw (22cm or more if possible), a length of 7–8mm accessory cord or tape, thread hook if available.

Method

The ice is the weakest point of this structure, so ensure that the thread will not be compromising the strength of the area in which you wish to work.

■ The ice screw is wound into the ice at 45 degrees horizontally to the surface and at an angle of about 90 degrees to the vertical, in as far as the eye of the screw will allow.

■ Withdraw it and repeat the process in the opposite direction a sufficient distance away, just enough so that the teeth of the screw emerge into the bottom of the previously drilled hole. It may help to insert the thread hook into the first hole as this could be used as a guide by eye for getting the second hole angle correct. When completed, the two holes should meet at an internal angle of around 90-degrees.

■ The accessory cord or tape is manoeuvred through the two holes, most easily with the use of a specifically manufactured tape hook, and a thread created, with the threaded material being tied off with a suitable knot such as a double fisherman's.

COACHING NOTES

Testing the thread by pulling on it with the rope and a couple of people helps to show its strength. Obviously, ensure that anyone doing the pulling is in no danger of injury if the ice should fail – this includes factors such as ensuring they are not wearing crampons, and that there is no danger of them slipping and hitting boulders if the ice should fail. Make sure that it is being pulled in the correct direction of loading, which will be along the surface of the ice and not outwards.

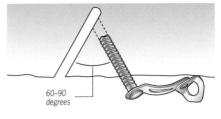

The Abalakov thread

TIP
You may find it tricky to thread the tape or cord through the hole. There are special hooks on the market for solving this problem, or you can make one yourself from a wire coat hanger. Make it about 30cm long with a loop at one end for carrying and bend the other end back on itself to make a small hook. This can be sharpened into a tight angle with pliers and then finished off with a file to give it a bit of a point. Carrying it may best be done down the inside of your longest ice screw.

An Abalakov thread hook

TIP
If you do not have a supply of threadable tat, you could unpick a Prusik loop or use a sling – this latter idea works well if the thread is to be used as an anchor rather than a point of retreat. Finally, if you are abseiling and have run out of tat, you could thread the rope itself through the Abalakov, ensuring that it will not freeze into place and will still be retrievable.

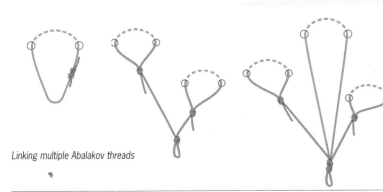

Linking multiple Abalakov threads

TIPS

TIPS

If you are going to abseil from a single Abalakov, you may wish to back it up until the last person descends. You can do this by placing an ice screw (probably the one you used for constructing the thread in the first place) a suitable distance above it and clipping an extender between the screw and the abseil rope. Have the heaviest people descend first, leaving the lightest to abseil last, once they have removed the screw and extender.

Sometimes, natural ice threads will be seen, such as where an icicle reaches and bonds with the ground. These features may be threaded, but great care must be exercised when assessing their strength – they will generally be far weaker than a thread constructed from solid ice.

An Abalakov thread using a sling as an anchor

Pitons

Pitons, or 'pegs', are included here for completeness. However, they are often a contentious item of gear and their use should be carefully considered. They have lost much of their following in summer due to the way that they scar the rock during retrieval but are still used by many climbers in winter as they are often the only reliable protection that can be gained. Take care to find out the local ethics for the area in which you are going to climb, as in many places they are, for example, discouraged from use on summer routes under winter conditions.

A variety of pitons

Two angle pitons stacked

TIP

In winter, clean as much of the ice from a potential placement as you can. Be very aware that a piton may appear to have been well placed but could be sitting between two layers of ice in the crack, causing it to fail when loaded. Generally speaking, angles and leepers are better at cutting through ice on rock than knife blades and kingpins, but never underestimate just how hard a layer of ice on the rock can be.

There are a variety of types and a small selection will often be carried on winter routes. RURPs' knife blades, kingpins, lost arrows, leepers, angles and bongs are all types of piton, with the first and last being the least-seen on a winter rack.

The piton should be hand-placed for around 50–75 per cent of its length (making allowances for iced up cracks) with the eye down-most for most types. When being hammered in, the noise of the blows should be rising in pitch, showing that the piton is being placed well. If it goes in with a series of dull thuds, particularly into icy cracks, remove it and try another place. Horizontal placements will generally be much stronger than those in vertical cracks.

It is important that the piton is driven right into the crack, so that the eye is flush. If not, and you are convinced that the placement is good or there are just no alternatives, you will need to tie the piton off to reduce leverage. This can be done by clove-hitching a sling around the piton in the same manner as for an ice screw. Be aware that the striking surface of a piton can often become burred and sharp, so make sure that the sling you use cannot be cut if it is loaded.

Some shapes of pitons are capable of being stacked, particularly angles. If the crack is a bit too wide for one piton, match another to it and drive them in together. In this instance, it will normally be the bottom piton that is clipped in to, thus needing to be placed flush with the rock.

Piton Removal

Remove the karabiner from the piton and knock it a few taps in one direction parallel to the crack, then a few in the other. Repeat this until it can be removed by hand. It is this removal that damages the rock, as the piton gouges a channel around its placement, hence their use being frowned upon in many areas and by many climbers.

TIP

It is easy to lose a piton during removal, as it suddenly 'pings' out and down the route. You should never leave one of your climbing karabiners attached to it as it could be damaged by the hammer. However, you could clip in an old karabiner, or use a small 'accessory' karabiner, that has a short length of cord attached to it. Alternatively, thread a piece of old cord through the eye and use that. This will allow you to remove the piton and avoid dropping it.

Snow Shelters

The following pages show a variety of snow shelters. The majority of these are emergency bivouacs, and are reserved for when there is simply no alternative but to dig in. There is also a snow hole shown, which is designed for a planned night out, the construction of which is quite lengthy but can provide comfortable accommodation for a number of people.

■

EMERGENCY SNOW SHELTERS

What is an Emergency Snow Shelter?
This is exactly as it sounds – only for use in an extreme emergency. The decision to spend the night out in the mountains under winter conditions must not be taken lightly. It will be seen that the construction of a snow shelter is a very tiring task, expensive on both time and energy, both of which may be better utilised making your way down the mountain if at all possible.

When and Where do we Use it?
We could only recommend the use of a shelter in the case of injury, benightment in foul weather, lost in poor visibility on dangerous terrain, and so on, when all other options have been exhausted.

EQUIPMENT
Anything to hand, such as an ice axe, deadman, lunchbox, helmet, bivi bag, trekking poles and, best of all, a shovel and a snow-saw.

Lean-to Sitting Bivi
This is the most practical of all the bivis shown, and meets the basic requirement of seeking shelter from the wind. It is the recommended method of sheltering from the weather during an enforced stopover.

A wedge-shaped slot slightly over shoulder-width is cut into the snow bank, with the depth sufficient to ensure the person is below the level of the snow surface. A seat can be fashioned at the back of the slot from debris, and insulated

with spare kit and rope. The slot needs to be roofed over in some fashion. This can be done by weighing down a bivi bag or group shelter with snow blocks around the edge, supported across the roof of the slot by trekking poles if possible.

In the right snow conditions, it is far better to cut a series of snow blocks, slightly longer than the width of the bivi, which can be placed over the shelter to provide a roof. This, of course, will take a little more time and energy, but will be not only more substantial, but also thermally more efficient. The narrower the width of the shelter, the easier it will be to cut blocks to fit. As with any emergency shelter, it is important to mark your position somehow, by weighing down a bivi bag for instance, or by placing your ice axe or trekking poles in the snow above your shelter.

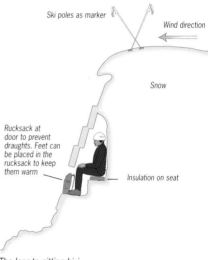

The lean-to sitting bivi

Sitting Bivi
This bivi requires a steep bank of snow for construction, the steeper the better, such as that found at the edge of streams and re-entrants. Start by tunnelling in and slightly up-slope, before turning and digging straight up. The distance in is dictated by the snow-pack angle and strength – in a vertical drift and good snow this may be as little as 30cm.

Imagine yourself sitting on a chair – this is the internal shape that you are looking for; a small seat can be fashioned out of debris from the vertical section. Allow room enough to enable you to sit up straight, with a couple of inches clearance above your head. Smooth across the roof of the sitting area to help prevent drips. You may wish to fashion a ventilation hole in the wall in front of your face by using the shaft of your axe. Although when completed this may appear to be the same as the lean-to bivi, it is in fact much more awkward to construct as you end up in a position of having to dig upwards and excavating above your head – a sure way to get covered in snow with the knock-on effect of damp and heat loss.

TIPS
1 Excellent lightweight shovels are available which split into sections for carrying if required. These are handy when out on a trip, and absolutely essential when leading a group. Those with a curved blade tend to be more efficient at digging and snow removal than the straighter design.
2 It is important to mark your location, whichever type of shelter you use. Trekking poles are ideal, and if you can tear a strip from an orange bivi bag and attach it to the end, it would assist location immensely.

Mousehole Bivi
The mousehole bivi, or 'shovel-up', is a reasonable option for a relatively flat area, as long as the wind will not cause the snow to blow away during construction. Place all of the groups' rucksacks on the ground and cover them with a bivi-bag. Pile as much snow as possible on top of the sacks to create an igloo-shaped structure. The effect of moving the snow from one place to another helps the consolidation process. Lightly firm the snow down with shovels, hands etc if necessary, and dig in a small entrance on the leeward side. Remove the bivi-bag and rucksacks, and sculpt the inside to shape. Smooth the roof to prevent dripping.

Snow Grave
Intended for use on flat terrain, the snow grave is the least practical and pleasant of the methods shown here. However, it does have its place and has been used in the high mountains, hence its inclusion. It is reliant upon the snow having a layer of hard slab or thick crust. Using the axe pick, cut out an outline of approximately 60cm x 120cm on the ground. Divide this into 30cm x 60cm slabs, and carefully lift them out. Scoop out the snow underneath, hollowing out an undercut section for the feet. Ensure that you leave a lip for the slabs to rest on when they are replaced. Carefully put back two of the slabs, climb underneath, and lower the final slabs down on top. Ensure that there is sufficient ventilation. Use all available kit to help minimise body contact with the snow.

Snow

Insulation: Rucksack, rope etc

Snow grave side and top views

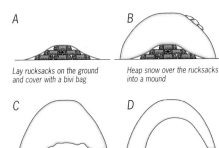

A Lay rucksacks on the ground and cover with a bivi bag

B Heap snow over the rucksacks into a mound

C Tunnel in on the leeward side and remove the rucksacks and bivi bag

D Enlarge the centre and smooth off the ceiling to prevent drips

Mousehole bivi

COACHING NOTES

It is an extremely valuable experience for people to try digging a shelter. Allow about thirty minutes for the exercise, and get them to sit/lie in it after completion. It is also worthwhile spending time with a map, helping people identify areas that may be suitable as bivi sites. It should be made clear that life is far easier if a shovel is available, and a group's kit should always include one. An avalanche probe, which should also be part of the group's kit, is useful in determining the depth of a bivi site before construction starts.

OBSERVATIONS

1 There are a whole variety of possibilities for biviing out, often using a hybrid of the methods given above. Large boulders often have soft drifts behind them, these can be scooped out relatively easily and shelter found there. Below the tree line, the lower branches of trees can often support snow but leave a sheltered area underneath.

2 The important things to remember are: get out of the wind; insulate yourself from the snow; ensure adequate ventilation; mark your position; keep up your morale.

3 The most important factor in any bivi situation is to minimise the amount of your body touching the snow, otherwise heat is wicked away at an alarming speed. A good deal of insulation would be needed to prevent this from happening if you were in the prone position, such as in the snow grave; for that reason the lean-to sitting bivi would always be our first choice. Insulation can be provided by sitting on your rucksack, rope, etc, and the sitting position is far comfier than any other for an extended period of time.

TIP

If at all possible, urinate before going into your shelter. This is for two reasons. Firstly, once you are in your shelter you should not come out any more than is necessary – this will lose you a lot of body heat, and there is a chance that you may not locate your shelter again in bad visibility. If you need the toilet while you are inside, do it where you are.

Secondly, if you have been missed in the valley and a search is in progress, not only does dehydration-coloured urine stand out in the snow as a locator, but it gives a search dog a large scent target to head for.

SNOW-HOLE CONSTRUCTION

What is a Snow Hole?

A snow hole, as opposed to a snow shelter, is a well-constructed place for a pre-planned stay of one or more nights. They can range in size from the most basic, which will sleep one or two people, up to those sleeping twelve or more.

When and Where do we Use it?

The snow hole is a pre-planned activity, thus it can be used almost anywhere the snow build-up is sufficient as a base for climbing, walking or, for many people, as an experience in its own right.

EQUIPMENT

Ice axe, shovel, snow saw; an avalanche probe is useful but not essential.

Method

The hole site needs to be selected carefully, not only from a safety point of view, but also for ease of digging. Lee slopes in a variety of forms will hold sufficient snow, and the steeper the snow the better, re-entrants and the lee of moraine deposits are ideal. There are a number of ways to construct the hole. The following is the one that we find to be most efficient in time and effort in the majority of cases.

Mark out a shape on the steep slope in front of you, approximately 60cm wide and 120cm high. This will be your entrance passage-way, the size of it can always be reduced at a later stage. For now, it makes life easier having room to work. Tunnel in and slightly up. The distance in will be dictated by the strength of the snow, the angle of the slope and the size the finished hole needs to be. The thickness of the wall may be around 60–90cm on steep ground, but much thicker if the slope is at an angle.

The inside of the hole can then be constructed, which is done by digging out an area large enough for you to lie down in. This will normally be at 90 degrees to the entrance tunnel, and the floor of the sleeping area needs to be fashioned so that it is higher than the access level. Building it this way allows for warm air to be trapped in the living space, and allows easy removal of debris while digging. This inner area can be wedge shaped, and care should be taken to ensure that the floor ends up with a

1 The slopes which are ideal as snow-hole sites are also those that will be holding a large weight of snow, thus possibly avalanche prone. More than one person has been carried off by an avalanche while looking for a suitable place to stay, so be aware of your surroundings, the nature of the terrain and the state of the snow-pack. Test for the stability of the slope if in any doubt.

2 A well-organized snow hole will generally be a comfy one, so there are a couple of things that you can do at the construction stage that will make life more pleasant later on. The storage of gear is important, so a couple of long shelves can be fashioned by digging into the walls. It would be a good idea if the kit stored here was not left loose, as it would tend to attract moisture from the atmosphere when the interior temperature warms up from body heat or cooking. Kit placed into plastic bags or boxes will stay dry. Consideration should be given to the area in which cooking will take place. This is not only a very time-consuming process, but also can be a little messy if care is not taken. It therefore makes sense not to have the stove in the centre of the hole in case of any spillage. The best location for it will be near the entrance tunnel – this not only keeps it out of the way, but also allows poisonous vapours created by the cooking process to sink to the outside and not be trapped in the hole itself. Lighting is also another essential, and the effect of having a candle will lift not only the amount of light, but also the temperature and morale. A single candle will appear very bright, as the light will be reflected off the snow. The best position for this is in a triangular slot near the cooking area, the back of the recess shaped to reflect light.

3 When dug into a lee slope, care must be taken that the entrance to the snow hole does not drift over during the night. If winds or snow are forecast, it may be necessary to get up as often as once every hour to dig out the front of the hole to ensure that ventilation is maintained. Cooking becomes an extremely hazardous operation when there is no ventilation, as poisonous fumes are given off, and cooking should not be undertaken if there is no fresh air. This is particularly important in the morning, when the temptation is to light the stove and roll over back to sleep while it heats up – any ventilation may have disappeared during the night.

4 Leaving the snow hole for any reason must be thought through, especially if needing to answer the call of nature during the night. You may be tempted to go outside for a couple of minutes, but in windy or misty weather the snow-hole entrance can be impossible to relocate once left and the chances are that all of your warm clothing will still be inside. On a clear still night, the glow of a candle from inside the hole can be seen from some distance, but in bad weather great care must be taken. A climbing rope can be used to link a number of hole entrances, so that location is made easier, and it can be tied around any person needing to venture outside, and used like a lifeline. The rule here is that if you do not have to venture outside in bad weather, don't. If you have to, ensure that you have a torch and warm clothing on, and avoid the temptation to 'nip out' lightly clad.

5 Snow holes and snow-hole sites must be left spotlessly clean. Any debris left behind will not only be distasteful for any subsequent occupiers, but will also be left when the snow melts. Matches and candle stubs are but a small example. Consideration must be made to carrying out human waste. If left, this is not only extremely unpleasant and unsightly, but also presents a large problem with the pollution of waterways and local habitat. Crapping into a plastic bag, then placing this in a stout screw-top plastic container for later disposal at a lower level is the best remedy, and is to be encouraged. Some mountain areas have a human-waste disposal system in place, whereby they provide you with hygienic bags and carrying containers, along with a designated disposal point back in the valley. Take time to investigate if one has been set up at your intended destination, and use it.

1 Digging a snow hole is extremely damp work, and if nothing more than your gloves get wet you are doing well. It is worth wearing waterproofs with a minimum of clothing underneath to save perspiring too much, with your spare clothing packed away but easily to hand for when the digging stops. Gloves will get sodden, so having an old pair to use for the digging is a good idea, keeping your better pairs dry for the rest of the trip.

2 A handy way to remove debris is to lay a plastic bivi bag on the floor of the hole beneath where you are digging. The debris will fall onto this, and it can then be easily dragged out.

3 Following the actual construction of a snow hole, cooking is the next longest process. Make things comfortable for yourself by ensuring that all the required food and utensils are to hand. You can then get into your sleeping bag and operate from there. Avoid the temptation to carve out large pieces of your snow hole to melt for water, have a pile of snow ready cut into chunks. Start with a little and, once there is some water in your pan, add pieces slowly. Placing the stove on a flat piece of rock or small piece of plywood carried for the purpose will stop it melting itself into the floor of the snow hole quite as fast as otherwise it might – care should be taken with boiling liquids for this very reason.

smooth and level surface. The walls and ceiling should also be smoothed over, using either a gloved hand or the back of the shovel, sometimes both, to reduce the likelihood of drips when the temperature within the hole rises.

If there are two of you able to dig at the same time, you may elect to dig two tunnels initially. Start about 1 to 2 metres apart and dig in for a suitable distance, then curve round and join up. Team-work will let you enlarge the holes and dispose of debris, then one of the tunnels can be blocked up by the final blocks of excavated snow, leaving just the one entrance.

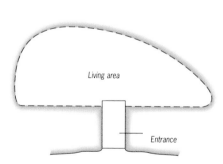

Snow hole: cross-section from front

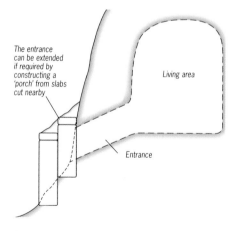

The entrance can be extended if required by constructing a 'porch' from slabs cut nearby

Snow hole: cross-section from side

Gear Lists

The following lists are for guidance and interest only. There will be, of course, huge differences in people's personal preferences and aspirations. The use of any particular manufacturer's product name is not designed to promote a particular brand, but denotes the type, shape and quality of the piece of equipment desired.

Recommended Lead Rack: Summer

The following list of equipment gives a good idea of what a lead rack should consist of. It allows for most single- and multi-pitch applications, where best-practice and personal safety are prime considerations.

Helmet
Harness
Rock boots
Rope

ON HARNESS

Belay device on HMS karabiner.
2 or 3 spare HMS screwgates.
1 x D-shape screwgate with 2 Prusik loops, made from 6mm kernmantle, 50–55cm long when tied with a double fisherman's knot.
For longer routes: penknife on small snapgate or screwgate karabiner.
For working with groups: selection of elastic bands or hair ties to hand out if required.

ON RACK

Wires, i.e. rocks, sizes 1 to 9, doubled up.
Rockcentrics, sizes 6,7,8,9, tied with 9mm kernmantle. The 6 rockcentric takes over in size from where the 9 rock leaves off, making a logical size progression.
Extenders x 8. Not too long, pre-sewn approx 15cm long.
Spring-loaded Camming Devices (SLCDs), set of four, flexible stem, sizes 1/2,1,2,3.
Nut key, with pullers for releasing jammed camming devices.
Snap karabiners, straight gates (or some bent gates), to use with all the above.
1 x 16ft (240cm) sling with HMS screwgate.
2 x 8ft (120cm) slings with 1 HMS screwgate each.

For longer routes: 1 extra 16ft (240cm) sling and HMS krab, 2 x 4ft (60cm) slings with two D-shape screwgates on each.

Recommended Lead Rack: Winter

A winter lead rack is very hard to design, due to the vast variation in route types, climbing styles, weather conditions etc. For instance, a rack for climbing icefalls on Ben Nevis will vary somewhat from a rack for climbing buttress routes in the Cairngorms. The rack below is therefore a very personal view, and is seen by the authors as the sort of rack they would take out on a 'let's go and see what's in nick' sort of day. Much of what is listed may be chosen to be left at home. Huge variations are possible, apart from the more practical aspect of having to carry it all!

Helmet
Harness
Rope
Axes to suit
Crampons to suit

ON HARNESS

As for summer kit.
Penknife.

ON RACK

4 extenders.
Wires 1–9, doubled up.
Rockcentrics 6,7,8,9 on 9mm kernmantle.
SLCDs, size 2 & 3.
3 drive-in warthogs, useful for frozen turf.
3 ice screws, various lengths.
Rock pegs. A selection of knife blades, angles and kingpins will be found useful, about eight in total.
Snap karabiners with straight gates, to use with the above.
4 x 4ft (60cm) slings, each with 2 karabiners on (may be snap gates).
2 x 8ft (120cm) slings, each with an HMS screwgate.
1 x 16ft (240cm) sling with HMS screwgate.
2 x 3m lengths of tape, to be used for abseil retreat, repairs etc, can live in rucksack.
2 x 1.5m lengths 8mm kernmantle, used for rigging Abalakov threads, can live in rucksack.
Abalakov thread hook.

Gear Lists

Summer-walking Rucksack Contents

The list below is a recommended selection of kit for the summer recreational walker. It is assumed that some high terrain will be covered, and that the walker will not be responsible for the safety of others in his charge. Personal choice will dictate the final selection of contents, but the following should be carefully considered:

rucksack, of around 30–40 litres, with hip belt
waterproof trousers
waterproof jacket
spare fleece (in addition to one being worn)
woollen or fleece hat and spare
gloves x 2 pairs
survival bag or bivi shelter
small sit-mat
first-aid kit
food
hot or cold drink
any personal medicines
headtorch with spare bulb and battery
map, covered with plastic. Taking a second as a spare is a sensible precaution if walking alone
OHP pen, useful for making notes on a map
compass
whistle
sun hat
sun cream
insect repellent
small amount of high-energy emergency food
sunglasses
mobile telephone
GPS
these last two items, if carried, should be switched off, padded and left at the bottom of the rucksack and are for emergency use only.

Winter-walking Rucksack Contents

All of the 'Summer-walking Rucksack Contents', plus:
ice axe
crampons
long neoprene strap with buckle for crampon repairs
ski goggles with anti-mist lenses
balaclava from fleece or similar material
extra fleece or down duvet
thick gloves or mitts
hot drink.

Summer-leader's Rucksack Contents

The rucksack of a summer mountain leader should contain adequate kit for not only himself, but a few extra essentials for group use. It cannot be expected that a leader carries enough kit for all of the group, and a lot of emphasis must be put into briefings prior to departure from base to ensure that participants are properly equipped. A final check of their rucksack contents should be made just before departure, making sure that clothing that you have specified as needing to be waterproof is not just 'showerproof'.

It is quite acceptable that one or two of the group items are carried by the group members themselves, as long as it is not hindering their own pace. All equipment listed for 'Summer-walking Rucksack Contents', plus:
2 extra pairs of gloves for group use
30m 9mm kernmantle rope
16ft (240cm) sling and HMS karabiner
group shelter, large enough to accommodate all group members
large first-aid kit
group vacuum flask containing hot juice rather than tea
duplicates of group members' personal medicines
list of contact names and addresses
spare map
spare compass.

Winter-leader's Rucksack Contents

The extra kit needed for winter group walking can also be shared out amongst the group. All of the 'Summer-leader's Rucksack Contents', plus:
ice axe
crampons
crampon spares kit, containing 2 long straps with buckles and a combination crampon spanner/screwdriver
helmet, depending on terrain and objectives.
spare fleece or down duvet
snow shovel
avalanche probe.

United Kingdom Mountain Training Schemes

Mountain Leader Training
Hyfforddi Arweinwyr Mynydda

There are a number of walking, climbing and mountaineering awards available in the United Kingdom, administered by Mountain Leader Training (MLT). All of the schemes require registration with the home-nation training board and consist of a training course (or in some cases exemption for very experienced candidates), a consolidation period and an assessment. Candidates are expected to have some experience prior to registration, and all relevant experience is entered into a log book kept by the candidate. These awards are outlined below, and full details can be gained via the website at www.mltuk.org.

■

CLIMBING WALL AWARD (CWA)

This scheme is for climbers who are in a position of responsibility when supervising climbing activities on indoor or outdoor climbing walls, artificial boulders and towers. It is primarily concerned with ensuring good practice, leading to the safe enjoyment of climbing activities, and to an understanding of the sport. It covers the supervision and management of activities including bouldering, the teaching of basic movement skills and roped climbing and the avoidance of common problems but excludes the teaching of leading. There is an add-on element, which is often run in conjunction with the standard course, which covers top roping and abseil sessions.

Training course duration: minimum 12 hours + 4 hours for the top roping and abseiling module
Consolidation period: recommended minimum of three months
Assessment course duration: minimum 6 hours + 2 hours for the top roping and abseiling module

SINGLE PITCH AWARD (SPA)

This scheme is for those who are in a position of responsibility during single pitch rock climbing activities. It is primarily concerned with good practice, leading to the safe and quiet enjoyment of the activity. For the purposes of this scheme, a single pitch route is one which: is climbed without intermediate stances; is described as a single pitch in the guidebook; allows students to be lowered to the ground at all times; is non-tidal; is non serious, having little objective danger and presents no difficulties on approach or retreat (such as route finding, scrambling or navigating). Topics covered include: personal climbing skills, use of climbing walls, group climbing and abseiling, and the avoidance and solving of related common problems.

Training course duration: 20 hours
Consolidation period: recommended minimum of six months
Assessment course duration: 20 hours

CLIMBING WALL LEADING AWARD (CWLA)

This scheme is for holders of the SPA or CWA awards who are in a position of responsibility when instructing and coaching the skills required to lead routes on indoor or outdoor climbing walls and towers, with fixed protection. It is primarily concerned with ensuring good practice, resulting in the safe development of leading skills, and to an understanding of the sport. It covers the introduction, coaching and ongoing development of the technical and movement skills required to lead routes safely. It excludes the skills associated with leading on natural crags and sport climbing venues, such as placing protection (or using non-fixed pre-placed traditional protection) and the judgement required to lead routes on natural rock.

Training course duration: 12 hours
Consolidation period: recommended minimum of three months
Assessment course duration: 6 hours

United Kingdom Mountain Training Schemes

WALKING GROUP LEADER (WGL)

The WGL is the basic award for leaders of hill walking groups in defined terrain and conditions. WGL has been designed to complement the long established Mountain Leader Award (ML), which trains leaders with the skills to lead walking groups in all mountain areas of the United Kingdom and Ireland.

Training course duration: 30 hours
Consolidation period: dependent upon completion of syllabus requirements
Assessment course duration: 30 hours

SUMMER MOUNTAIN LEADER AWARD (ML)

The Mountain Leader Award (ML) was established to promote the safe enjoyment of the hills and mountains. ML provides training and assessment in the technical and group management skills required by those who wish to lead groups in the mountains, hills and moorlands of the United Kingdom and Ireland, in anything other than winter conditions. It integrates experience, training, and assessment in a variety of testing conditions in mountainous country.

Training course duration: 60 hours
Consolidation period: dependent upon completion of syllabus requirements
Assessment course duration: 50 hours

WINTER MOUNTAIN LEADER AWARD (WML)

The Winter Mountain Leader award scheme provides training and assessment of the skills and techniques necessary to lead walking parties on the hills and mountains of the UK and Ireland under winter conditions, excluding roped climbing on technical terrain. The demands made on the leader in winter are much greater than in summer, therefore the Mountain Leader award is a prerequisite for all candidates and it builds on many of the skills already acquired.

Training course duration: six days
Consolidation period: dependent upon completion of syllabus requirements
Assessment course duration: five days

MOUNTAIN INSTRUCTOR AWARD (MIA)

The Mountain Instructor Award (Summer), known as the MIA, is for instructors working in summer conditions in the UK and Ireland and covers multi-pitch rock climbing, scrambling and related mountaineering skills.

Training course duration: nine days
Consolidation period: minimum of 12 months
Assessment course duration: five days

MOUNTAIN INSTRUCTOR CERTIFICATE (MIC)

Available to MIA holders, the Mountain Instructor Certificate covers the additional skills required for winter mountaineering and winter climbing. It also includes elements of training and assessment which the MLT feels are necessary for those advising and directing other courses of training or related activities.

Training course duration: five days
Consolidation period: dependent upon completion of syllabus requirements
Assessment course duration: four days

INTERNATIONAL MOUNTAIN LEADER (IML)

The International Mountain Leader Award (IML) provides comprehensive training and assessment for individuals who aspire to work as leaders in Europe and further afield. It integrates training, experience and assessment in a variety of realistic situations. The Award provides training and assessment in the skills required for leading and educating groups worldwide in summer conditions and also on easy snow-covered, rolling, Nordic-type terrain in the 'middle mountains' in winter conditions. The scheme does not involve the techniques and equipment of alpinism or glacial travel.

Training and assessment requirements: varied, details from MLT.

BRITISH MOUNTAIN GUIDE (BMG)

This scheme trains and assesses experienced mountaineers in the skills required for the provision of instruction and guiding services in climbing, skiing and mountaineering on rock, ice and snow in all conditions and all seasons at BMG and IFMGA international standards. The award is administered by the British Association of Mountain Guides and is valid world wide.

Training and assessment requirements: varied, details from www.bmg.org.uk

MOUNTAINEERING AWARDS OF THE UK

Personal experience requirements increase as candidates progress to higher awards.

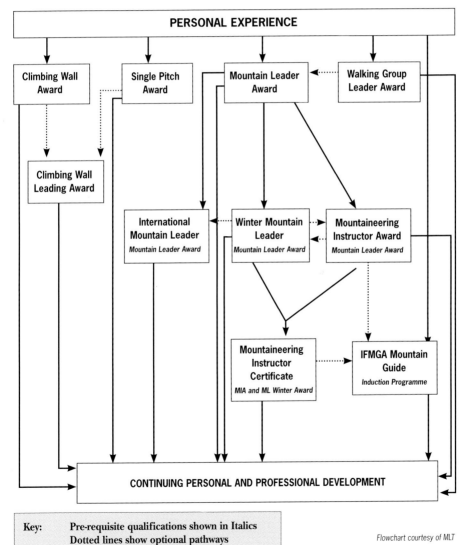

Key: **Pre-requisite qualifications shown in Italics**
Dotted lines show optional pathways

Flowchart courtesy of MLT

United Kingdom Mountain Training Schemes

Pete Hill, MIC, FRGS

Pete has climbed in many continents and countries across the world, including first ascents in the Himalayas. He is holder of the MIC award, the highest UK instructional qualification, and has been delivering rock and mountain sports courses at the highest level for a number of years. He is a member of the Alpine Club, Honorary life member of the Association of Mountaineering Instructors and a Fellow of the Royal Geographical Society. A lack of common sense has found him on the north faces of the Eiger and Matterhorn in winter, as well as a number of other extreme routes climbed in extreme conditions in the European Alps, Africa, Nepal and India.

Pete lives in Scotland and has two daughters, Rebecca and Samantha. A frequent contributor to various magazines and websites, he is author of *The International Handbook of Technical Mountaineering, Sport Climbing, Rock Climbing* and *The Complete Guide to Climbing and Mountaineering*. He runs summer and winter skills courses from beginner through to advanced, as well as treks and expeditions to countries worldwide. A lot of his time is spent delivering ML (Mountain Leader), SPA (Single Pitch Award) and CWA (Climbing Wall Award) courses, and he can be contacted via his website at www.petehillmic.com.

Stuart Johnston, MIC

Stuart is one of Britain's foremost mountaineering instructors and trainers, running summer and winter courses for all levels of enthusiasts, from beginner to aspiring leader and climbing professional. A member of the Association of Mountaineering Instructors, and since 1993 holder of the UK's highest qualification in the field: the Mountaineering Instructors Certificate (MIC).

Stuart is also a consultant adviser on outdoor health and safety and consults with many UK based high profile organisations. He is a qualified Wilderness Emergency Medical Technician and is a member of the WEMSI Europe teaching faculty.

He is an active member of Scottish mountain rescue and holds a voluntary post of training officer for The Mountain Rescue Committee of Scotland. Today, Stuart runs a successful mountaineering company from his base in Aberfeldy, Scotland, delivering courses from summer and winter mountain leader training and assessment to recreational mountaineering/climbing holidays. He also designs mountain safety products including the highly acclaimed Felpro Shelter (www.felpro. co.uk). Stuart is co-author of the 'Hillwalkers Guide to Mountaineering' and writes for various outdoor publications including 'Trail' magazine. Stuart can be contacted at www.climbmts.co.uk.

The Association of Mountaineering Instructors

The Association of Mountaineering Instructors (AMI) is the representative body of professionally qualified mountaineering instructors in the British Isles. AMI is committed to guaranteeing quality and promoting good practice in all mountaineering instruction.

AMI members are highly experienced mountaineers who have undergone rigorous training and assessment to qualify under the Mountain Leader Training UK (MLTUK) Mountain Instructor Scheme. They are trained not only in technical mountaineering skills but also in the personal skills of teaching and mountain leadership. Only instructors holding the MIA (Mountain Instructor Award) or the MIC (Mountain Instructor Certificate) qualifications are permitted to become full members and display the AMI logo.

The AMI ensures the continuing development of instructors through a series of workshops and training courses, which means that members remain at the forefront of technical and coaching developments.

Further information about the AMI can be found on its web site at www.ami.org.uk.

Acknowledgments

We are very grateful to a number of people who helped in the production of this book.

Eric Pirie, Steve Blagbrough and Shaun Roberts have been invaluable in shaping its outcome. They are all mountain instructors, qualified to the highest level, and have burnt a large amount of midnight oil proof-reading the text for us, for which we are eternally grateful.

Nigel Williams, as well as writing the foreword, provided us with much-needed inspiration throughout the writing process, and without his guidance our task would have been far more difficult.

Our thanks must go to Rab Carrington Ltd, who provided the clothing that we used in the photographs, and which was also used during our technical work-shopping sessions for the diagrams. Our days out with a camera and note book were made far more comfortable due to them, and their excellent kit stood up to the worst weather that a Scottish winter (and summer!) could throw at us. Details of Rab products can be found on their web site at www.rab.uk.com.

Thanks must also go to our long-suffering families, who have put up with months of neglect while we both giggled and grinned our way through the text, in shadowy computer-screen-lit rooms across the country.

Pete Hill & Stuart Johnston

Acknowledgments for the Revised Edition

This update has been possible due to the very valuable contributions from a number of people. In particular, Malcolm 'Ginge' Lee MBE MIC, Jonathan Preston MIC BMG, George McEwan MIC, Chris Pretty MIA, Di Gilbert MIC, James Hotchkis, Steve Long MIC BMG, Sean Cattanach and Paula Griffin have all added to the quality of the new book, and to them we are very grateful. There have also been myriad other acquaintances, both long and short term, who have given us ideas for additions and changes, and to all of you our heartfelt thanks.

Our thanks also go to Nigel Williams MIC, Head of Training at Glenmore Lodge National Outdoor Centre, for doing us the honour of providing an updated foreword.

We are also very grateful to MLTUK for allowing us to use some of their syllabus information, and to equipment manufacturers Petzl and Beal for allowing us to use some of their facts and figures, and to re-create information from their very informative websites at www.petzl.com and www.bealplanet.com.

Index